THE MOST
EVIL
DICTATORS
IN HISTORY

SHELLEY KLEIN

MICHAEL O'MARA BOOKS LIMITED

First published in Great Britain in 2002 by
Michael O'Mara Books Limited
9 Lion Yard
Tremadoc Road
London SW4 7NQ

A CIP catalogue record for this book is available from the British Library

ISBN 1-84317-071-X

www.mombooks.com

Designed and typeset by Design 23

Printed and bound in Singapore by Tien Wah Press

CONTENTS

INTRODUCTION

Every time a dictator dies, or an atrocity is perpetrated, or details of the torture endured by those who lived through one regime or another escapes to the outside world, invariably the cry goes up that this must never be allowed to happen again. The unsavoury fact is, however, that it *does* happen again, over and over, from one continent to another. Even though we have reached the twenty-first century, around the world today people still suffer at the hands of individuals whose psychopathic nature or ideological passions require either the subjugation or annihilation of those over whom they rule. The motives that inspire dictators never die; sadly the same cannot be said of the dictators' victims.

Interestingly, of the men who appear in this book, Josef Stalin has to be not only the most terrifying of individuals (although quantifying what accounts as 'most terrifying' is well nigh impossible), but also by far the most influential. No other dictator either living or dead has been hero worshipped to the extent that Stalin has been – and not just in his own country, but all over the world. Stalinism was (and is) a doctrine that still exercises tremendous influence over people from all walks of life. Fortunately, the same cannot be said of any other dictator, although Hitler did (in the form of Oswald Mosley) and does (in the form of several European far-right groups such as Britain's National Front and France's Front National headed by Jean-Marie Le Pen) still have his admirers. But, unlike Stalin, Hitler's influence is less ideological, more simply racist.

Naturally, given the scale of the Holocaust combined with its cruelty and the cinematic footage that was taken by both American and British soldiers as they liberated the death camps, Hitler's reign of terror is perhaps the one most commonly associated with the word 'evil'. In its systematic approach to the murder of millions of men, women and children, by an apparently civilized nation, it was truly horrifying. How could an entire country let itself be governed in such a manner? How could a whole nation not have known what was occurring on its very own doorstep? Was Germany populated by millions of little Hitlers – men and women who all, in their own way, harboured the same resentments as their Führer? The debate over this has raged and will no doubt continue to rage for years to come, but that there is the potential for evil within all of us, is surely one of many conclusions that can be drawn.

When it comes to the psychopathic side of human nature, however, and to the different types of torture to which all the men in this book at some stage resorted, alongside the enjoyment they derived from their crimes and the bloodlust they displayed, surely that separates out the good from the bad. Hitler, Pol Pot, Idi Amin, Stalin, Papa Doc Duvalier, Saddam Hussein; all in their own way committed crimes against humanity for which there is neither excuse nor justification. Stalin is said to have taken a 'sickening interest' in how his victims died, and Papa Doc is reported to have enjoyed watching the torture of innocents within the confines of his own home. In addition, it has recently come to light that under Saddam Hussein, victims were regularly filmed while being tortured so that the tapes could be played back to him and his family as light entertainment. Who in their right minds would want to know of, or sit down and watch, such material? But therein lies yet another question for the world to answer. Were, or are, these despotic individuals certifiably insane? It would be easier for all of us to believe that they were (and in the case of Idi Amin and to some extent, Robert Mugabe, Pol Pot and Saddam Hussein we might be justified in so thinking), but surely this is too simple an explanation. Surely there are other characteristics that might explain their actions.

Having studied all fifteen men in some depth, it has been interesting to note that a lack of education, or a failure to complete their education, seems to be a common factor in several of these dictators' lives. Saddam Hussein and Idi Amin were both bordering on the illiterate while Adolf Hitler, Pol Pot, Kim Il Sung and Nicolae Ceausescu never completed their studies and Hitler's failure to gain entrance to Art School certainly left him with a massive inferiority complex. Education is also a common denominator when it comes to dictators' pet hates. Pol Pot, Mao Tse-tung and Idi Amin, for example, all persecuted and killed those they thought to be 'intellectual', no doubt because they saw them as a threat to their respective regimes. In a dictatorship there can be no dissent, no questioning the authority of the ruling party for, rather as in fairy tales when water is thrown on the witch and she shrivels up and dies, few dictators can withstand rigorous investigation by those properly equipped to interrogate them.

So how would these men, who have come to stain the world with the blood of their victims, have justified their crimes? Were there any whose ideologies or policies were developed solely to benefit the people rather than to damage and torture them?

In the case of the three earliest dictators in this volume, Herod the Great, Genghis Khan and Shaka Zulu, it could be argued that, given the period within which they were operating, their actions weren't as heinous or unlawful as those later down the centuries. After all, all three despots' enemies would have been behaving along much the same lines, slaying their opponents at any given opportunity. Life wasn't as sacrosanct in Genghis Khan's or Shaka Zulu's time as it is today. The Romans (who are regarded as a huge civilizing influence over the Western world) were, of course, as barbaric in their practices as ever Herod the Great might have been. As all the best comedians say, timing is everything and where these three jokers were concerned, that is very much the case.

Sadly the same cannot be said for the rest of the group. Their reasons or excuses are of a far different ilk, especially with characters such as Augusto Pinochet who believed that without his intervention to break up Salvador Allende's left-wing government, his country would have fallen into dire economic straits. Similarly, several other dictators believed that, at the time of their taking over control, they were doing the best for their countries. It was only subsequent to their respective coups that they failed to live up to the promises they had made. Certainly, in the case of Nicolae Ceausescu, Papa Doc Duvalier and even to some extent Stalin and Mao Tse-tung, this was so. Ideologically speaking, they all set out with the belief that their policies could help their countries either sociologically, economically or both. That this never happened is surely testament that no policy, or dream, or social ideal, when taken to an extreme will ever succeed; quite the contrary, it will turn into a nightmare.

Which brings us neatly to the likes of Saddam Hussein, Idi Amin and Anastasio García Somoza – men whose sole purpose in succeeding to government appears to have been the lining of their own pockets and the subjugation of their people as some kind of sick entertainment. Undoubtedly, Somoza didn't slaughter as many citizens as Hussein or Amin; nevertheless his was a dictatorship which financially benefited no one more than himself. Hussein and Amin, on the other hand, made no bones about their respective greed, nor did they appear embarrassed by, or regretful of, the blood that was spilled in their names. Both boasted of their crimes, teased the world with their bombastic rhetoric, and together tortured and slaughtered whomsoever they pleased.

In contrast, a far more shadowy and mysterious figure than any other dictator who appears in this book is Kim Il Sung. He also amassed vast wealth and tortured his citizens, but because Northern Korea is such an insular, almost hermetically sealed country, it has been impossible to know the true extent of the damage he wreaked on his people. What *is* known is that, like many of his fellow dictators, Kim wished to pass his bloodied crown on to his son. In fact, this is a recurrent theme throughout the lives of most of these men. Dictators often want the role to be hereditary.

Anastasio Somoza, Papa Doc, Kim Il Sung, Nicolae Ceausescu and Saddam Hussein all groomed their sons to take over from them after they died. Perhaps this is because, at the height of their megalomania, they viewed themselves as royalty and therefore their children had a 'blood' right to rule in their wake. Or perhaps they believed that if their offspring took over their mantels, they themselves would achieve immortality? This second explanation is far more likely for no one, let alone megalomaniac dictators, finds it easy picturing a world without themselves in it. Besides which dictators, having exercised complete control when they were alive, must want to believe that they can continue to do so even after they are dead. What better way to achieve this than by passing the baton on to your sons? In this respect the Romantic poet, Percy Bysshe Shelley, wrote a very prescient poem pointing out not only the lunacy, but also the pointlessness of such an exercise. Called 'Ozymandias' it sums up perfectly even the most powerful of men's total inadequacy in the face of Time.

> I met a traveller from an antique land
> Who said: Two vast and trunkless legs of stone
> Stand in the desert...Near them, on the sand,
> Half sunk, a shattered visage lies, whose frown,
> And wrinkled lip, and sneer of cold command,
> Tell that its sculptor well those passions read

Which yet survive, stamped on these lifeless things,
The hand that mocked them, and the heart that fed:
And on the pedestal these words appear:
'My name is Ozymandias, king of kings:
Look on my works, ye Mighty, and despair!'
Nothing else beside remains. Round the decay
Of that colossal wreck, boundless and bare
The lone and level sands stretch far away.

Given recent events, namely the toppling of Saddam Hussein's regime and the consequent dismantling of his own giant statue, the above could not be more appropriate. Nevertheless, it is of little comfort to anyone who has had to suffer at the hands of one of these despots that one day his palaces will crumble and his offspring will expire. Instead what is needed is an assurance that such events can't and won't happen again. Needless to say, mankind has yet to reach a point where this can be imagined. In the meantime, a handful of present-day dictators are still enjoying the spoils of their respective regimes, and there are undoubtedly several 'would-be' dictators patiently waiting in the wings...

HEROD THE GREAT

Slaughterer of the Innocents

The reign of Herod, who was effective ruler of Judaea and much
else from 37BC to his death four years before the Christian era, is
an episode in Jewish history with which Jewish historians, no less
than Christian ones, have found it difficult to come to terms.
Herod was both a Jew and an anti-Jew; an upholder and
benefactor of Graeco-Roman civilization, and an oriental
barbarian capable of unspeakable cruelties.

A History of the Jews,
Paul Johnson[1]

The story of the birth of Christ is said to be the greatest story of them all.
Throughout Christendom it is certainly amongst the most treasured, re-
enacted at Christmas in churches, schools and community centres. Joseph
and Mary arrive at the inn, only to be turned away and sent to a manger where, during
the night a child is born; a child who shortly afterwards is attended by three wise men
and three shepherds. It is a joyful occasion, a birth that heralds many good things. But
as with all such events, darkness looms in the background, for the coming of Christ
was not received by everyone in Judaea as heralding a new dawn. One man in
particular greeted the news with trepidation; his name was Herod the Great.

Born circa 74BC in the Land of Edom[2] (which is now commonly referred to as
Negev or Negeb), a small desert region to the south of Judaea, Herod was an Edomite
by birth. His father was called Antipater and his mother, who was of Arab descent, was
called Kupros (sometimes spelt Cypros). Antipater was a supporter of Hyrcanus II,
who had come to the throne after Julius Caesar defeated Pompey in 49BC. Both
Hyrcanus and Antipater, realizing that an allegiance with the superpower that was
Rome would serve them and their families well, then supported Caesar during further
civil strife. As a result, Hyrcanus was given overall control of Judaea which in turn
yielded significant benefits for Antipater, who was able to secure high-ranking
positions for his sons. One of them, Phasael, was made Prefect of Jerusalem while
Herod, who was only sixteen at the time, was given the job of Prefect of Galilee, a
fertile region to the north of Judea and Samaria that would later bear witness to the
ministry of Jesus, himself a Galilean.

One of Herod's first acts as Prefect appears in many ways typical of how he would
later treat all of his subjects, i.e. he was both fair yet tyrannical, both civilized yet

barbaric. On coming to power he ran to ground a group of semi-religious guerrillas, who had refused to pay the taxes and obey the laws of the Herodian administration. The rebels were led by a man called Hezekiah and, once Herod had captured the rebels, he then tortured Hezekiah prior to executing him and his co-conspirators without any form of Jewish religious trial. Naturally, this infuriated the more traditional Jews who not only pointed out that Jewish government allowed for no separation between church and state, but also informed Herod that he had committed a capital offence under Jewish law. Suddenly, Herod was arraigned to appear before the Sanhedrin (a Jewish court). Being brought before the Sanhedrin was a serious matter; normally people would humble themselves in front of the judges and beg their forgiveness. Not Herod. It is said that he arrived at the court surrounded by a coterie of armed guards. He is also said to have turned up wearing brightly coloured, flamboyant clothing, striding into the courtroom without once acknowledging the judges. Herod would, undoubtedly, have been found guilty but a sudden and unexpected command came through from Rome ordering that Herod be released without charge. When he left the Sanhedrin, Herod was triumphant, returning to Galilee an even more arrogant man.

On 15 March 44BC, Julius Caesar was murdered by Marcus Junius Brutus and Gaius Longinus Cassius. In the ensuing mayhem Herod's father, Antipater, waited anxiously to see who would replace the old emperor.

The Herodians, as Herod's family was always referred to, relied on Rome for their position in life, for despite being Arabs by blood and Jews by religion, Rome presented Antipater and his family with the best opportunities to improve their lot. Subsequent to Caesar's death, therefore, Antipater watched carefully as events unfolded in Rome to see who would seize power. Marc Antony and Octavius wanted to avenge Caesar's death, as a consequence of which Brutus and Cassius turned to Judaea to furnish them with enough money to mount a war against their enemies. Antipater had no option but to concede and ordered each of his Prefects to raise a portion of the funds through taxation. This was never going to be a popular move, but Antipater made the situation worse by extracting these new taxes through brute force. One collector, a man by the name of Malichus, refused to do as he was ordered in the hope that this would make Antipater look bad in front of the Romans. Both Antipater and Cassius were furious. They arrested Malichus and were on the verge of having him executed when Hyrcanus stepped in and revoked the death penalty. Shortly afterwards, a huge feast was held which both Antipater and Cassius attended. Antipater is said to have picked up a goblet of wine from which he drank; then fell down dead, poisoned. All evidence pointed towards Malichus and both Herod and his brother Phasael vowed revenge, but in the event it was Cassius who ordered an armed guard of Roman soldiers to execute the assassin. This stood Herod in very good stead in Rome. Cassius, however, was not so fortunate and was defeated shortly afterwards in battle (circa 42BC) by Marc Antony and Octavius. Downhearted and exhausted, Cassius committed suicide by throwing himself on his sword, leaving Marc Antony to take over as ruler of the eastern half of the Roman Empire.

At almost the same time, Herod and Hyrcanus came under attack by yet another group of Jewish rebels, but once again Herod swiftly defeated the uprising. As a reward for his loyalty, Hyrcanus arranged for Herod to marry his granddaughter, Mariamme. Herod already had one wife, an Arab woman by the name of Doris, but this didn't stop him taking a second. This was not, of course, against the law and Herod could see great advantage arising from the union. After all, Mariamme was a princess and related to one of the most influential men in the district.

Over his lifetime Herod married no less than ten wives and is thought to have fathered twelve or fourteen children. Despite this, it appears that it was always Doris and Mariamme who were closest to his heart and whose children benefited most from their father's success. Doris had one son; a boy by the name of Antipater and Mariamme had two children, Alexander and Aristobulus.

Herod worked hard at forging an alliance with Rome and also in established a solid dynasty through his sons, but after Cassius's death he realized that he would have to win over Marc Antony if he was to maintain good relations with his 'employers'. Some of Herod's enemies had tried to persuade Marc Antony to oust Herod from his position in Judaea and on hearing of this, Herod rushed to speak to Marc Antony. The leader of the eastern Roman Empire was swift to assure Herod that he had no reason for concern. Marc Antony acknowledged that Herod was a good friend to Rome and, although Herod had supported Cassius, Marc Antony knew this was a sign of Herod's loyalty to the Empire.

In fact, Marc Antony and Herod had a lot in common. Both enjoyed the good things in life; they loved drinking and feasting and although Marc Antony could be very warm and effusive, there was also a cruel, brutal side to his nature. This came to the fore when he ordered the execution of hundreds of Jews who opposed Herod. He then appointed Herod and his elder brother, Phasael, joint rulers of Judaea. Hyrcanus was deeply unhappy about this turn of events for, in effect, this made him little more than a puppet king. Nevertheless, he didn't have long to brood over his loss as shortly afterwards his kingdom became embroiled in a new war.

Born around 74BC, Herod lived to the age of 78, although latterly he became increasingly infirm with symptoms some thought to be psychosomatic, brought about by his many evil deeds. One scholar even described Herod's ailments as 'Herod's Evil'.

Around 40BC one of Rome's fiercest enemies, the Parthians (Parthia comprised an area that today covers Iran and part of Iraq) invaded Syria, which was part of the Roman Empire. Huge legions of Roman troops marched westwards to reclaim their territory and repel the invaders. Presented with an opportunity to attack Herod whilst his 'protectors' were otherwise engaged, the Jews, headed by a man called Antigonus, mounted an offensive against their reviled overlord. Antigonus further inflamed the situation by promising the Parthians overall control of Judaea if they could drive Herod out or, better still, kill him. Antigonus and his men invaded Judaea and took control of Jerusalem. During the fighting, Herod managed to escape to Masada, but his brother Phasael and Hyrcanus were captured. It is said that Antigonus then had the ear (or ears) of Hyrcanus cut off after which he gave the body parts to the Parthians as a trophy of war. Hyrcanus, meantime, was left not only to bear the pain of such an attack, but also its long-term effect on his status because, since he had been mutilated, he could no longer act as a High Priest. Phasael didn't fare well either. Deeply distressed at having been captured, it is thought that he either killed himself by smashing his head against the prison walls or that he was poisoned by Antigonus and his men.

Meanwhile, Herod's followers gathered at Masada which in Hebrew means 'fortress' – an apt name, for the whole construction sat 1,300-feet high on top of an isolated outcrop of rock overlooking the Dead Sea. Because of its position and height, approaching Masada was very difficult to reach; indeed the Jewish historian Flavius Josephus (born AD37 – died circa 101) said it could only be accessed by means of a 'snaky path', thus making it the ideal place in which to hide. Before seeking sanctuary in the fortress, however, Herod first took advice from one of his brothers:

> **'And when he was come to Idumea, at a place called Thressa, his brother Joseph met him, and he then held a council to take advice about all his affairs, and what was fit to be done in his circumstances, since he had a great multitude that followed him, besides his mercenary soldiers, and the place Masada, whither he proposed to fly was too small to contain so great a multitude; so he sent away the greater part of his company, being above nine thousand, and bid them go, some one way, and some another, and so save themselves in Idumea…but he took with him those that were the least encumbered, and were most intimate with him, and came to the fortress and placed there his wives and his followers, being eight hundred in number…'[3]**

Herod stayed at Masada for a short time before leaving his wives and most of his followers in order to travel to Rome, some say via Egypt where he met with Cleopatra. Once he arrived at his ultimate destination, he pleaded with the Senate to bestow upon him the title King of the Jews and allow him to return to Judaea and re-establish Roman sovereignty. The Senate agreed, conferring upon him the formal title '*rex socius et amicus populi Romani*', 'allied king and friend of the Roman people'. Herod and

36,000 Roman troops then marched first on Galilee, where they subdued all resistance, before moving on to Joppa. Then Herod returned to Masada to liberate his loyal followers. Finally, he marched on Jerusalem where he besieged the city for several weeks before scaling the walls to capture the city. With victory assured, Herod, together with his Roman soldiers and those Jews still loyal to him, massacred much of the city's population in order to establish their authority over Jerusalem's remaining citizens. In addition, the Romans also looted gold, clothing, jewels and any other items of value from the city until Herod begged them to stop and promised to pay them handsomely from his own coffers.

Meanwhile, Antigonus, who had been captured by Herod, was swiftly delivered to the Romans at Antioch where he was strung up on a cross and whipped until he lost consciousness. Then he was beheaded.

Throughout the rest of his reign, Herod displayed all the signs of a great politician by ensuring that he always enjoyed the unstinting support of whoever was in power in Rome. When Mark Antony's star was rising, for instance, Herod duly pledged his allegiance but when Antony fell, Herod swiftly changed tack, making a close ally of Octavius Caesar. Herod swiftly became one of Rome's most loyal 'satellite kings'.

From the start, Herod wished to make his mark on Judaea and stamp his authority on all sections of society. Bearing this in mind, he ordered the execution of forty-six (out of a total of seventy-one) members of the Sanhedrin because, to Herod's way of thinking, they were meddling in secular matters, which were *his* jurisdiction. Thereafter, the Sanhedrin was strictly a religious court. Herod then further emasculated the Jewish population by reforming the High Priesthood, whom he regarded as a legitimate threat to his position as ruler. Normally, the role and title of High Priest was hereditary, but after Herod took control he both appointed and dismissed many of their number, a move that infuriated the Jews who thereafter regarded the position of High Priest as being tainted by Rome. But there was one High Priest who won the people's approval. His name was Ananelus and, despite being appointed to the position by Herod and in spite of the fact that he was only seventeen at the time, it is said that the Jews openly approved of his ministry, praising him wholeheartedly. Naturally, this didn't play well with Herod who had already begun to display deep-seated signs of paranoia. Accordingly, he prepared a grand feast to be held at Jericho and invited Ananelus to attend. The day was sweltering hot and most of the party retreated to some bathing pools nearby where, it is said, Ananelus was taken to a shaded part of the ponds and drowned by Herod's cronies.

The Jews were shocked grief-stricken when they heard the news of the High Priest's death. Ananelus's mother, Alexandra, along with several others, suspected foul play, if not outright murder. To them, this was another sign of an Arab desecrating their rights. Enraged by what had happened, Alexandra journeyed to Egypt where she sought and received counsel from Queen Cleopatra. Cleopatra was deeply sympathetic to Alexandra's plight and promised her that she would do everything in her power to rid Judaea of Herod.

When three visiting wise men came to ask him about a newborn 'King of the Jews', Herod was furious. He regarded himself as King and could not countenance the existence of an infant usurper. He ordered all male children up to the age of two years in Bethlehem and the surrounding area to be put to death. The massacre became known as The Slaughter of the Innocents. It is estimated that up to 10,000 children were murdered.

As was the wont of many later dictators (Stalin, Ceausescu, Papa Doc, to name but a few) who made it their duty to build up large networks of spies in order to keep an eye on their enemies, Herod now employed similar tactics. He stationed informants everywhere, but in particular in the large marketplaces and public baths where people would openly exchange news and pass the time of day. Consequently, before Cleopatra or Alexandra could put any of their plans into action, Herod heard of their plotting. Forewarned by her own spies, Alexandra fled Jerusalem hidden in a coffin.

Meanwhile, as every good student of English literature knows, Cleopatra was busy casting her spell over Marc Antony. The latter was smitten by the Egyptian queen and the two began plotting to overthrow Octavius (who commanded the western half of the Roman Empire) and move the capital from Rome to Alexandria in Egypt. Marc Antony ordered all those loyal to him to line up and fight Octavius, but fortunately (or so it turned out) Herod was too busy fighting his own battles to participate. As a result, Herod escaped the defeat of Antony and Cleopatra off the coast of Greece in the Battle of Actium in 31BC. As soon as he heard the news Herod, always with one eye trained on the main chance, immediately swore an oath of allegiance to Octavius.

Herod also organized the Actian Games to celebrate Octavius's victory. The games were Graeco-Roman in nature and included such entertainments as chariot racing, musical interludes and wrestling. The games, however, were yet another snub to the Jews, particularly as much of the musical material contained bawdy language offensive to those of the Ultra Orthodox persuasion.

Nor were the games the only element of Greek culture that Herod introduced to Judaea for, at this point in his life, he was smitten by all things Hellenistic. Before the death of Alexander the Great in 323BC, the young soldier had spread Greek customs throughout the East and, although by Herod's time the Greeks were in decline, the Romans were still heavily influenced by them. When Herod rebuilt the seaport town of Strato's Tower, re-naming it Caesarea, he also fortified the city of Samaria and renamed it Sebaste (a Greek translation of the name Augustus).

Having disposed of Ananelus because he saw him as a possible threat, and secure in the knowledge that Rome was now very much behind him, Herod then turned his attention to one of his oldest 'enemies', Hyrcanus. Miraculously, Hyrcanus had survived Antigonus's bid to overthrow him and, though mutilated, had since become a High Priest in Babylonia. Fearful that Hyrcanus might one day return and reclaim his throne, Herod saw fit to have him assassinated. At this point, several sources (including a version found in the Talmud) would have us believe that Mariamme, devastated by her grandfather's untimely death, committed suicide and that her body was preserved in honey. Many people, however, believe she was executed at a later date by Herod, who suspected her of having been unfaithful. Take this account from Robert Graves's novel *Claudius the God* which, although a work of fiction, is based on a monumental amount of historical research.

'When Mariamme found out about these secret orders she naturally became resentful and said things in the presence of Herod's mother and sister which she would have been wiser to have left unsaid. For they were jealous of Mariamme's power over Herod and repeated her words to him as soon as he returned, at the same time accusing her of having committed adultery in his absence as an act of spite and defiance – they named the Chamberlain as her lover. Herod had them both executed.'[4]

Despite his taste for blood, Herod did have a more constructive side to his nature and during his reign built or re-built (as mentioned above) a great many new towns, towers and palaces including the Phasael (later known as the 'Tower of David'), the Antonia fortress, the Macharus and in particular the Second Temple in Jerusalem (erected, it is said, on the remains of King Solomon's temple), a building upon whose steps Jesus would later preach. The construction of the temple, under Herod's guidance, was undertaken with great extravagance. According to accounts found in the Talmud, it was built from yellow, white and blue marble and parts of it were gilded with real gold. 'To strangers,' wrote Josephus in *The Jewish War*, 'as they approached it seemed in the distance like a mountain covered with snow; for any part not covered with gold was dazzling white.' Josephus also recorded that while it was under construction it only rained at night, taken as a sign from God that work should not be hindered. Herod had more than 10,000 men and 1,000 priests working on the project and made a monumental effort not to offend orthodox Jews by, for instance, using unhewn stone to construct the altar so that the blocks would not have been touched by iron.

The temple took forty-six years to complete and when it was finished it resembled a city within a city. There were cloisters, inner temples, forecourts, inner courts, bridges, etc and it attracted thousands of people including priests, scribes, musicians, moneychangers and engineers. But, despite the painstaking craftsmanship, despite its elegance, grandeur and importance to Jerusalem, in AD70 the Romans, while crushing a Jewish revolt, razed the temple to the ground. (Today all that remains are sections of the outside western wall, better known as the Wailing Wall, which is a holy site for Jews who insert prayers between the crumbling stones.)

Herod made one fateful mistake while constructing the edifice, though, for above the main entrance he placed a golden eagle – a symbol of Roman authority. In an instant he disenfranchised all those pious Jews he was attempting to placate. A group of Torah students led by a young man by the name of Judus, climbed the temple, removed the eagle and smashed it to pieces, an act Herod saw as a direct threat to his sovereignty. He had the students hunted down, captured and taken in chains to Jericho where they were tried in one of the Roman amphitheatres and afterwards burned alive.

With the construction of the Second Temple Herod had hoped to be remembered long after he was dead. Indeed, under his rule vast amounts of money were spent on erecting buildings in his honour. Herod's private expenditure was also vast and, like many despots after him, most of his money came from exploiting his subjects. Herod confiscated the estates of his enemies and pocketed the profits himself. He also taxed the populace, raking off most of the proceeds. But as the historian Paul Johnson notes, working in Herod's favour is the fact that under his rule the country was very prosperous 'thanks to external peace, internal order and expanding trade.' With Herod, however, the negative aspects of his regime always outweighed the positive. When it came to upsetting the Jews and offending their sense of tradition, he was second to none. In addition to the eagle fiasco, several buildings were constructed on Herod's orders that he knew would upset the Jews, pagan buildings such as theatres and amphitheatres which went directly against Jewish law.

But if Herod could upset the Jews *en masse*, it was nothing to the way he upset his own kith and kin.

Mariamme had had two sons by Herod: Alexander and Aristobulus, but Herod had also taken other wives and two of their children, Salome and Pheroras, believing Herod favoured their two half-brothers, began spreading ugly rumours to the effect that they

This illustration shows Herod cowering in terror from the ghost of his wife, Mariamme, who had been falsely accused of adultery and plotting against him. Herod had both Mariamme and her alleged lover put to death.

wanted to kill their father and seize control of Judaea. Yet another of Herod's children, his eldest son Antipater, fuelled the disputes even more. Eventually Herod, terrified of what was being said, asked Rome to put Alexander and Aristobulus on trial for treason. This was done and the two men were taken to Berytus where they were swiftly condemned by an assembly of judges after which, on their father's orders, they were starved to death.

But Antipater didn't escape punishment either. After his two stepbrothers had died, he was sent on a mission to Rome. During his absence Herod discovered his plotting and on his return Antipater was also condemned to death.

It seemed as if there was no escape either from Herod's wrath or his paranoia, the latter of which spawned an atrocity most famously recorded in the Gospel of Matthew (although it doesn't appear in any other canonical gospel or secular historical account unless you believe that events recorded in Jeremiah, 31:15 refer to the Massacre, 'Thus saith the LORD; A voice was heard in Ramah, lamentation, and bitter weeping; Rachel weeping for her children refused to be comforted for her children, because they were not.') The incident became known as the Slaughter of the Innocents. When Herod received the three wise men and heard them ask, 'Where is he that is born King of the Jews? For we have seen his star in the east, and are come to worship him', he was enraged. After all, who would dare to refer to himself as king of the Jews when Herod rightfully owned that title? Herod brooded over what the wise men had imparted and finally decided on a drastic course of action, namely the slaughtering of every male child in the kingdom under the age of two. Subsequently an angel 'of the Lord' appeared to Joseph in a dream, '…saying, Arise, and take the young child and his mother, and flee into Egypt, and be thou there until I bring thee word: for Herod will seek the young child to destroy him.

> 'When he [Joseph] arose, he took the young child and his mother
> by night, and departed into Egypt:
> 'And was there until the death of Herod: that it might be fulfilled
> which was spoken of the Lord by the prophet, saying, Out of
> Egypt have I called my son.
> ' Then Herod when he saw that he was mocked of the wise men,
> was exceeding wroth, and sent forth and slew all the children that
> were in Bethlehem, and in all the coasts thereof, from two years
> old and under, according to the time which he had diligently
> inquired of the wise men.'[5]

That this was the action of a tyrant can be in no doubt, although estimates of the number of infants slaughtered varies from between 10,000 to 150,000. Whatever the actual number of murders committed, the act itself marked Herod out as a particularly loathsome individual who would stop at nothing to hold on to power.

With his sons dead and the blood of innocent children on his hands, Herod's already dubious position within Judaea grew even more unstable. His health had also begun to suffer although no one knew precisely what it was that ailed the old man. Josephus described Herod as suffering variously from coughing, itching, fever and worms. Another very vivid description of his illness can be found once again in Robert Graves's *Claudius the God*:

'I never heard that it had any name but *Herod's Evil* or that anyone else had ever suffered from it before him, but the symptoms were a ravenous hunger followed by vomiting, a putrescent stomach, a corpse-like breath, maggots breeding in the privy member, and a constant watery flow from the bowels. The disease caused him intolerable anguish and inflamed to madness an already savage nature.'[6] However, still more scholars have speculated that perhaps Herod's illness might have been psychological. After all, this was the man who had ordered that his own wife and sons be put to death. What isn't in dispute is that Herod had grown into a very frail old man. Towards the end of his life it is said that he changed his will three times and disinherited many of his surviving children. Immediately after his death, Rome swept down on Jerusalem and in AD 6 Judea, at the Jews' request (they were terrified that one or other of Herod's surviving sons might take over where their father had left off) became a Roman province. Despite the Jews' hatred of their lord and master, however, Herod was buried in an exceptionally lavish ceremony, best described by Josephus: 'There was a solid gold bier, adorned with precious stones and draped with the richest purple. On it lay the body wrapped in crimson, with a diadem on the head and above that a golden crown, and the sceptre by the right hand. The bier was escorted by Herod's sons and the whole body of his kinsmen, followed by his Spearmen, the Thracian Company, and his Germans and Gauls, all in full battle order, headed by their commanders and all the officers and followed by five hundred freedmen carrying spices.'[7]

Herod was perhaps the first despot the world had ever had the misfortune to experience. Sadly he would not be the last.

[1] *A History of the Jews*, Paul Johnson, Orion Books, 1993.

[2] As referred to in the Book of Obadiah, from the Old Testament

[3] *Jewish Antiquities*, Flavius Josephus, translated by W. Whiston, www.ccel.org/j/josephus.

[4] *Claudius the God*, Robert Graves, Penguin Books, 1943.

[5] Authorized (King James) Version of the Holy Bible, St Matthew, 2: 14-16.

[6] *Claudius the God*, Robert Graves, Penguin Books, 1943.

[7] *The Jewish War*, Flavius, translated by G.A. Williamson, New York, Penguin Books, 1959.

GENGHIS KHAN
Oceanic Warrior

Perhaps the route to power pursued by Genghis Khan seemed for so long like an act of bravado against reason or like a miracle that we only consider the external circumstances and the apparent equilibrium of powers. However, he was as logical and calculating as the next man, and he operated only within the realm of the possible and based his plans on that reality.

From *L'Empire Jaune de Gengis Khan* (*The Yellow Empire of Genghis Khan*), by Joachim Barckhausen, Paris, 1935.

It was the Chinese who, during the Tang Dynasty, in annals written around the 7th century, first mentioned the word 'Mongol' in respect of nomadic groups who camped around Siberia's Amur River. Geographically, Mongolia was sandwiched between China and Russia in Central Asia. It was a tough terrain; a mixture of mountainous highland and wide-open plains. To the south stretched the Gobi desert which the nomads used as they travelled between China and Iran; to the north stood high mountain ranges with fast-flowing rivers, although the dense forests there at least provided some shelter.

The people of Mongolia were not an organized society; they were a pastoral people who, although they often gathered together during annual migrations, never otherwise gathered as a single mass. The only common factor affecting them all was a shared religion, one that focused on natural deities such as sky-gods, tree-gods and river-gods. In this respect, they were similar to the Japanese who practised Shinto. In spite of their religion, however, the Mongols lived in a state of constant anarchy for many centuries, although there was a myth that by the beginning of the 12th century a man would appear to unite their number and lead them to a great destiny.

Genghis Khan was born around 1155-62 on the banks of the Onon River which is near the present-day border between Mongolia and south-eastern Russia. His father was a Mongol chieftain by the name of Yesügei and came from the Borjigin clan. His mother was a woman called Hö'elün who came from the Märkit tribe. Genghis Khan was born with the name Temujin which in translation means 'iron worker'. There are many stories surrounding his birth, including one that he was clutching a blood clot when he was born thus presaging that he was destined to become a great leader of men. Other stories attributed him a supernatural birth; that he was the offspring of a brown doe and a gray-blue wolf or that he was a descendant of Alan Qu'a, a woman who had been impregnated by a ray of sunlight.

Although very little is known about Temujin's childhood, it is believed that as a young boy he was engaged to be married to a girl called Börte, the daughter of another chieftain. However, at the age of about nine or ten, Temujin's father was killed, poisoned by a rival tribe. The young Temujin subsequently attempted to persuade his own tribe that he should now become chieftain in place of his father, but his plan was rejected and Temujin, his mother, his three brothers and sister were expelled from the group. Life on the plains without the support of a clan was tough. Food was difficult to come by and it is believed that an early example of Temujin's ruthlessness occurred during this period, when he caught one of his brothers attempting to steal food from the family and killed him. Of course, this story quickly established Temujin's reputation as a hard taskmaster, someone who shouldn't be crossed, no matter who you were. Another story dating from this period related how, while out hunting one day, he was ambushed and kidnapped by an enemy clan who took him back to their camp and imprisoned him. But Temujin killed his guard, escaped and, although the enemy clan went in search of him, due to his excellent survival skills Temujin evaded capture and returned to the family group.

Eventually, having lived on the plains in virtual exile from his father's tribe, Temujin went in search of his childhood fiancée's father who belonged to the Qongirat clan. He was well received and the marriage between himself and Börte went ahead as planned. (In future years Genghis Khan would take many wives and concubines, but it was always Börte, his first wife, who remained the principal female in his life.) Börte gave birth to Temujin's four most famous sons; namely Jochi, whose own son Batu is said to have founded the empire of the Golden Horde in Russia and eastern Europe; Jagatai who ruled in Central Asia; Ögödei who after Genghis Khan died ruled in northern China; and finally Tolui who followed his father into battle and razed the city of Merv to the ground.

Temujin, who as a dowry was given a black sable coat that subsequently became the foundation of his huge fortune, now had the backing of his new wife's tribe and thereby achieved a certain status that he hadn't enjoyed since the death of his father. But at the same time he also wanted to re-establish links with his original clan and, therefore, visited a man by the name of Togrul who had been his father's sworn brother and the leader of the Kereit, a tribe in central Mongolia. Togrul promised Temujin that he would do everything in his power to re-unite the

Although legend has it that he was born of a brown doe and a gray-blue wolf, Genghis Khan was actually the son of a Mongol clan chieftan.

young man with his original group as well as with his father's relations. But before this could occur a group of Märkit kidnapped Börte.

Initially, Temujin was forced to flee to the mountains where he remained hidden for several weeks, but eventually he regrouped with Togrul and another young chieftain by the name of Jamuka and together the three of them rescued Börte and defeated the Märkit. Word of Temujin, Togrul and Jamuka's bravery then spread far and wide and increasing numbers of Mongols joined them so that, as a group, they could defeat their common enemies. And, for a time, this strategy worked. Temujin, Togrul and Jamuka remained friends, setting up their respective camps in close proximity to one another, herding their animals together and generally living in peace side by side. But sadly, the peace was short-lived for the three men fell out. This split in allegiances mirrored the greater political picture of the time; one in which friendships and alliances were in a constant state of flux and where you could never be 100 per cent certain of where your friends' loyalties lay. The split between Temujin, Togrul and Jamuka was then further exacerbated when around 1195-96 chieftains of several different Mongol tribes called a *khuriltai* (an assembly) and announced Temujin their Khan, in addition to which they gave him the name, Genghis. There is some debate as to the translation of this name, but generally it is believed to stand for one of the following: either 'precious warrior' or 'spirit of light' or most likely of all, 'oceanic warrior'. The latter translation

The barbarous, anarchic reputation of Genghis Khan's cavalry soldiers belied the sophisticated organisational structure of his army.

derives from the Turkic word *tengiz* meaning, 'a large body of water' and although it has not been universally accepted, the fact that the ocean symbolizes both breath and depth of wisdom leads many scholars to believe this is the closest source. Whatever the translation, however, the meaning was obvious – Temujin was from now on to be hailed lord of all he surveyed.

Genghis Khan now set about laying down a series of laws that, over a period of years, became known as the *Ih Zasaq* or *Yasaq* (the Great Law). Sadly, little remains of the original codes, but they are thought by many scholars to have strongly relied on ancestral traditions and to have been moral in content so that they could be referred to in all matters when a judgement was required. Take as an example this description by the historian Juvaini:

'In accordance and agreement with his own mind, he established a rule for every occasion and a regulation for every circumstance; while for every crime he fixed a penalty. And since the Tartar peoples had no script of their own, he gave orders that Mongol children should learn writing from the Uighur [a Turkic people], and that these "yasas" [laws] and ordinances should be written down on rolls. These rolls are called the Great Book of "yasas" and are kept in the treasury of the chief princes.'[1]

Despite Temujin having been appointed Khan, there were still a handful of Mongol tribes who were not overjoyed at his election for, according to tradition, they believed there could only be one emperor on earth, just as there was only one god in heaven. First and foremost amongst this number was Temujin's friend and ally Togrul, leader of the Kereit. Temujin, in a rare offer of friendship, gave Togrul the chance to lay down his arms and surrender to him and his men, an offer Togrul declined. Instead, several bloody battles ensued resulting in the destruction of the Kereit army. When Togrul was caught, he asked Genghis to execute him without spilling any of his blood. Genghis obliged and had Togrul beaten and suffocated. After this defeat and execution, it is said that the last Mongol tribe who questioned Genghis Khan's leadership was defeated circa 1204.

In 1206, for the second time, a *khuriltai* was convened and Genghis Khan was once again proclaimed leader of all the Mongols. This was probably a more serious assembly than the previous one, given Genghis Khan's new reputation as a slayer of men. Genghis Khan then resolved to conquer as much land and as many people as possible and build up an empire over which he could rule. Below is a small prose/poem, which has been attributed to Genghis Khan and which sums up his new headstrong, bloodthirsty attitude.

> The greatest happiness is
> To vanquish your enemies,
> To chase them before you,
> To rob them of their wealth,
> To see those dear to them
> Bathed in tears, to clasp to
> Your bosom their wives
> And daughters.

In the beginning, Genghis Khan's army was exclusively cavalry. Being nomads, this was, of course, a natural choice as most Mongolians learned to ride from an early age and were excellent equestrians. The horses also allowed Genghis Khan's army to travel vast distances, in particular because the Mongolian stock on which they rode was a typically hardy breed which could cover the huge open plains on very little food. But it soon became clear to everyone that cities could not be vanquished using horses alone. Instead, Genghis Khan began to build up a huge arsenal of weapons including mangonels, which were a medieval form of machine for catapulting stones. He also trained his men to use javelins and smaller catapults than the mangonels which could be used by individual soldiers. A lot of this weaponry was, in fact, invented by Chinese engineers and later, when Genghis Khan invaded the Iran/Afghanistan territories, he also took on board several of their weapons including ballista which were similar to the mangonels but shaped like crossbows for firing extremely large arrows over huge distances.

But perhaps Genghis Khan's greatest gift to his troops was the great organizational skill he brought to bear on them. In particular, he based his army on the decimal system. The largest unit was called a *tjumen* and consisted of 10,000 fully trained troops. A normal army would be made up of three *tjumens*, one of which would be solely infantry whose job it was to engage in close combat. The other two troops would be cavalry whose job it was to encircle the enemy from both left and right. Each *tjumen* would then be made up from ten regiments, each consisting of 1,000 men. These 1,000 units were named *mingghan* and each of these in turn consisted of ten squadrons of 100 men which were called *jaghun*. The *jaghun* were further divided into 10 units of 10 men each called *arban*. With reference to the structure of command, each *arban* would elect their leader by majority vote and each of the 10 elected *arban* leaders would afterwards vote for a commander of each *jaghun* and so on upwards, although Genghis Khan alone was responsible for naming the commanders of each *mingghan* and *tjumen* who were then given the title of *noyon*. All appointments were made, not by social rank or age, but on ability alone and it is also worth mentioning that while each man was intended to participate in major offensives in a co-ordinated manner, he was also expected to be self-sufficient and have within his means the capacity for independent thought. In this way Genghis Khan built up his army, but the organization of the troops was only one innovation that he brought with him, for Genghis Khan was also a great tactician and introduced many new military manoeuvres to his men. One of the most strategic of these was based on the concept of retreat. It is an old Asiatic principle that one must be yielding when one's opponent is strong, but go on the offensive at the first sign of weakness. Indeed, Genghis Khan's men developed this technique into a fine art, often retreating at the first sign of trouble only to lure their opponent into a false sense of security, thus revealing their weak spots, after which the Mongolians would attack in earnest.

Another manoeuvre was to spread five squadrons of men as widely apart as was possible. Two squadrons would take forward positions, three would stay further back, but when fighting commenced those in the rear would surge forward shooting hails of arrows at the enemy. After this offensive the rear troops would fall back and ensure that none of the enemy escaped while the front two ranks would charge and deliver the decisive blow – often through close combat with knives, swords and occasionally martial art techniques. On top of this 'two/three' strategy, encirclement was also used as a means of crushing the enemy. This required mobility and a fleetness of foot, but the Mongols were experts in both, in particular because they wore very light armour. All of the above techniques were employed by the great Khan's troops and so practiced did they become in the art of war that they were rarely defeated.

In 1207, Genghis Khan launched a crusade to conquer vast areas of China.

At this time, China was divided into three separate kingdoms: the Tangut and Jin kingdoms in the north and the Sung kingdom in the South. Genghis began his attack on the Jin, but it was heavy going and it took almost two years before any progress was made. In the meantime, he took advantage of the slowness of this campaign to conquer a second territory, Manchuria, which was no mean feat as it measured 386,000 square miles. Finally, Genghis Khan attacked and conquered Peking – without doubt one of his finest achievements – after which both the Tangut and Jin kingdoms fell under his control. However, the fighting had not been without heavy casualties and it was recorded by the Taoist monk Ch'ang-ch'un that the battlegrounds were so thick with corpses, he could still see evidence of them nine years after the war had finished.

Leaving one of his most trusted generals, Mugali, in control of the Chinese campaign, Ghenghis Khan now turned his attention to the Mongolian border with Khwarizim, a vast empire that today encapsulates Turkmentistan, Uzbekistan and Tajikistan as well as Afghanistan and most of Iran.

During this period, Khwarizim was under the control of Ala ad-Din Muhammad, who was better known as the Shah of Khwarizim. Many scholars indicate that the origins of this war were due to the slaughter of a Mongolian caravan together with a large deputation of Mongolian ambassadors by Ala ad-Din Muhammad's men at Otrar on the Syr Darya River. Subsequently, Genghis Khan ordered that the Shah be turned over to the Mongolians, otherwise there would be bloodshed. Of course, this request was denied and war was declared.

Setting out for Khwarizim, Genghis Khan and his army spent most of the summer of 1219 on the Irtysh River, only arriving in Otrar later that autumn. He then left a large platoon of his men to besiege Otrar (in point of fact it fell after only two days), while he continued westwards with the main body of his army (approximately 120,000 men) to attack Bukhara. This he did in 1220, but much as in Otrar, the army met with very little resistance after which Genghis Khan, eager to make good progress, marched his men towards Samarkand where they also met with little or no opposition.

But this didn't stop the Mongolian army from looting and pillaging and then burning everything in their wake. Far from it; this was part and parcel of their whole campaign for they recognized that any survivors would then spread the word and tell the world how ruthless and terrifying it was to go to war against Genghis Khan's army.

Having taken Samarkand, Genghis Khan now went after his ultimate prey, the Shah himself, but the latter fled in terror, finally ending up on an island in the Caspian Sea where it is said he died in despair around 1220-21.

This wasn't the end of the dispute, however, for the Shah's son pursued the battle and succeeded in inflicting a defeat on the Mongol forces at Parvan, just north of Kabul, after which he drove them out of Sogdiana. Tragically for Iran and Afghanistan, Genghis Khan then released the full force of his wrath on both territories and between 1221-22 whole districts were wiped out. Cities were burnt to the ground; entire populations were put to the sword. In Merv (which alongside Baghdad, Cairo and Damascus was one of the most important capitals of Islam and which was often referred to as the 'Queen of Cities'), Genghis Khan's son, Tolui, is said to have reduced the buildings to rubble, killing over 700,000 men, women and children. And near Bamiyan in Afghanistan's Hindu Kush there are the remains of two towns, Chahr-I Golgola (the City of Sighs) and Chahr-I Zohag (the Red City) both of which were razed to the ground by the Mongols. According to Juvaini the following then occurred: 'A quarrel, which gave no respite, was discharged from the town [Bamiyan] and hit a son of Chaghatai, the favourite grandchild of Chingiz-Khan. The Mongols made the greater haste to capture the town, and when it was taken Chingiz-Khan gave orders that every living creature, from mankind down to the brute beasts, should be killed; that no prisoner should be taken; that not even the child in its mother's womb should be spared.'[2]

Indeed, so devastating was the destruction wreaked by Genghis Khan and his armies that some scholars have likened it to present-day nuclear warfare. Cities, towns, villages were obliterated, deserts were overrun by crowds of people fleeing from the devastation and as the army marched on, often the only living creatures that remained in their wake would be flocks of vultures and other birds of prey.

Nor was Genghis Khan's personal reputation much better. Although several portraits show him as a grandfatherly man with a long white beard and laughter lines round his eyes, these were painted after his death, in particular by the Yüans of China and the Il-khans of Iran, who were fascinated by the man who had conquered their forbears. This image stood in direct contrast to the reality of the great Khan. So brutal was he that it is well nigh impossible to imagine the depths to which he and his men would sink in the name of victory. Some of the legends surrounding his methods of torture and execution were no doubt exaggerated for propaganda purposes, but there are others that are certainly not unfounded - such as when he had prisoners thrown into pots of boiling oil, decapitated or tied to horses and dragged over miles and miles of rough terrain.

Despite all these horror stories, Genghis Khan was also said to have a more reflective side to his nature, showing a considerable amount of interest in religion and philosophy. Take, for example, the following description:

'Being the adherent of no religion and the follower of no creed, he [Genghis Khan] eschewed bigotry, and the preference of one faith to another, and the placing of some above others; rather he honoured and respected the learned and pious of every sect.... And as he viewed the Moslems with the eye of respect, so also did he hold the Christians and [Buddhist] idolaters in high esteem. As for his children and grandchildren, several of them have chosen a religion according to their inclination, some adopting Islam, others embracing Christianity, others selecting idolatry and others again cleaving to the ancient canon of their fathers and forefathers...'[3]

Nevertheless, when it came to fighting, Genghis Khan would not bend to anyone's will or accept defeat. In the case of Shah Mohammad's son, Shah Jalal ad-Din Mingburnu, the great Khan drove him and his forces as far back as the Indus Valley that lies in the western part of South Asia in what today is Pakistan and western India. By the end of 1221 Shah ad-Din Mingburnu had abandoned the fighting and fled. Once again, Genghis Khan had succeeded in winning the battle, although he didn't pursue Shah ad-Din Mingburnu into India's heartlands, some say because he knew his troops couldn't survive or function adequately in such a hot climate.

Meanwhile, those of Genghis Khan's troops who had remained in Iran after the defeat of Shah Mohammad had to make their way back to Mongolia, but rather than cross the Caucasus Mountains, they travelled instead via Georgia. At this point the Georgians were in the ascendant. They had enjoyed several decades of strong independent rule - firstly under David the Confessor (1089-1129) and also during the reign of Queen Thamar (1184-1213) and were, therefore, a force to be reckoned with. Genghis Khan's troops, under the dual leadership of Jebe and Subotai, first met with the Kipchak Turks who, on seeing the strength of the Mongol army, turned for help to several Russian princes. The Russians' war tactics, however, were no match for the Mongolian troops and shortly thereafter the

Genghis Khan's ruthless reputation was enhanced at Merv, known as the Queen of Cities and one of the most important Islamic centers, in 1221. Khan's forces, under his son Tolui, destroyed the city and massacred 700,000 men, women and children.

Kipchak Turks and Russians were defeated at the Kalka River. Jebe and Subotai then led their men around the Caspian Sea and rejoined Genghis Khan in central Asia.

In the space of four years Genghis Khan and his men had travelled a distance of approximately 12,500 miles and defeated five of the greatest nations in the world. His empire now stretched from the Pacific Ocean to the Baltic and the Mediterranean (in essence covering more than 11,500,000 square miles or 30,000,000 square kilometres, which is a territory almost three times the size of North America). The Mongol influence also affected territories to the south of India where the various rajahs were said to have recognized Genghis Khan's authority. But victory comes at a price, if not for the conquerors then for those they have defeated and the massive destruction that accompanied Genghis Khan's onslaughts became legendary.

Although some descriptions, as has already been mentioned, were exaggerated for propaganda purposes, most scholars believe that the Mongols were amongst the fiercest and most bloodthirsty of all fighting forces. The following extract is from a letter written to the archbishop of Bordeaux by Hyon de Narbonnes:

'Their leaders feed on cadavers like it was bread and leave to the vultures only bones…. Old and ugly women were given to these cannibals…to serve as their nourishment during the day. As for those who were pretty, they abstained from eating them but, despite their cries and their lamentations, they smothered them under multitudes of violations that they made them submit to. They sullied virgins until they gave up the ghost, then cutting off their breasts that they reserved for their chiefs as a delicacy, they dined on the remains with gluttony.'[4]

Genghis Khan is believed to have arrived back in Mongolia around 1225. After so many years of battle, he had aged badly and his health was further affected by a riding accident that had both injured and exhausted him. But great leaders of men do not have time for rest and recuperation. He had a vast kingdom to rule and armies to manage and Tangut, whom he had vanquished so many years previously and who had promised to rally behind him, had failed to do so. Genghis Khan couldn't let this pass without punishment.

The winter of 1225-26 saw the great Mongol leader crossing the Gobi desert with the mainstay of his army. The journey was arduous, but Genghis Khan, determined to crush the Tangut, marched without let-up. Finally battle commenced and although there is not a great deal of information about the fighting, most scholars agree it was a short-lived affair, the Tangut being swiftly defeated. On what happened afterwards, however, opinion is divided, for some scholars believe Genghis Khan died during the battle and never saw his enemy vanquished, while others insist he died after the fighting was over in an accident while out hunting.

Whatever the case, all are agreed that on his deathbed he divided his kingdom between his surviving sons, telling them, '…my life was too short to achieve the conquest of the world. That is left to you.' The year was 1227 and the whole Mongol nation was plunged into despair. Their great Khan was dead and the only thing left for them to do now was to bury him with honour and with the most flamboyant funeral rites. To this end, the thousands of captured Tangut soldiers were slaughtered, after which some scholars believe Genghis Khan's body was carried back to the place of his birth, north-east of Ulaanbaatar. According to legend, anyone who laid eyes on the funeral procession was executed so that no one would know of the great Khan's death until a successor had been named. Another legend has it that the cart carrying his body became stuck in boggy ground in the Ordos region of China and only became free again after prayers were made to Genghis Khan's spirit not to abandon all those who worshipped him. Afterwards the Mongols built a shrine at Ordos and today the Genghis Khan Mausoleum is located in the middle of the Ordos grassland. No one knows the exact location of the great Khan's grave, but holy pilgrimages are made to this site every day and holy ceremonies are held here four times a year to honour his memory.

After Genghis Khan's death, his son Tolui (1193-1232) was charged with overall responsibility for the Mongols. Always a favourite of Genghis Khan's, particularly because he had acquitted himself so well during the Merv campaign, he was often referred to as the 'Prince of Fire'. Nevertheless, although Tolui tried his utmost to live up to his father's reputation, no one could be expected to succeed to the extent that the great Khan had done. In fact, several civilizations attempted the same – that is, to create or recreate the glory of the Mongol Empire – but, like Tolui, each in turn failed. Firstly there was Tamerlane (1336 – 1405) who, after Genghis Khan himself, was the most influential military leader of the Middle Ages. Later came his descendants, the Timurids, who founded the Great Mughal Empire in India (which was later inherited by Queen Victoria). There was also the Manchu who established the Ch'ing dynasty in China, but none of the above could claim anything like the influence of Genghis Khan. After all, this was a man who had extended his territory from Poland to Siberia, from Moscow to the Arabian Peninsula and from Siberia to Vietnam. There was no one like him, not even his grandson the great Kublai Khan (Tolui's son) who was immortalized by Samuel Taylor Coleridge in his famous poem of that name, could come close in comparison. Even today we speak of the great man, referring to anyone displaying fascist tendencies as someone a 'little to the right of Genghis Khan'. For someone who lived as far back as the 12th century, that is quite an achievement.

[1] *The History of the World Conqueror* by 'Ala-ad-Din 'Ata-Malik Juvaini,
    trans John Andrew Boyle, Manchester University Press, 1958.
[2] *Genghis Khan: The History of the World Conqueror*, by 'Ala-ad-Din 'Ata-Malik
    Juvaini, trans unknown.
[3] *Genghis Khan: The History of the World Conqueror*, by 'Ala-ad-Din 'Ata-Malik
    Juvaini, trans unknown.
[4] *Genghis Khan and the Mongol Empire*, by Jean-Paul Roux,
    Thames & Hudson, 2003.

SHAKA ZULU

An African King

Round his bare head he wore a circlet of otter skin, bearing
within its circumference bunches of gorgeous red loury plumes,
and erect in front, a high glossy blue feather, two feet in length, of
the blue crane. Hanging over his shoulders and chest was a fringe
three inches long of manufactured "tails" of spotted genet and
blue grey monkey fur. Depending from the hips almost to the
knees, and completely circling the body, was a kilt of numberless
similar "tails" of the same furs.

The Annals of Natal: 1495-1845,
by Henry Fynn (compiled by John Bird), 1966.

After Nelson Mandela, it is probably safe to say that the most famous South
African in history is Shaka Zulu. Known throughout the Zulu kingdom as a
fierce warrior who killed a leopard at nineteen, who built up an invincible
army from a core of less than five hundred men and who, over the course of his twelve-
year reign, was responsible for the murder of over one million people, Shaka Zulu, or
'King Shaka' as he is sometimes also known, was a ruthless leader who wielded
incredible power.

Shaka Zulu was born around 1785-87, the illegitimate child of a woman called
Nandi (a member of the Langeni tribe) and Senzangakona who was a young Zulu
chieftain. As a consequence of this unfortunate start in life, Shaka grew up in a less
than welcoming environment, for his mother was shunned by her tribe and, according
to legend, Shaka was teased and ridiculed because of his bastard origins.

At an early age, Shaka was put to work as a shepherd in E-Langeni-land, but even
while tending his flock, other children took great pleasure in bullying the young boy.
Throughout his childhood it is said that he cut an extremely lonely figure.

Nonetheless, by the age of nineteen, Shaka was already a formidable fighter, a fact
backed up by the story in which he kills a leopard. The leopard had been 'treed' (that
is chased into a tree in order to be killed). Shaka threw the first spear, but the weapon
didn't lodge in the animal's heart, instead the leopard jumped out of the tree and
advanced towards Shaka who, rather than retreating, waited until the animal was upon
him before clubbing it to death.

Perhaps because of this show of strength or perhaps because he had grown up to
be well-liked and respected, at the age of twenty-three Shaka Zulu was called to serve
as a soldier for the Mtetwa tribe.

'His regiment had its own kraal [homestead], *Ema-Ngweni*, and their captain was

Buza. Shaka was issued with an oval shield measuring 5ft 9in by 3ft and three throwing *assegais* [spears]. He wore the uniform – white oxtails at ankles and wrists, a kilt of fur strips, a skin cap with black widow-bird plumes, and ox-hide *ixi-xatuba* sandals.'[1]

He must have cut an imposing figure and for the next six years he acquitted himself admirably within his unit. At the same time he also began to seek better, more efficient tactics and weapons with which to kill the enemy. To this end Shaka is said to have designed a new type of blade for his spear, one that was stronger than the previous lightweight *assegais*. Shaka wanted to use freshly smelted or virgin iron so that the new spearhead could be beaten into the exact shape he required. The blacksmith to whom he went is said to have built a new bellows and furnace for the purpose, after which a clean bar of iron was beaten out using granite blocks. The result was exactly as Shaka had dreamed, a spear of great beauty and effectiveness. Indeed so lethal was the new weapon that Shaka gave it its own name, the '*Ixwa*' and although there is no direct or indirect translation of this word, some people have wondered whether it wasn't onomatopoeic, describing the sucking sound the blade would have made when it was pulled from the flesh.

Shaka Zulu also introduced heavier shields made out of cowhide and later showed his men how best to use their new weapons. For instance, he demonstrated that by using the new shield's left side to hook the enemy's shield to the right, it could expose the enemy's ribs to such an extent that they could be stabbed much more easily. Finally, in order to toughen the troops up, Shaka made them train and fight with bare feet. He argued that not only would this strengthen their reserves, it would also make them swifter. So for hours they ran over the desert, over hot rocks and thorn bushes until the soles of their feet were tough enough to withstand any amount of pain or discomfort. And Shaka's new weaponry and new tactics must have worked, for in several encounters with rival tribes his reputation as a warrior was second to none. In 1810 Shaka, in a battle against the Butelezis tribe, is said to have single-handedly struck down several opponents with his new, broad-bladed spear, after which the remaining Butelezis

As well as being revered as a great warrior in his own right, Shaka Zulu rigorously trained and disciplined his men, turning them into a formidable fighting force.

fled in terror. Many myths arose around Shaka Zulu, the most colorful of which is the tale of the Mad Giant.

This man of enormous stature was said to have built himself a kraal on the side of a hill within the boundaries of one of Shaka's fellow warrior's land. The giant was wrecking havoc, stealing livestock and terrorizing local women and children and if anyone challenged him he would charge at them with an axe, muttering evil spells as he did so. Everyone was afraid of the Mad Giant, until Shaka Zulu came forward and felled him with a single blow.

Whether this story is true, it does serve to illustrate how, over the next several years, Shaka built up a reputation within his small fighting unit to such an extent that when discussions were held as to who should succeed after his father, Senzangakona, to the Zulu chieftainship, Shaka's name was presented as one of the strongest contenders. Meantime, Shaka was given overall control of the Zulu army, a position he relished and one that allowed him to refine his battle tactics and leadership qualities. He trained his warriors rigorously, punishing them for the slightest disobedience and drilling into them that they were answerable only to him as their commander-in-chief. It was a system that worked well and soon Shaka was in command of a formidable fighting force.

By 1815 Shaka Zulu's father was on his deathbed. Early the next year he died. As was the Zulu custom when burying a chieftain, his body was wrapped in the hide of a black bull after which it was kept in a hut guarded by five warriors. A fire outside was kept constantly alight. After a period of some days, Shaka Zulu's father was buried in the Mpembeni Valley (*Makosini* – The Place of the Chiefs). At the burial ceremony his two chief servants were executed so that they could accompany their master on his journey.

Shaka had been earmarked to succeed his father as Chieftain. However, after the burial ceremony he learned that this was not to be so. Instead, one of Shaka's half-brothers by the name of Sigujana took over that mantle. Shaka was furious, as were his men, but it took another of Shaka's half-brothers, Ngwadi (son of Nandi by a marriage to Gendeyana), to put an end to Sigujana's usurpation. Shaka Zulu now took over the role of leader of the Zulus and without further ado entered his dead father's kraal. He began reshaping the whole Zulu clan, summoning all of the men and enrolling them in his 'army'. The older men, those between thirty and forty years of age, were formed into the *Ama-Wombe* regiment, the younger men were brigaded into the *Jubingqwanga* regiment and finally there was Shaka's own regiment, the *U-Fasimba,* whose warriors were made up of mainly twenty-year-old youths. Shaka built each unit a new kraal, which acted much like a garrison or barracks does today. Such organization was unknown to the Zulus and yet everyone complied knowing that their new leader was not a man to be crossed.

The first true act of aggression instigated by Shaka Zulu in his new role of chieftain was against the *E-Langeni* – the same tribe he had grown up with and therefore the same men, women and children who had subjected him to years of bullying. Shaka had never forgiven his tormentors; now, as a chieftain in his own right, he decided to seek retribution. It was a dangerous task given that Shaka's forces numbered only 500 men and many of the other tribes were stronger than his own. And yet Shaka had several things in his favour, including the *Ixwa* spear and his own meticulous attention to detail. He trained his men hard, taking them out on manoeuvres, showing them how to ambush their enemies and how to put their spears to good use. Finally, having taught his men all that he could, he made a night march of twenty-five miles over the Mtonjaneni Heights towards his prey. By dawn Shaka and his men had surrounded not only the Esiweni kraal in E-Langeni land, but also the E-Langeni chief. At first light Shaka commanded that the E-Langeni surrender, which they did immediately without the slightest attempt to fight back. Shaka put on trial all those people against whom he still held a grudge. He cited a whole list of crimes from his childhood days for which he held them responsible. Shaka then divided the group into two, those whom he would pardon and those whom he could never forgive for their crimes. This second group were then brutally killed by being impaled on long poles and then burnt. The executions over and done with, the E-Langeni chieftain submitted to all Shaka's demands, one of which was that all the remaining male members of the tribe join Shaka's troops. No sooner said than it was done. Suddenly Shaka Zulu had doubled his forces.

Shaka Zulu returned to his home kraal, his reputation greatly enhanced. Neighbouring clans such as the Qungebeni, Sibiya and Gazini then began sending their own young men to join Shaka's troops, all of whom were subsequently put through a vigorous training period. Nor did it take long for Shaka to mount his second big attack, this time against a chieftain called Pungashe whose Butelezi clan lived to the west of Shaka's land. The fight when it came was like a short, sharp shock to Pungashe whose forces had never faced such organized, well-trained troops. In fear, they ran for cover amongst their women folk, but Shaka's men were out for blood and, closing in on the soldiers and civilians, slaughtered every last one. Naturally a handful of women and children escaped, but Shaka ordered that they be hunted down and captured alongside the Butelezi's cattle. Only Chief Pungashe managed to flee and later he sought refuge with another chieftain, of the Ndwandwe tribe.

Shaka returned to his homeland with the captured Butelezi women in tow. Those who weren't married (who numbered between 100-150) became Shaka's property and subsequently he divided them into three groups or 'seraglios' one of which was appointed to each of his military kraals. The fight against the Butelezi had been a great victory. In point of fact, under Shaka's rule the Zulus had almost quadrupled their territory and the Zulu army had grown in strength to such an extent that it numbered almost 2,000 soldiers.

According to E. A. Ritter in his book on Shaka Zulu, the next few months of his life were relatively tranquil, until, that is, he suspected his troops were harbouring witch doctors amongst them who were in danger of bringing bad luck to him and his men. Concerned at the implications of such an occurrence, Shaka summoned five witch-finders to inspect his kraals and 'smell out' the offenders.

'Nobela was the leader of the group. Her face was an evil mask streaked with white clay paint, which also covered her arms and legs. An assortment of dried and inflated bladders and snakeskins adorned her head and arms. Claws and teeth of leopards and hyaenas, and goats' horns hung from her neck, and over her shrunken breasts grinned the skulls of two baboons.'[2]

As might be expected everyone was terrified, not just by the sight of the witch-hunters, but also at the consequences of being accused of being a witch doctor, for everyone within the condemned man's kraal would be executed. Eventually, Nobela chose eleven men to be put to death and ordered that their kraals should also be wiped out and burnt, as was the law. But even then Nobela wasn't finished, for shortly afterwards she accused two of Shaka's closest friends of harbouring evil spirits. In an act that was almost unprecedented, it is said that Shaka challenged Nobela to prove her accusations were correct and that she and her co-witch-hunters weren't acting out of jealousy or spite. After much prevarication Nobela confessed that she and one of her group had indeed used their powers incorrectly. Shaka pardoned them, but thereafter made it known that he wouldn't countenance the 'indiscriminate use of power by diviners' and that he would have the final say in whether someone was guilty or not. In addition he also ruled that no one serving in the army would ever be subjected to a 'smelling out' again.

Subsequent to this ruling, Shaka's reputation as a ruler of great wisdom spread far and wide, not just within his own tribe, but further abroad. Huge numbers of people outside Shaka's territory began moving into Zululand so that they too could benefit from the protection of the laws of the wise warrior king. The men joined Shaka's growing army and none too soon for, shortly afterwards, war broke out between the Zulus and an opposing tribe called the Ndwandwes, led by a very powerful chieftain whose name was Zwide.

Zwide's tribe resided in a domain north-east of the Black Umfolozi River. He was a very ambitious warrior and had swelled his own army's ranks by subduing smaller tribes (including the Ema-Newangeni tribe) and combining them with his own.

Nevertheless, with approximately 3,600 heavily armed and well-trained men, Shaka Zulu marched northwards over the Umfolozi River towards Zwide's capital. All along the way Shaka looked after his troops, ensuring they were properly fed by butchering cattle they had brought with them expressly for that purpose. After a second day's march Shaka's men reached the upper waters of the Um-Mona River, which was a tributary of the Black Umfolozi. They were nearing their quarry and early the next morning one of Shaka's scouts reported seeing Zwide's troops near one of his principal kraals. Finally, Zwide manoeuvred his men onto a steep ridge near Nongoma. It was a strong position, one which Shaka Zulu instinctively knew he would have to break. He decided the best course of action would be to lure some of Zwide's men away from the ridge and attack them, after which Zwide would come to their rescue, giving Shaka ample opportunity to ambush his foe. The scheme worked and Shaka overwhelmed his opponents after which a dreadful slaughter ensued. The Ndwandwes, although formidable, didn't have either the iron discipline or the rigorous training that Shaka's troops enjoyed and within ten minutes it is said that over 1,000 of their number were killed. Despite this set-back, the Ndwandwes were not about to give up and once again they advanced on the Zulus and once again they sustained many injuries and loss of life. Eventually, the Ndwandwes decided to retreat, but Shaka, realizing victory was his, commanded his men to pursue the enemy and slaughter them as they ran. This was the Zulus' first great battle (known as the battle of Quokli) and under no circumstances

Lieutenant Farewell, a member of Henry Fynn's 1824 trading expedition, negotiating the barter of goods with Shaka Zulu.

was Shaka going to relinquish an inch of ground. In the event, he lost approximately 1,500 warriors, but the Ndwandwes lost far in excess of that number (in the region of 7,500). Moreover, those left wounded on the battlefield were quickly despatched by the Zulus after which their bodies were disembowelled.

It was shortly after this great battle that a young man called Mzilikazi Kumalo, who in the future would found the Matabele nation, joined Shaka's ranks. Training then continued even more rigorously than before and included several new tactics such as the 'buffalo' formation. In effect the 'buffalo' consisted of four troops of men who were divided into the two horns, the chest and the loins of the beast. During an attack the 'chest' of the buffalo would strike the enemy's front line while the 'horns' would strike the enemy's flanks thus encircling them. The 'loins' would remain hidden and would only be used when reinforcements were required. As for Shaka himself, he would operate the buffalo from afar – normally standing on high ground so that he could see all of the action – and with the aid of foot soldiers who acted as messengers, he conducted the fight. Every day, Shaka's men would be put through their paces, marching forty or fifty miles at a time, practicing army manoeuvres and, although Shaka looked after his men well, if anyone fell out of rank during these marches they were ruthlessly executed on the spot by a rearguard hand-picked by Shaka for this very purpose.

But Shaka's enemies were also training hard, in particular Zwide, who had escaped from the battle of Quokli. In fact, Zwide's fortunes were on the up, for several distinguished warriors (namely Soshangane and Zwangandaba) now decided to join his ranks, along with men from both northern and eastern territories.

Never one to leave anything to chance, Shaka had placed a spy in his enemy's camp, a man by the name of Joluju (in translation the 'Honey Man'), who in time told Shaka of a planned invasion of Zululand. In the meantime, however, Shaka had a different battle to fight, this time to the south of Zululand with the Quabe tribe whose chieftain, a man by the name of Pakatwayo, Shaka said had offended him.

The battle commenced in midwinter of 1818 and was swiftly won by the Zulus who, within less than an hour, had captured Pakatwayo. He subsequently suffered some type of fit and died.

Shaka's territory now measured some 7,000 square miles, stretching as it did from the White Umfolozi River in the north to the Tugela River in the south. In addition to this, Shaka had brought together over thirty disparate tribes and united them into one large military unit. By anyone's standards, this was an enormous achievement. Shaka also began revolutionizing agricultural production so that his people were never left short of food and he introduced a cadet branch to his army so that boys who were over the age of puberty, but under the age to become warriors, could begin training and serve the community at one and the same time.

Shaka now turned his attention back to Zwide. Only two small tribes stood between him and Shaka, the Dlaminis and the Zungus and it was only a matter of time before all-out war commenced and much blood was spilt. By May 1819 Shaka had ordered his citizens to begin storing grain in caves and forests dotted all round the kingdom and later the next month he ordered his spy, Joluju, to lead Zwide and his troops on a wild goose chase so that by the time Shaka attacked, the Ndwandwe troops would be too exhausted to fight. Zwide fell for the trick and despatched 18,000 troops to hunt Shaka down. They crossed the White Umfolozi River into Zululand, but they had only taken three days' supply of food with them, thinking that they could raid the Zulus grain stores and replenish themselves as they went. It was a huge mistake for Shaka (as noted above) had hidden all his grain away and not an ounce remained for the invading Ndwandwe to eat. The majority of Zulus had also disappeared into the mountains and forests, leaving their kraals empty. Those who remained then began teasing the Ndwandwe by pretending to steal the oxen they had brought with them and by so doing drew the Ndwandwe across the Tugela River. But the Ndwandwe chieftain wasn't a naïve man and began to suspect that he and his men were being led into a trap. He decided to retreat, a maneuver that prompted Shaka to pursue his enemy and stage an attack. Suddenly the two armies were engaged in combat and, as had been the case in all Shaka's previous fights, the battle was short-lived, Shaka defeating the Ndwandwe troops in a matter of hours. But the fight didn't end there, for Shaka was determined to pursue and kill all those Ndwandwe warriors who had fled the battlefield as well as the men, women and children who had remained behind in Zwide's kraal. To this end he sent two of his best fighting forces in pursuit of the enemy and, true to form, they indiscriminately slaughtered anyone connected to the Ndwandwe. They also captured the Ndwandwe livestock and afterwards burnt all the kraals down to the ground. Frustratingly for Shaka, however, Zwide had once again evaded capture, though Zwide's mother, Ntombazi, was caught and a few days later put on trial in lieu of her son. Sitting in front of her, Shaka asked the old woman many awkward questions, all of which she threw back in his face until ultimately Shaka sent her back to her hut, the interior of which was pitch black owing to the fact that there were no windows within the structure. As her eyes became accustomed to the gloom, Ntombazi realized that she was sharing the space with a wild hyena, an animal known for its ferocious nature.

'Ntombazi was at last able,' writes E.A. Ritter, 'to see quite clearly nature's undertaker who would dispose of her body partly alive, and partly dead, but altogether very thoroughly.'

After Ntombazi died, Shaka and his warriors celebrated their great victory over the Ndwandwe by feasting and drinking. Shaka Zulu was now the undisputed leader of Zululand; he was in an unassailable position and yet his fighting days were not over for in the winter of 1820, in a bid to unite the Zulus with a tribe called the Tembus, another bitter battle ensued. To begin with it didn't look as if things were going to go Shaka's way. The Tembus were equally as well equipped as the Zulus and they had just as many warriors. Indeed, the first part of the battle was an all-out victory for the Tembu chieftain who was called Nguni. A messenger was sent to tell Shaka the bad news and was promptly executed for his pains. Thereafter, Shaka ordered his men to fight twice as hard and by the end of the day their fortunes had turned and the Zulus were victorious. Despite this, Shaka wasn't satisfied that all his warriors had fought to the best of their ability and he therefore demanded that all his men, in order to show they had not shirked while fighting, bring forth spears from those Tembu they had slain. If a warrior could not show any spoils of war then he would be punished. In total, fifty or so men were executed in full few of their comrades.

After this last victory, Shaka Zulu went about building a new capital for Zululand. He chose a beautiful spot on the southern side of the lower Umhlatuze valley, which he named Bulawayo. Shaka concentrated on re-organizing his citizens and their agricultural output. He also set up a Zulu court of justice which was initially built in the shade of a giant fig tree that stood in the courtyard of Shaka's Great Council hut. The court was presided over by Shaka himself, together with a handful of trusted councillors. However, the councillors didn't have a great deal of say when it came to passing judgement, for this was Shaka's territory alone and he would put people to death for the slightest misdemeanours. Executions were commonplace and took the form of strangulation, stabbing, impaling on spears, setting on fire and clubbing to death. In this way many men and women lost their lives, but Shaka was absolute monarch of all he surveyed and his word was law. Every Zulu citizen swore allegiance to him, besides which everyone could see that he was building up a strong Zulu nation with a single Zulu language so, despite the fear and the bloodshed, they stood behind their great leader.

The Zulus' way of life, however, was about to change forever. In 1824, a white British colonial adventurer by the name of Henry Francis Fynn, along with several others, was sent out on board the *Julia* to meet and set up a trade agreement with the Zulu King. The British had created a small settlement near Port Natal (now better known as Durban) having already established a small colony on the Cape. They were in search of ivory, animal hides and other exotic objects, but initially Shaka refused to grant an audience to these interlopers. It was only when Fynn decided to travel across Natal in search of his quarry that Shaka sent spies out to assess the situation. His informers reported back that the white men appeared friendly, besides which they carried with them a wealth of goods. His curiosity roused, Shaka saw no alternative but to invite the white men to meet him and Henry Fynn made his way towards Bulawayo. Fynn wrote:

'We were struck with astonishment at the order and discipline maintained in the country through which we travelled. The regimental kraals, especially the upper parts thereof, also the kraals of the chiefs, showed that cleanliness was a prevailing custom, and this not only inside their huts, but outside, for there were considerable spaces where neither dirt nor ashes were to be seen.'[3]

Eventually, the English party arrived at Shaka's enclosure and were warmly welcomed. Fynn found Shaka Zulu to be a dignified leader and in turn Shaka informed Fynn of his wealth, not only in terms of land and cattle, but also his military force, of which he was extremely proud. Fynn also recorded that Shaka Zulu was interested to

Modern day Zulus carry shields and weaons representing those of their illustrious ancestors during the festival held to celebrate King Shaka Day.

learn about King George IV. He wanted to know about his form of government, how many cattle and wives he owned, how much land made up his kingdom and the size of his capital city. Later, according to Fynn, he then 'changed the conversation to the superiority of their arms, which, he said, were in many ways more advantageous than our muskets. The shield, he argued, if dipped into water previous to an attack, would be sufficient to prevent the effect of a ball fired whilst they were at a distance, and in the interval of loading they would come up to us at close quarters…'

Fynn's visit continued amid much festivity and exchanging of goods and information until eventually Fynn and his men, having made friends with the Zulu King, decided to go back to Port Natal. This was the first time Shaka had met with any European, but it certainly wouldn't be the last. In fact E.A. Ritter reports that Henry Fynn was present during October 1827 when Shaka's mother, Nandi, by whose side he had stood through the years, fell ill and died. Fynn reported that Shaka was inconsolable and began ordering the execution of citizens. 'Towards afternoon,' he wrote, 'I calculated that not fewer than 7,000 people had fallen in this frightful indiscriminate massacre.' The stream which ran through the kraal soon became blocked because of the number of corpses and everywhere blood was spread over the ground. Later that same day, Nandi was buried in the presence of approximately 12,000 warriors. Afterwards, Shaka ordered his troops to go out into the countryside and execute anyone they found guilty of not having properly mourned his mother's passing away. In fact, Shaka's violent behaviour escalated to such an extent during this period that no one was safe. One whole harem of women was clubbed to death and several young male children are said to have met the same end after having displeased their King. Other atrocities quickly followed. A group of boys was accused of suckling cattle whose calves still required the milk, and on being found guilty; the boys were sentenced to death by the spear. Fynn wrote later that he tried to dissuade Shaka from this type of atrocity, but to little avail.

From being a much-revered King, Shaka Zulu, now in his forties, was no more than an evil despot who couldn't control his darker emotions. Killing sprees continued apace and the Zulu nation cowered under his rule for almost another full year until, in September 1828, two of Shaka's half-brothers, Mhlangana and Dingane, with the aid of an aunt (Mkabayi) who believed Shaka's incessant warring was beginning to weaken the kingdom, began plotting his downfall. Finally, on 22 September they put their plan into action and while Shaka was holding talks with his councillors, the two assassins hid behind a reed fence, awaiting their opportunity. When the councillors left the chamber, Mhlangana thrust his spear into Shaka's body, swiftly followed by Dingane doing the same. It was a terrible sight, nonetheless with the deed done, they quickly spread a rumour that a group of messengers who were bringing Shaka gifts had in fact assassinated their brother. Subsequently, Shaka's body was wrapped in the skin of a black bull and buried in a pit.

All his life Shaka Zulu had struggled to attain the kind of power that, as a boy, he could only dream about. In twelve short years he successfully created, from what was once a small principality, a huge Zulu homeland. In the beginning Shaka was King of a mere 100 square miles, but by the end of his reign he commanded over 200,000 square miles. His troops had swelled from a paltry 500 warriors to a formidable army of 50,000 well-armed, highly disciplined soldiers. It was an enormous achievement, yet one built on the deaths of thousands of men, women and children.

And as for Shaka's murderers, Dingane decided the best course of action would be to kill his co-conspirator, Mhlangana, after which he ascended to the Zulu throne, but the Zulus were never quite the same fighting force as they had been under Shaka's rule and today Shaka Zulu's reputation stands as Africa's fiercest warrior and King.

[1] *Shaka Zulu*, E. A. Ritter, Granada Publishing Limited, 1958.
[2] Ibid.
[3] Ibid.

JOSEF STALIN
Russia's Uncle Joe

There was one on the house-front immediately opposite. BIG
BROTHER IS WATCHING YOU, the caption said, while the dark
eyes looked deep into Winston's own…In the far distance a
helicopter skimmed down between the roofs, hovered for an instant
like a bluebottle, and darted away again with a curving flight. It
was the police patrol, snooping into people's windows. The patrols
did not matter, however. Only the Thought Police mattered.

1984, by George Orwell.

Perhaps more than any other dictator either living or dead, the name Josef Stalin conjures up an image of George Orwell's 'Big Brother' – a ruthless tyrant never seen by the majority of the people other than on posters or in the newspapers, but himself all-seeing, presiding over an Orwellian super state where terror, betrayal, murder, death and destruction were everyday occurrences. In fact, of all the dictators who came to power after World War I, Josef Stalin was arguably the most successful. Not only did he rise to a position of ultimate authority in the world's second most powerful nation, not only did he kill more people than even Hitler managed, but he also lived well into his seventies, dying in 1953. At his funeral millions of Soviet citizens, young and old, grieved openly. After all, this was the man who had led the Soviet Union to victory against Adolf Hitler and Nazi Germany, this was the man who had dragged the country from a peasant state to an industrialized nation. But behind the pomp and circumstance, behind the great pronouncements made by those who survived him, lay a much darker picture in which millions died in labour camps, in prisons or simply of starvation. A brutal despot, Stalin thought nothing of eliminating all those he thought posed a threat to his regime and even rewrote history books and tampered with photographs in order to eliminate all trace of those who dared to oppose him.

Iosif Vissarionovich Dzhugasvili was born on 21 December 1879 in the Caucasian town of Gori, Georgia, in southern Russia. His father, Vissarion Dzhugasvili was a cobbler, but he had made little headway in his chosen career and had turned instead to alcohol. Returning home drunk most nights, Vissarion used to beat his wife, Yekaterina, who, given her husband's inability to bring home an adequate wage, took in washing and sewing to make ends meet. It was a hand-to-mouth existence made all the more difficult by Stalin's childhood illnesses. Yekaterina had to nurse her young son through a bad case of smallpox that left his face slightly disfigured, and later he suffered septicaemia which left his left arm weaker than the right. Yekaterina had little more to rely on than her religious beliefs to carry her through the bad times. She was a deeply devout woman and as Stalin grew up she became more and more determined to see her son enter the priesthood. In 1888, at the age of nine, Stalin was enrolled at the local Orthodox school in Gori and later (in 1894) he won a scholarship to the Orthodox theological seminary in Tiflis. It was while attending this last establishment that Stalin first became interested in politics and during his fourth year he joined a radical group called Mesame Dasi who were demanding independence for Georgia and who followed a socialist doctrine. Unsurprisingly, Stalin's political shenanigans landed him in trouble and in 1899, much to his mother's displeasure, he was expelled from the seminary. He tried to find work as a private tutor and, when that failed, as a clerical worker, but neither suited his newly-adopted political ambitions. In 1901 he joined the Social Democratic Party of Georgia in Tiflis where he began organizing strikes and demonstrations. At this time in his life Stalin liked to be called by the nickname 'Koba' ('Indomitable') after a Georgian folk hero, but later in 1913 he adopted his preferred soubriquet of 'Stalin' ('Man of Steel').

On 18 April 1902 Stalin, having come to the notice of the authorities, was arrested for the first time and sent to a labour camp in Siberia. Never one to bow down to authority, he escaped and reappeared in Tiflis two years later. It was then that he turned his mind towards a new branch of politics, Bolshevism, which espoused a highly disciplined, centralized administration, something Stalin swiftly identified as his path to power. Excited by this new movement (which was led by Lenin) Stalin began to propagate Lenin's ideas by writing about them in secret pamphlets and newspapers which were then clandestinely distributed throughout Tiflis and the surrounding area. Despite all the frenetic political activity, Stalin still found some time for a private life and in June 1904 he married a young peasant girl called Yekaterina Svanidze. Sadly, the union was short-lived as Yekaterina died three years later, leaving a son, Yakov, for Stalin to bring up. Fatherhood, however, didn't suit the young revolutionary and instead of devoting himself to his son, he once again threw himself into his political work, even organizing bank raids in order to raise funds for the Bolsheviks. Over the next few years his life was a mixture of political activism followed by long spells of imprisonment, but his hard work for the Bolsheviks did eventually pay off when, in 1912, Lenin personally appointed him one of the leaders for important underground propaganda work. By this time, Stalin had moved to St Petersburg and, amongst other duties, he set up *Pravda*, the new Bolshevik newspaper, the first edition of which appeared on 5 May 1912. Lenin also asked Stalin to join him and several other colleagues on a trip to Vienna where, during the early months of 1913, Stalin wrote the first of many studies of Marxism. Slowly, Stalin was working his way into the very heart of the Bolshevik party although, as has been noted by many scholars, it was his organizational skills and fanaticism for detail rather than his intellectual ability that endeared him to Lenin.

By 15 March 1917, when Tsar Nicholas II abdicated from the Russian throne, World War I had been raging for three years and the Russian people were tired and demoralized. Stalin, who had been serving yet another prison term in Siberia, couldn't believe his luck when, on the Tsar's abdication, the prison guards allowed their wards to go free. Stalin immediately returned to St Petersburg, but although he was now quite prominent within the Bolshevik party, he was still not as well-known nor as well-respected as either Lenin or Trotsky, both of whom were great politicians and versatile orators. Stalin did succeed in being elected as one of nine members of the party's Central Committee and, although he wasn't a key player in overthrowing the temporary Russian government (under the control of Alexander Kerensky), he did eventually agree that it was the best course of action for both the party and the country.

In fact, it was Leon Trotsky who was the major player behind the October Revolution, although in later years Stalin would re-write the history books and portray himself as its main instigator. Indeed, this 'revision of history' – as it became known – was not only to become a favourite pastime of Stalin's, it became almost his trademark, for he doctored hundreds of official documents with the sole purpose of making himself look better. He also tampered with photographs, often having those he'd killed removed from the pictures with acid or other substances and at one point, having portrayed himself as Lenin's closest friend, he hung a fake photograph of the two of them on the wall of his country house in Kuntsevo.

The Bolsheviks finally came to power on 7 November 1917 but it was neither a smooth transition nor a smooth ride once they were in power, for when Russia withdrew from World War I in 1918, the Bolsheviks had to fight a bitter civil war with the White Army who were Tsarist sympathizers.

It was during this time that Stalin was given a series of relatively minor positions such as acting Inspector General of the Red Army and Cabinet Minister for Nationalities. These were not posts of any great influence and would not have brought him much notice within the party, but he worked at them methodically and, as ever, enjoyed the organizational side of each job. In fact later historians have argued that it was the very mundanity of his early career that ultimately led him to take over the Bolshevik party because none of his rivals took him seriously, thus allowing him to work quietly in the background, biding his time. Another reason why Stalin was so successful during this early period was that he never deviated from Lenin's policies – quite the opposite, in fact. Stalin made it his duty to back Lenin in everything he said and did. And this ploy worked, for in March 1919 he joined Lenin, Leon Kamenev (the chairman of the Central Executive Committee), Trotsky and Kretinsky on the inner directorate of the party, which was by then called the Politburo. Rather than push himself forward, Stalin instead preferred to remain in the background and thus was quite happy heading up the *Orgburo* (Organizational Bureau) whose main concern was the appointment of party officials. Consequently, Stalin began promoting as many friends and political allies as he could, nearly always choosing men who came from humble backgrounds and who had little or no education because these men were more easily manipulated. Stalin also polished his skills as a master manipulator by playing on the rivalries between different colleagues, thereby encouraging them to oust one another from the party.

It was also during 1919 that Stalin married his second wife, Nadezhda Allilueva. Twenty-three years his junior, Nadezhda was the daughter of an old political friend of Stalin's from Georgia. Despite the age difference, theirs seemed a happy marriage and by the end of 1919 Nadezhda had given birth to a son, Vasili. Nadezhda also encouraged Stalin to pursue greater and greater goals, although she no doubt had little idea where this would lead. Soon Stalin began a series of secret investigations against every party official to whom he had taken a dislike. This gave him enough evidence with which to blackmail certain individuals who stood in his path. By whatever means came to hand, Stalin slowly began to climb his way up the party political ladder. In 1922, perhaps realizing that Stalin was a force to be reckoned with and believing it better to keep your enemies close, Lenin appointed him General Secretary of the party.

It was a fatal mistake, but before Lenin could right the situation he suffered a series of strokes. This gave Stalin the opportunity he had always craved and with Lenin incapacitated he swiftly took charge of the party. With ruthless efficiency, he obtained an order from the Central Committee giving him the authority to keep Lenin in total isolation from both news of the party and of the outside world. Finally Lenin, realizing just how misguided he had been in thinking Stalin would make a good leader, managed to dictate a letter to one of his secretaries. Lenin intended this statement to be read out loud during the next party congress, but as fate would have it, he suffered a fatal brain haemorrhage on 21 January 1924 after which Stalin swiftly delayed the conference and suppressed the offending document.

Over the next five years a protracted battle commenced for the party leadership, a battle that saw Stalin initially align himself to the right of the party and then shift to the left. Between times he instigated the removal of practically everyone who stood in his path, including Trotsky (who was deported from the country and later assassinated), Zinoviev and Kamenev (who were both expelled from the party and later executed), and Bukharin who was put on trial for treason. By 1929 Stalin had achieved ultimate power. The country

In June 1904 Josef Stalin married his first wife, a peasant girl named Yekaterina Svanidze but the marriage was tragically short-lived as Yekaterina died just three years later leaving Stalin with a son, Yakov.

was now his and for the next twenty-four years he never once loosened his grip.

From the very beginning, what Josef Stalin had in mind for Russia was a complete conversion from a near total nineteenth-century agrarian society to a more modern, twentieth-century industrialized one. He wanted Russia to catch up with the West whom he regarded as ten times more advanced than the USSR.

With this in mind, he put into operation a Five-Year Economic Plan that, amongst other things, forced all peasants to join state-owned farmers' co-operatives where they had to pool all their machinery, livestock and grain after which they either relied on the government for their wages or had to survive on what was left over after the government had taken its cut. The results were appalling. Rather than hand over what was lawfully theirs, a huge percentage of peasants took to burning their land and killing their livestock. This led to a nation-wide famine, although those in the south were particularly badly hit. It is estimated that approximately three million people were affected in the Ukraine alone and it is said that some parents even resorted to eating their dead babies. Sadly, however, Stalin didn't stop there. As well as forcing peasants to work on his state-run farms, those peasants who were somewhat wealthier than the rest (the *kulaks*) and those who opposed collectivisation were deported and murdered in their hundreds of thousands in order that the state could take over their land. Nor were those who escaped this death toll much more fortunate for they were either forced to work in the new state-controlled factories or sent to labor camps where they were worked into the grave. The factories were hardly an easier option, being more akin to large conveyor belts where workers were little more than cogs in a wheel. Each factory that was taken over by the state was given a target which it had to meet every year over a period of five years. The targets were calculated and set by teams of workers in Moscow who were employed by a state-run organization called *Gosplan*. Over half-a-million workers did nothing other than set targets for each and every factory throughout Russia. They would also check that the targets had been met. Naturally, this put a huge amount of pressure on the men and women who ran and worked in these units. Managers were frequently executed for not meeting their targets and employees soon had to work longer and longer shifts in order to complete their quotas on time. Taking sick leave or a day off work, no matter what the excuse, became a crime punishable by law and, because Stalin demanded increasingly unrealistic targets, managers began tampering with the figures to cover their shortfalls. The phrase 'hell on earth' might well have been coined to describe the condition in these factories and as for the gulags (the word is an abbreviation that in translation means, 'Central Board of the Reformatory Concentration Camp') no description on earth could convey the misery that they inflicted. Mostly located in the harshest regions of the Soviet Union such as Siberia, the temperatures in these camps often fell well below freezing, yet the prisoners were expected to live in unheated huts and were forced to build roads, canals and factories. They had to exist on the most meagre of diets and if anyone made even the most minor of mistakes the guards would often shoot them on the spot or beat them to death.

To make matters worse, only the smallest percentage of the inmates were actually criminals in the old-fashioned sense of the word – the others were all political prisoners. Doctors, teachers, scientists, artists were sent in their thousands to the camps for 'opposing' the regime and if one member of a family was arrested, it was more than likely that his or her relatives would be similarly detained and convicted. Stalin also harboured anti-Semitic ideas and when he came to power the pressure on the Jews increased. He eliminated all Jews from senior posts within the regime and had Jewish citizens closely monitored by the Secret Police. 'Is it true,' wrote Trotsky to Bukharin on 4 March 1926, 'is it possible, that in *our party*, in *Moscow*, in *Workers' Cells*, anti-Semitic agitation should be carried out with impunity?'[1] But Stalin didn't care. Far from it. The more death and destruction, the better it seemed. 'The greatest delight,' he once told one of his victims, 'is to mark one's enemy, prepare everything, avenge oneself thoroughly, and then go to sleep.' For him the end justified the means and what he had in mind was the subjugation of an entire people to *his* will alone.

For those closest to Stalin these must have been turbulent, even terrifying, times and for one person in particular it all proved too much. On the evening of 8 November 1932, having attended a dinner party to celebrate the 15th anniversary of the Bolshevik Revolution, Nadezhda Allilueva went up to her room where her body was later discovered lying on the bathroom floor. The official version of events was that she had died of appendicitis, but she had actually been insulted by Stalin at the dinner party, gone upstairs, fetched a gun and shot herself through the head. Stalin was said to be devastated by his young wife's suicide and the author Simon Sebag Montefiore goes as far as to suggest that her death was the catalyst that set Stalin on a course of mass terror. Stalin was said to sit alone for hours spitting at a wall, promising to wreak revenge on all those responsible (naturally he never thought to accuse himself of this crime). Whether Montefiore's theory is correct or not, the fact remains that between 1933 and 1939 Stalin began to purge the party of everyone who had opposed him over the past few years. Some were genuine enemies, but he also began to hunt down imagined enemies leaving only 'yes' men surrounding him, those too frightened to speak up or speak out. It was also during this period that Stalin began to build up an elite force of secret policemen (much like Ivan the Terrible's *Oprichnina*) called the NKVD. In return for services rendered these henchmen were given flats, dachas, country homes, cars and chauffeurs, but in order that none of them betrayed his trust and to keep them in line, Stalin would murder a handful of them each year.

By 1934, at the seventeenth Party Congress, over 300 delegates were so disaffected by Stalin that they voted against him as Party Leader in favour of the more popular Sergei Kirov (leader of the Communist party in Leningrad). Stalin was devastated, enraged by what he saw as a mass betrayal, and less than a year later Kirov was mysteriously murdered – probably on Stalin's orders – although there is no direct evidence linking him to the death. Stalin took control of the ensuing investigation and immediately built the Party Congress dissent into a major conspiracy against the state, thereby giving him precisely the excuse he needed to rid himself of even more

In November 1932, Stalin so insulted his second wife, Nadezdha Allilueva, at a dinner party celebrating the 15th anniversary of the Bolshevik Revolution, that she went upstairs to her bathroom and shot herself in the head.

opponents. The campaign of terror that followed culminated in the huge show trials of 1936-1938, where over 1,000 delegates (out of 1,200) from the 1934 Congress were executed or sent to the gulags and 98 out of a total of 130 Central Committee members were shot. These included the likes of Bukharin and Kamenev who were tortured into confessing to ridiculous crimes before being tried and shot. In addition, between 1934-1938 it is estimated that at least 7,000,000 people 'disappeared', including most of the senior officers within the Red Army (Stalin killed three out of five marshals, fifteen out of sixteen commanders, 60 out of 67 corps commanders and all seventeen commissars), not to mention those from the Red Navy as well. Lorries marked 'Meat' or 'Vegetables' would be packed full of victims who were driven out into nearby forests where long pits had been dug. The victims would be lined up by the pits and shot so that their bodies would fall backwards into the 'graves'.

It has also become increasingly apparent that Stalin enjoyed learning exactly how his opponents had died, and several of his trusted lieutenants would often act out how

In November 1943, Stalin met with US President Roosevelt, British Prime Minister Winston Churchill and their delegates at a conference in Teheran to discuss the progress and aftermath of World War II.

his victims had begged for their lives before they were shot. In the Lubyanka prison in Moscow detainees were sometimes beaten so viciously 'that their eyes literally popped out of their heads'.[2] Over the years, Stalin grew increasingly cruel and increasingly paranoid and even some of those men and women with whom he had enjoyed, if not close personal contact, then at least close political friendship, ended up dead. Nor did he trust members of his own family. Huge numbers of the Svanidzes and the Alliluevas were executed for 'betraying' either him or the state. Neither were the families of his closest political associates safe. Polina Molotov, the wife of his foreign minister, was sent to prison for ten years.

The only person who grew close to Stalin and who saw him not as a tyrant but as a kindly father figure was his daughter by Nadezhda, a little girl by the name of Svetlana. After her mother's death, Stalin encouraged his daughter to become his 'little mistress' and to all intents and purposes she ruled his heart. His other children, sadly, did not fare so well. His first son, Yakov, was variously bullied then ignored by his father to such an extent that he tried to kill himself. The fact that he didn't succeed only caused Stalin to mock him further. Eventually, Yakov died in a Nazi concentration camp, some say due to Stalin's unwillingness to bargain with the German authorities for his life. Stalin's second son, Vasili, didn't fare much better. Growing up in his father's shadow, it is said he turned into a weaker version of Stalin, but with just as strong a cruel streak. Vasili became an alcoholic and eventually died of the disease.

By 1939, the bulk of Stalin's political purges were over and done with but this was by no means the end of the death and destruction in Russia. Despite having signed a treaty of non-aggression with Hitler that, in effect, sanctioned Germany's invasion of Poland, on 22 June 1941 Hitler launched Operation Barbarassa and invaded the USSR. Stalin was taken almost completely by surprise and, due to the purges of the Red Army and the Red Navy during the 1930s, his armed forces were lacking the quality of leadership required to combat such an onslaught. As a result, the Red Army suffered virtual annihilation at the hands of the Nazis who were better trained, better equipped and better led. In less than six months nearly four million Russian troops had been captured, not an insignificant number if one calculates that it took only three million German troops to bring this about.

Yet, surprisingly, Hitler failed to capitalize on his huge victory and declined the suggestion that 800,000 Russian volunteers might be put to good use fighting for Germany. Instead, he alienated the Russians by allowing his troops to commit violent and vile atrocities all over the country, so that by the time the Germans marched on Leningrad and held it under siege, the Russians were in no mood to surrender. Stalin grabbed his opportunity and appealed to the people to fight the enemy and throw the Nazis out of Russia once and for all. Miraculously, this seemed to galvanize everyone into action and, with the Germans ill-prepared for the onslaught of a Russian winter, the tide eventually began to turn. Nonetheless, in the midst of this pain and suffering Stalin was unrelenting in his own personal torment of the people. Ordering special NKVD units to follow in the wake of Russian troops, any soldier who was caught trying to retreat was shot on the spot by the secret police. Stalin also let it be known that if any member of the armed forces decided to surrender to the enemy then that person's family would either lose their state allowances or be arrested and executed.

By 1945, the Red Army was in the ascendant and had pushed back Hitler's forces to the extent that in May Russian troops entered Berlin. It was a great moment, but one that was later marred by Stalin who, anxious that his troops might have been seduced by western ideas, ordered that all those returning from Germany be sent to the gulags for re-education. In addition, Soviet citizens who repatriated to Russia having been in detention in foreign prisons and work camps were deemed by Stalin to be traitors and, as they stepped off the ships and trains, were hurried into large yards where they were either executed or sent to the gulags. Family after family was wiped out, generation after generation.

Nor was the West spared from the suffering, for directly after World War II finished, the forty-year Cold War began with the 'iron curtain' descending over eastern Europe. All those countries occupied by the Russians were turned into 'satellite states' governed by puppet administrations that were directly answerable to Stalin for their every decision. All along, Stalin had wanted to isolate Russia and other eastern bloc countries from what he saw as Western contamination; now his dream had come true. Russia's fate was sealed.

In 1946, Stalin initiated his fourth, Five-Year Plan that, just as before, demanded ever-increasing productivity from Russia's citizens. Nobody could meet the targets, yet despite their desperate circumstances, despite the threats made against them, Russians didn't rise up against their leader. Instead, they worshipped him as if he were some sort of god. The worse Stalin treated his people the more they seemed to revere him. In schools pupils were made to recite poems extolling his virtues. Posters with slogans such as 'Thank you Comrade Stalin for a Happy Childhood' appeared everywhere. The most ubiquitous of these images was a photograph of Stalin holding a little girl – six-year-old Gelya Marikova – with the words 'Friend of the Little Children' printed above it. Ironically, Gelya's father was later accused of spying for Japan and executed on Stalin's orders and, later still, Gelya's mother was murdered. But the cult of personality that Stalin built up around himself seemed impregnable. Nobody questioned his authority; instead Russians spent large parts of their day thanking comrade Stalin for the gifts he had bestowed on them, the food he had provided, the education he had given their children. Artists were 'persuaded' to produce works only in the Socialist Realist style, i.e. one that promoted Stalin's own ideas of the benefits of industrialization and the power of the individual as part and parcel of the larger socialist state. On Stalin's seventieth birthday an image of his face was projected against the sky over the Kremlin. It was as if Stalin was a god and Stalinism a new type of religion.

Although everything appeared to be going Stalin's way, although he had succeeded in vanquishing the Germans, although he had rid himself of all his opponents, he grew more and more unhappy, more and more paranoid. He saw enemies where there were none and at one point employed fifteen personal food tasters, so scared was he of being poisoned. If Stalin appeared in public, which became increasingly rare, then more often than not it was in a bullet-proof car, the windows of which were three inches thick. Tunnels were dug between his office and other government buildings so he could make a quick getaway should anything go wrong, and in the gardens of his country residence telephones were installed every few yards or so, in case Stalin suffered a heart attack or was set upon by assassins.

But his paranoia didn't stop at the extensive measures he took to ensure his personal safety; it also took the form of the continued persecution of fellow party members. In 1949 another wave of Stalinist purges swept the country and anyone suspected of even the slightest transgression was put to death. Stalin's anti-Semitic tendencies also came to the fore during this period, both in his personal life and in the country as a whole. Svetlana, his beloved daughter had fallen in love with a Jew, but Stalin would not countenance such a relationship and labelled him a British spy after which he was sent to a labour camp. In February 1953 Stalin also began the construction of four huge prison camps in Kazakhstan, the Arctic North and Siberia. Most researchers agree that, in a ghastly echo of Hitler's Final Solution, these camps probably signalled a new terror campaign, this time directed solely at the Jews, for since 1948 Stalin had stepped up his anti-Semitic campaign closing down Jewish theatres, synagogues, newspapers and publishing houses. His campaign also targeted Jewish doctors whom he accused of trying to poison their non-Jewish patients or of killing them on the operating table. It was paranoia taken to an extreme and this was especially the case when, having had a medical check-up with his own doctor, Professor Vinogradov, and not liking the results, he had the professor arrested for being an 'agent of international Zionism'. This led indirectly to Stalin's own death, for when Stalin eventually had a stroke whilst staying in his countryside dacha, the doctors who were called to his bedside were unfamiliar with his medical history and could do little to save him. On 5 March 1953 at 9:50pm Josef Stalin died, some believe as a result of a cerebral haemorrhage, while others more circumspectly believe as a result of having been poisoned.

Whatever the case, the news of Stalin's demise wasn't publicly broken until 6 March when it was announced that 'The heart of the comrade-in-arms and continuer of genius of Lenin's cause, of the wise leader and teacher of the Communist Party and the Soviet Union, had ceased to beat.'[3] Leaflets were handed out on the streets of every town and city for those who didn't have access to the radio. Meanwhile, Stalin's body was being prepared for an autopsy. Nurses washed him down and his corpse was taken in a white car to the mortuary. After doctors had examined it, his body was then given to embalmers so that it could lie in state for up to three days without decomposing. Stalin's corpse was put on display in the Hall of Columns. Despite the sub-zero temperatures, queues immediately formed to view the body; everyone wanted to pay their last respects and as the crowds grew denser several hundred people were killed, trampled underfoot or rammed against barricades.

Finally, on 9 March, the coffin was lifted from the Hall of Columns, put on a gun carriage and taken to Lenin's tomb in Red Square. Georgy Malenkov, Lavrenty Beria and Vyacheslav Molotov all made speeches after which Stalin's coffin was laid to rest inside the tomb. For some it was too much to bear and they wept and mourned openly for their 'Uncle Joe' as if he had been the kindest of patriarchs. For others it was nothing short of a miracle that this time it was he who had died, for during Stalin's rule approximately 20 million citizens lost their lives, up to 14.5 million due to starvation. One million were executed for political offences and at least 9 million were exiled or imprisoned in the gulags.

1   *The Prophet Unarmed: Trotsky 1921-29*, by Isaac Deutscher, Oxford, 1965.
2   *Stalin: The Court of the Red Tsar* by Simon Sebag Montefiore,
       Weidenfeld & Nicolson, 2003.
3   stalin.narod.ru/

ADOLF HITLER
A Twentieth-Century War Lord

There are three things central to the future of Germany [the third
of which is]…The anti-Semitic concept: it confirms the racial
rejection of what is essentially hostile to all that is German.
Nationalism is above all inoculation against a bacillus, and the anti-
Semitic concept is the necessary defence, the antibody if you like
against a pestilence which today has a grip on the whole world.

Hitler speaking in Munich, 29 January 1923[1]

On 20 April 1889 in the tiny village of Brasnau on the Austro/Bavarian border,
a child was born who was destined to preside over one of the most evil
periods of history mankind has ever experienced. Dictator of Germany for a
little over twelve years, on his orders six million European Jews were murdered along
with thousands of communists, gypsies, homosexuals and the mentally and physically
impaired. This tyrant also plunged the world into a war in which over 40 million men,
women and children lost their lives, over half of them civilians. In short, if ever a
nightmare took the shape of a man, Adolf Hitler was it.

As a young boy, Hitler did not enjoy the most stable of childhoods. His father, Alois
Hitler was a customs official, a cog in a very large wheel, someone who suffered from
a huge inferiority complex. He had been married twice (siring three children) before
he met Adolf's mother, Klara Pölzl, who was twenty-three years his junior. The age gap
led Alois to treat Klara with contempt and when Adolf was a young boy he witnessed
his father's boorish, violent behaviour on more than one occasion. Fiercely protective
of his mother, Adolf felt unable to go to her aid and this left him feeling vulnerable and
inadequate.

After a few unremarkable years at school, Adolf finally moved out of the family
home, gave up on his studies (without securing his School Leaving certificate) and
travelled to Vienna. Shortly after arriving there he applied for a place at both the
Vienna Academy of Art and the Vienna Academy of Architecture, but to his life-long
fury, both rejected him. Dispirited, he moved lodgings to a dingy hostel near the river
where he scraped together a living by drawing advertisements and posters for small
business ventures. It was, by anyone's standards, a grim, hand-to-mouth existence, but
always a loner, Adolf found comfort in being rejected by the type of bourgeois society
he had come to despise. He withdrew further and further into himself, though on the
rare occasions when he did speak, it was often to rant and rave about politics. Reinhold
Hanisch, a friend of Hitler's from this period, recalls, 'Hitler went to a cinema where
Kellermann's *Tunnel* was being shown. In this piece an agitator appears who rouses the

working masses by his speeches. Hitler almost went crazy. The impression it made on him was so strong that for days afterwards he spoke of nothing except the power of the spoken word.'[2] In fact the impression it left on the young Hitler must have spanned not just days, but decades, for he was always more at ease giving speeches than writing them.

In the spring of 1913, at the age of twenty-four, Hitler left Vienna in order to escape conscription into the Austrian army. He travelled to Munich where he continued his somewhat isolated existence, living very much in his own fantasy world. It was also in Munich where he began to formulate what would later become his life-long obsession concerning the Jews. In *Mein Kampf* Hitler wrote that it wasn't until he was an adult that he became aware of the 'Jewish problem', but there is a wealth of evidence to suggest that his father Alois was vehemently anti-Semitic and no doubt passed these views on to his child.

Whatever the case, at the time when Adolf lived in Munich the Jews were an easy target, fleeing in droves as they were from pogroms across Russia and Eastern Europe and in particular from Poland and Hungary. It wasn't difficult to feel resentment towards them, but Hitler's anti-Semitism went further than most, combining as it did

Hitler enjoys the adulation of the Nazi faithful lining the route as he drives into Wildenau in Sudetenland after his troops annexed or 'united' it with Germany in October 1938.

pseudo-scientific theories to support his belief that the Jews were of an inferior race. To add insult to injury he believed they were responsible for every evil on earth.

Take for example this excerpt from *Mein Kampf*:

'The black-haired Jewish youth lies in wait for hours on end, satanically glaring at and spying on the unsuspicious girl whom he plans to seduce, adulterating her blood and removing her from the bosom of her own people…The Jews were responsible for bringing Negroes into the Rhineland with the ultimate idea of bastardising the white race which they hate and thus lowering its cultural and political level so that the Jew might dominate.'[3]

But, though obviously fascinated by this and other such dubious theories, Hitler had to put his life on hold for a short time when, on 28 June 1914, Franz Ferdinand was assassinated, an act which precipitated World War I. Despite being an Austrian citizen, Hitler managed to join a Bavarian infantry regiment (another recruit in this same group was Rudolf Hess). Hitler was given the role of *Meldegänger* (a runner), i.e. someone whose job it was to carry messages from the trenches to Company HQ and vice versa. For the first time in his life, Hitler worked hard at something and when under pressure was found to be more than adequate. In fact he acquitted himself so well that he earned two Iron Crosses for bravery, but sadly the medals were the only good thing to come out of Hitler's war experience for the conflict served only to entrench his already dubious ideas and prejudices.

On leaving the army Hitler returned to Munich where, rather than go back to his ramshackle existence as an artist, he was instead determined to pursue a career in politics. Above all else, Hitler wanted to create a grassroots movement, one that would break the back of Social Democracy in addition to breaking the hold that the Jews had on the country. His timing could not have been much better, for Germany, having signed a Peace Treaty and having agreed to pay substantial war reparations, was left feeling broken and humiliated. The new government, the Weimar Republic, was therefore an easy target for much backbiting and rivalry and the German populace was restless for change. Hitler was in his element. He knew the time was ripe for someone to lead the disgruntled masses away from the main political parties; all that was needed was a new political vehicle. Step into the breach, The German Workers' Party.

Hitler joined this small, understaffed, under-ambitious outfit in 1919 and shortly afterwards was put in charge of a subject very close to his heart: propaganda. Immediately he undertook a gruelling tour of beer cellars, halls and auditoriums to spread the new word and, as Alan Bullock points out in his biography of Hitler, he 'came to know Germany and the German people at first hand as few of Germany's other leaders ever had. By the time he came to power in 1933 there were few towns of any size in the Reich where he had not spoken.'[4]

Soon the party changed its name to The Nationalist Socialist German Workers' Party and posters were to be found plastering walls throughout Bavaria with the swastika prominently on display. Despite all his efforts, however, progress for both his party (which was still a relatively provincial movement) and the country was slow. Four years after the end of World War I, Germany was still a sick and divided nation. The question of reparations hadn't been settled and the German Mark was practically worthless. Undeterred, Hitler pressed on with his all-encompassing vision, drumming up as much hatred as he could muster against the Jews whom he saw at work at the very heart of the Republic. He also began to organize mass demonstrations and riots against the state. He was imprisoned for high treason for his part in a demonstration that began on 8 November 1923 in the Bürgerbräukeller in Munich. The sentence handed down to Hitler was for a term of five years, but he was released after serving a little less than nine months.

On leaving prison, Hitler once again threw himself into politics, but since his short spell in prison, Germany had undergone a remarkable economic turnaround and where once there had been a disgruntled populace eager for change, now the majority of people felt financially better off and consequently less disaffected with the Republic. Now everything appeared to be working against Adolf Hitler. No matter how many speeches he made, or how many times he tried to stir up hostility towards the government, nothing worked. Not, that is, until 1930 when suddenly both Europe and America were plunged into the World Depression. Suddenly factories closed, people lost their jobs, businesses were forced into bankruptcy and by 1932 over six million people were recorded as being unemployed. If ever there was a time to go in for the kill then this was it. The Republic was weak and, taking full advantage of this fact, Hitler accepted an offer to form a coalition with the Right.

On the morning of 20 January 1933, after years in the political wilderness, after months of internecine wrangling, Adolf Hitler became Chancellor of the German Reich.

From the start Hitler's dictatorship used to its advantage the fact that the Weimar Republic was never officially annulled. This constitutional vacuum allowed Hitler to pass laws in as arbitrary a fashion as he wished. Within a few months he had broken the back of all opposition to either him or his party by banning both the Communists and Social Democrat Parties. These were extraordinary times for Germany and barely a year after he had come to power they were about to become even more extraordinary.

In 1934 Hitler decided to purge the German army of all those factions that he felt might be less inclined to do his bidding. One of his main targets was the head of the S.A. (*Sturm Abteilung*/Storm Troopers), Ernst Röhm, but there were countless other names on the list. The executions began on the night of 29 June and continued for two days. No one knows the final body count as most of the documents recording this purge have been destroyed, but it has been estimated that between 300-500 men lost their lives. As an early indication of the tactics Hitler would employ to ensure he remained in power, this ably demonstrates how ruthless he had become, how contemptuous he could be of human life and how indifferent he was towards law and order. From Hitler's point of view, life was about to grow even sweeter for, on 2 August 1934, President von Hindenburg died. Within an hour of his passing it was decreed that the office of President would now be merged with that of the Chancellor and that Hitler would not only be Head of State, but also Supreme Commander-in-Chief of the Armed Forces.

At a strategy conference in Munich in 1938, Hitler and his deputies met with their fascist allies from Italy. Pictured in the front row from left to right are; Hermann Göring, Benito Mussolini, Adolf Hitler and Count Ciano, the Italian Foreign Minister.

On 19 August 1934 the German people were invited to go to the polls to express their approval of Hitler's assumption of power. This wasn't an election – it was more a populist endorsement of the Chancellor's new role. Forty-five-and-a-half million voters took part and though more than thirty-eight million voted 'Yes', four-and-a-quarter million had the courage and wit to mark their ballot papers, 'No'.

One might have assumed that, on gaining power, Hitler would have thrown himself into the nitty-gritty of politics, but as several commentators have noted, he wasn't interested in the day-to-day running of government. Quite the contrary; he displayed a remarkable *laissez-faire* attitude, bordering on the downright lazy. Hitler was pre-occupied with two central ideas, the first being that of foreign policy. Ever since Germany's defeat in 1918 and the humiliation of having to pay reparations, he had yearned to rebuild Germany's confidence both at home and on the world stage. German nationalism was on the ascendant and part and parcel of this dream was to rearm the country so that it could compete on equal terms with other nation states.

The second central aim inevitably concerned the Jews. Laws (which later became known as the Nuremberg Laws) were passed that deprived anyone of Jewish blood from the right to German citizenship, banned marriages between Jews and Germans and denied Jews the right to hold office or even to vote. This was state anti-Semitism on a grand scale, the splitting of the country into two separate classes, the lower of which had no rights whatsoever – people who were regarded as sub-human.

'I shall have gallows erected, in Munich for example in the Marienplatz, as many as traffic permits. Then the Jews will be hanged, one after another, and they will stay hanging until they stink....As soon as one is untied, the next will take his place, and that will go on until the last Jew in Munich is obliterated. Exactly the same thing will happen in the other cities until Germany is cleansed of its last Jew.'[5]

But behind this and other vitriolic outbursts lay not only Hitler's personal loathing for the Jews, but also a cool, political calculation that this type of action would play very well with the majority of the German people. He was not mistaken, for after Hitler came to power, individual acts of violence against Jewish people escalated to the point where it felt as if a national effort were being made to scare Jews into submission. In November 1938 all the above came to a head in the *Reichskristallnacht* (the imperial night of crystal) where the S.A. were sent out in teams to burn down synagogues, smash and loot Jewish shops and businesses and attack anyone whom they believed to be of Jewish origin. Not long afterwards 20,000 Jews were sent to concentration camps for their 'own protection'.

During all this time Hitler's personal profile was going from strength to strength. The power he could cast over an audience has been likened to a witch doctor casting a spell or a magician hypnotizing a crowd. He was the master of mass emotion, able to manipulate people almost to the point of hysteria. Hitler also used every tool available at that date to promote himself and his policies. Albert Speer, Hitler's Minister for Armaments and War Production, spoke of this later when he was on trial for crimes against humanity.

'Hitler's dictatorship,' Speer said, 'differed in one fundamental point from all its predecessors in history. His was the first dictatorship in the present period of modern technical development, a dictatorship which made complete use of all technical means for the domination of its own country.

Through technical devices like the radio and the loud-speaker, eighty million people were deprived of independent thought. It was thereby possible to subject them to the will of one man.'[6]

Another commentator noted that several of the mass rallies, especially the yearly rallies in Nuremberg, were akin to attending a theatrical production. The sight of thousands upon thousands of soldiers all dressed in identical uniforms, all marching in unison to the same beat, roused the spirits in ways never before experienced. Hitler was a charismatic leader; Lloyd George – Prime Minister of Great Britain from 1916-1922 – said of him that he was, '… a born leader of men. A magnetic, dynamic personality with a single-minded purpose, a resolute will and a dauntless heart', a man who from very humble beginnings had transformed himself into a demagogue, a man who, as several historians have noted, was much admired by women. Yet, although many theories have been put forward regarding Hitler's sexual life, whether or not he was impotent for instance, or whether he suffered from syphilis, the truth is that very little is known other than that he had close relations with his niece, Geli Raubal, and later in life with a woman called Eva Braun.

Geli Raubal was the daughter of Hitler's half-sister, Angela Raubal. She came to stay with Hitler in 1925 in Munich when she was only seventeen years old and Hitler, who was thirty-seven at the time, promptly fell in love with her. Geli and Hitler spent a good deal of time together; he was mesmerized by her youthful beauty and proud to show her off to his friends, but soon he became very possessive of his niece and began to rule her life as though she were a chattel. Whether this was the reason for her suicide will probably never be known, but on 17 September 1931, Geli Raubal shot herself in Hitler's flat where she was staying at the time. One theory is that she had fallen in love with another suitor, but couldn't escape Hitler's tyrannical grip. Whatever the case, Hitler was said to be devastated by her death and a number of his associates later testified that Geli was the only woman Hitler had ever loved.

The second woman in Hitler's life was Eva Braun, the prototype of the kind of Aryan blonde, blue-eyed girl Hitler favoured. Eva worked as a shop assistant for a photography outfit and although Hitler showed some interest in her, it certainly wasn't love on the same scale as he had felt for his niece. But Eva was a very manipulative woman, and less than one year after Geli Raubal committed suicide, Eva attempted the same in a bid to force Hitler into recognizing her as his partner. Still raw from the memory of Geli's death, Eva's ploy worked and from then on she became his constant companion. However, the love of neither woman softened Hitler's heart or made him value the sanctity of human life any more than he had done in the past. Soon he began widening his hatreds, incorporating the mentally and physically handicapped.

Hitler's vision of a strong, healthy, pure-blooded nation did not extend to the 'feebleminded' or the sick, the insane or the needy. Nor did he look kindly upon Germany's huge population of gypsies. In fact, all of the aforementioned groups fell victim to vile medical programmes which included the sterilization of over 400,000 of their number. Worse, a Euthanasia Programme was also implemented as the following document outlines:

> 'Reichsleiter Bouhler and Dr Brandt are charged with the
> responsibility for expanding the authority of physicians who are
> to be designated by name, to the end that patients who, in the
> best available human judgement after critical evaluation of their
> condition are considered incurable can be granted Gnadentod
> [mercy death].
>
> SIGNED: **Adolf Hitler**'[7]

In effect, what this meant was that by the time World War II began, not only had policies been put into operation which foreshadowed the Holocaust, but to all intents and purposes the operational infrastructure was already in existence with which to carry out the killings.

Hitler was as deceitful on the international stage as he was despicable in the domestic arena. While voicing his determination for peace to the Allied leaders (and in particular the British Prime Minister, Neville Chamberlain), Hitler ruthlessly invaded three countries. On 11 March 1938 German troops marched into Austria and by 13 March it was announced the country would from then be 'united' with its German neighbor. Next, Hitler turned his attention on the Sudetenland which was 'united' with Germany on 1 October 1938 and finally troops marched into the Czech Republic which fell victim to the same annexation process on 15 March 1939.

Where would Hitler turn his attention next? This was the question on everyone's lips, the question that occupied every politician across Europe. Would it be Holland? or Switzerland? or perhaps Hungary or Poland? In the event, it turned out to be Poland. On 1 September 1939 Hitler's troops invaded Poland and on 3 September Britain and France declared war on Germany.

In the initial stages of this conflict, Germany was triumphant. After Poland, Hitler sent troops into the Netherlands, Norway, Belgium, Denmark, Luxembourg and France and in 1941 he declared war on America. At the same time, and with world attention preoccupied with fighting the Germans on all these different fronts, Hitler turned his mind to what chillingly became known as the Final Solution (*Reitlinger*).

Ever since he had assumed his position as Chancellor of Germany, the Jews had been deprived of more and more rights. Their movements had been restricted; they were made to wear a Star of David, black with a yellow background with the word 'Jude' in the centre. Jews were banned from public transport, not allowed to use public telephones (booths were marked 'Use by Jews Forbidden'). Humiliation after humiliation was heaped upon them, but with the invasion of Poland a new horror emerged. Suddenly Jews were being transported to labour camps where they were quite literally worked to death. Life expectancy was between six weeks and three months, a figure that didn't include those who committed suicide or died in accidents.

Yet, for Hitler, working the Jews into the grave was not a quick enough method of disposing of the 'vermin'. He therefore ordered the SS (his specially chosen elite force of soldiers) to experiment with different gases, ranging from carbon monoxide to the cyanide-based Zyklon-B. The first gas chamber to be built was at Brandenburg in 1939. It was erected as an experiment to see how effective the different gases were, and four insane men were its first victims. Thereafter further gas chambers were constructed and Hitler's Euthanasia Program was instigated, killing mainly the old, the sick and the needy. Finally, after Hitler's invasion of Poland, this program ran parallel to that of the Final Solution and apart from personnel, who changed from camp to camp, and perhaps the size of the killing chambers, the same methods and equipment were used in both.

At Auschwitz in Poland, four huge chambers were built, each of which could hold 2,000 people at a time. The victims were made to strip and then herded inside, at which point the doors were sealed shut and the gas (in Auschwitz/Birkenau it was normally Zyklon-B) was pumped in. It could take up to fifteen minutes for the victims to die – depending on where they stood in the crush. It was assembly-line genocide and although hundreds of thousands of people (on both sides of the conflict) lost their lives

in various ways during the war, nothing compared to the cruelty and inhumanity of this particular killing programme. Euphemisms were implemented, ranging from 'special actions', 'major cleansing actions', 'making free', 'appropriate treatment', in order to soften the reality of what was occurring. 'There were about 8,861,800 Jews in the countries of Europe directly or indirectly under Nazi control. Of these it is calculated that the Nazis killed 5,933,900, or 67 percent. Over two million Jews were killed at Auschwitz, 1,380,000 at Majdanel, 800,000 at Treblinka, 600,000 at Belzec, 340,000 at Chelmo and 250,000 at Sobibor.'[8]

In addition to the work camps and gas chambers, Hitler also sanctioned medical experiments on the Jews. The 'doctors' involved didn't allow the use of anaesthetics and according to later testimonies heard during the Nuremberg trials, they were either oblivious to the pain being caused or, worse, enjoyed seeing their victims suffer. The medical experiments included the 'patients' being subjected to freezing temperatures so that they froze to death. Alternatively some were exposed to such intense air pressure that their lungs burst. Patients were injected with various diseases in order to see how long it took them to die without medication. There were also reports of men being castrated.

To add to the inhumanity of all the ordeals the Jews, gypsies and communists experienced, after they had died gold fillings would be ripped from teeth, wedding rings and other jewelry would be collected and later melted down into gold bars.

But even though camps such as Auschwitz succeeded in gassing thousands of Jews per day, even this tally wasn't fast enough for the Nazi killing machine and orders were given that mass shootings should take place. Again, at the later Nuremberg trials, highly emotional evidence was given by eyewitnesses who saw what had occurred. In the final speech by Britain's Chief Prosecutor, Sir Hartley (later to become Lord) Shawcross, one such account of a mass execution of Jews by the *Einsatzkommandos* (Hitler's special forces) was read out, leading Albert Speer, who was one of those on trial, to reveal that it haunted him for the rest of his life.

'Without screaming or weeping, these people undressed, stood around in family groups, kissed each other, said farewells, and waited for a sign from another SS man, who stood near the pit...with a whip in his hand. During the fifteen minutes I stood nearby, I heard no...plea for mercy. I watched a family of about eight people, a man and a woman of about fifty with two daughters of about twenty to twenty-four and boys of about one, eight, and ten...The couple were looking on with tears in their eyes. The father was holding the hand of a boy about ten years old and speaking to him softly; the boy was fighting his tears...Then I heard a series of shots. I looked into the pit and saw that the bodies were twitching or...lying motionless on top of...those before them. Blood was running from their necks...'[9]

After the war ended, the German people, including those who lived closest to the camps, denied any knowledge of what had happened on their own doorstep. That this was disingenuous is an understatement, for over 900,000 Germans belonged to the SS alone, in addition to which no one could miss the huge numbers of Jews being transported to the camps by the railways. But no one would take responsibility, no one, it seemed, knew anything about Dachau or Auschwitz or any of the other killing zones, yet there was one man for whom the concentration camps were the logical conclusion to years of anti-Semitic bile: Adolf Hitler.

Despite later attempts by several right-wing politicians to prove Hitler had nothing to do with the extermination of the Jews, pointing out the lack of documentation linking the Führer directly to the camps, places such as Auschwitz were undoubtedly the realization of all Hitler's dreams.

However, though the Nazi killing machine was running smoothly and succeeding in its aim of bringing an end to the Jewish race, by mid 1944 the war was not going so well for the Germans. The Allies were pushing forward hard and fast. In May the Soviets, having freed Leningrad back in January, recaptured Sevastopol. By June the Allies had entered Rome and the D-Day landings had begun. Still Hitler battled on, even managing, on 20 July, to avoid an assassination attempt by Fabian von Schlabrendorff who had tried to blow the Führer up. But that was Hitler's only piece of luck in a campaign which, for the Germans, was looking increasingly grim.

On 25 August 1944 the Allies liberated Paris and by January 1945 the Soviets had captured Warsaw. Hitler realized his days were numbered and began behaving like a cornered animal. His language, according to those closest to him, grew increasingly crude, his ranting and raving became unbearable. This was the true Hitler, an uneducated, bitter, twisted man driven by hatred and malice.

It was at this point, knowing that the war was all but lost, that Hitler instigated a 'scorched earth' policy for Germany. His command was to 'reduce the land to ashes' but several of Hitler's closest advisers, including Albert Speer, tried to dissuade him. After all, the only people who would suffer would be the Germans themselves and surely the sign of a true leader was to show that, even in defeat, he was thinking of the best for his country. Hitler wasn't convinced. He wanted everything destroyed: bridges, factories, dams, railways and if anyone refused to comply they were to be shot on sight. Albert Speer did his best to sabotage the plans and in many respects succeeded by subtly altering the Führer's orders. Meanwhile, Hitler grew more isolated and increasingly desperate. By the beginning of April he was no longer able to keep in touch with his generals and though the Germans continued to fight, in particular in the East, there was no organization in what they were doing, no doubt because they knew their efforts were futile. Speer recalls spending an evening with Hitler around this time:

'I had never seen him in such a state before, nor ever again either. He talked about killing himself; that the last chance had gone; that the Luftwaffe and Wehrmacht had betrayed him…A little later he made a 180-degree turn – it was frightening. We would never capitulate, he said. We might sink, but we'd take the world with us.'[10]

As the Allies advanced, preparations were made for the government to move to a retreat in the Bavarian Alps, but at the last moment Hitler announced his intention to remain in Berlin. Eva Braun joined him there, declaring that she wished to remain with him to the end. Suddenly the curtain was falling. On 22 April 1945 Hitler invited a handful of men loyal to him (including Mr and Mrs Goebbels and their children) to join him in the 'Führerbunker', a concrete chamber buried fifty feet beneath the ground. Divided into eighteen rooms, six of them were sectioned off to provide Hitler and Eva with a private suite. Despite the relative safety of the place, it must have felt like a death trap, the last bolthole of a defeated man. The Russians were now in the city, bombs were being dropped night after night and, with no hope left, a meeting was convened at which it was decided on a mass suicide. Still Hitler had one last surprise up his sleeve for, on the morning of 29 April, he decided to reward one member of the remaining group with a particular honor. Eva Braun had always wanted to marry Hitler and now she was to have her way. Between 1am and 3am a brief, civil wedding took place in the bunker's map room. It was conducted by Walter Wagner, a civil servant who was brought into the bunker by Goebbels solely in order to unite the couple. Both Eva Braun and Adolf Hitler took an oath to swear they were of pure Aryan blood and afterwards champagne was drunk. Later that same day news arrived that Hitler's 'companion' dictator, Mussolini, had been executed by Partisans, along with his mistress Clara Petacci. This last piece of news must only have hardened Hitler's resolve to end his own life and on 30 April 1945, having eaten lunch, he and Eva retired to their private suite and closed the doors. Hitler shot himself in the mouth. Eva Braun took cyanide.

Hitler's body, according to the detailed instructions he had left for its disposal, was carried outside into the Chancellery Garden and laid alongside that of Eva Braun. Petrol was poured over both corpses and set alight. What happened to their ashes will never be known, but that the Third Reich was itself reduced to a similar state shortly after Adolf Hitler's death is a matter of historical record for, on 7 May General Alfred Jodl together with Admiral von Friedeburg signed an unconditional surrender of all German forces which was then presented to the USA, Great Britain, France and the USSR.

[1] Albert Speer: His Battle with Truth, by Gitta Sereny, Macmillan, 1995

[2] Hitler: A Study in Tyranny, by Alan Bullock, Penguin Books, 1990.

[3] Mein Kampf, by Adolf Hitler, (English translation by James Murphy), London, 1939.

[4] Hitler: A Study in Tyranny, by Alan Bullock, Penguin Books, 1990.

[5] Institut für Zeitgeschichte, Munich; quoted in Wistrich, Hitler's Apocalypse.

[6] Statement by Albert Speer during his final speech at his trial at Nuremberg, 1946.

[7] Albert Speer: His Battle with Truth, by Gitta Sereny, Picador, 1996.

[8] A History of the Jews, by Paul Johnson, Orion Books Limited, 1993.

[9] Albert Speer: His Battle with Truth, by Gitta Sereny, Picador, 1996.

[10] Ibid.

MAO TSE-TUNG
China's Revolutionary Leader

Although the bourgeoisie has been overthrown, it is still trying to
use the old ideas, culture, customs and habits of the exploiting
classes to corrupt the masses, capture their minds and endeavour
to stage a come-back. The proletariat must do the exact opposite:
it must meet head-on every challenge of the bourgeoisie in the
ideological field and use the new ideas, culture, customs and
habits of the proletariat to change the mental outlook of the
whole of society.

Sixteen-Point Decision of the Central Committee, August 1966

If we judge the extent of a dictator's power by the number of people over whom he wields control, then surely Mao Tse-tung would be at the top of the list. For over twenty-five years Mao commanded in excess of a billion people and his rule extended across a geographical area of over nine million square kilometres. In anyone's terms, these are impressive figures, but what makes them even more awe-inspiring is that in order to establish his stranglehold over China, Mao first had to defeat an army of over four million soldiers and in order to hold on to power, he probably killed far in excess of that number.

Mao Tse-tung was born in the tiny hamlet of Shaoshan in Hunan province on 26 December 1893. He was one of four children born to Mao Jen-sheng and his wife Wen Chi-mei. Mao's father was a strict disciplinarian of poor peasant stock who worked hard to drag his family from its working-class roots up to a more acceptable standard of living. From the start, however, the young Mao gravitated more towards his mother. 'There were two "parties" in the family,' Mao was later to recall. 'One was my father, the Ruling Power. The opposition was made up of myself, my mother, my brother, and sometimes even a labourer. My mother…criticised any overt display of emotion and attempts at open rebellion against the Ruling Power. She said it was not the Chinese way.'[1]

As a young boy between five and seven years of age, Mao was set light tasks to do on his father's land, and then was sent to primary school. His overriding memory of this time is of covertly reading Chinese romance stories, fittingly (as it would later turn out) about peasant rebellions. At age thirteen he left school and began working in the fields as well as tending his father's livestock. But as the young Mao grew up, his disdain for his father increased and eventually he ran away from home to live with a young law student. The break from his family was not to last long, however, and on his return home, probably in the hope of settling him down, the young Mao was presented with a wife (some six years his senior). Having gone back to his parents' house, Mao continued to work for his father for a further six years after which he became aware of a radical new school in Hsianghsiang, in which he enrolled. His studies were very successful and after a year he traveled to Changsha city to take the first of his exams. It was the summer of 1911 and the whole country was on the verge of an anti-imperial revolution for, ever since the 'Opium War' of 1840, when China was forced to open its doors to both European and Japanese merchants, the country had been reduced to little more than a semi-colony of the West. The Ching dynasty (the imperial rule of the Manchus) was despised and when forces, led by Doctor Sun Yat-Sen, overthrew it, Mao was swept up in the proceedings and felt so excited that he enrolled in the army. 'Among journals then dealing with the revolution was the *Hsiang Chiang Jih-pao*. Socialism was discussed in it, and in these columns I first learned the term. I also discussed socialism, really social-reformism, with other students and soldiers.'[2]

After a short time, believing the revolution over, Mao returned to his studies, some of the time attending school, but mostly teaching himself as he found the restrictions of most institutions unbearable. He read widely, enjoying works by, among others, Darwin and John Stuart Mill, as well as poetry and romances.

In the spring of 1913, Mao decided he had studied enough and began a course which would lead him to gaining a teacher's qualification but when he graduated, rather than take up a position in a school, he travelled instead to Peking and found himself a job working as an assistant to Li Ta-chao, the main librarian at Peking University. Li was a radical Marxist and later would become one of the founding members of the Chinese Communist Party (CCP). No doubt he wielded quite an influence over Mao, however, as was his wont, Mao didn't stay long in Peking.

In March 1919 Mao returned to Changsha to take up a teaching post in a primary school. He didn't relinquish his interest in politics and began lecturing on Marxism to anyone who would listen. He was also one of the founding members of the United Students' Association for Hunan province and when, in May 1919, students began demonstrating in Peking, he was fully behind the unrest. In the main, the students were against the concessions given to Japan under the Paris Peace conference, which in turn created bitter resentment towards China's new governing body who, although they had overthrown the old monarchy, had simply replaced it by designating various warlords as rulers. Mao was intent on changing this situation; he was determined to create a strong Communist opposition that would weaken and eventually overthrow these newest of China's oppressors. 'The old atmosphere of China is too heavy and suffocating,' he wrote to a friend in the New People's Study Society. 'We certainly need a new, powerful atmosphere in order to be able to change it. We must have a group of people, fearless of hardships and strong willed for the creation of this new atmosphere…'[3]

In 1920, Mao married his second wife (having discarded his first wife, with whom he had never lived). The second wife was a young woman by the name of Yang Kai-hui with whom he had fallen in love some years earlier. Together they rented a small cottage on the outskirts of Changsha. Yang was as politically minded as her new husband. She was a youth leader and an active communist who would later (in 1930) be executed by Hunan's anti-Communist Governor, Ho Chien, rather than relinquish her beliefs. In the meantime, the young couple worked towards the founding of a steadfast Communist Party. In the summer of 1921, Mao travelled to Peking with eleven other delegates to attend the 'First Congress' of the party. Up until now the new Republic of China had been dominated by the warlords and there was no central administration. The country was in turmoil; it needed strong leadership and Mao, determined to provide it, fully endorsed the Communist Party's decision to join with Sun Yat-sen's Nationalist Party, the Kuomintang (KMT). Mao was now made secretary of the Hunan branch of this new alliance and threw himself into organizing unions for the workers. It was also around this period that he decided that the base for a successful proletarian revolution in China was to be found in the countryside rather than in the industrialized cities.

'A revolution is not a dinner party, or writing an essay,' Mao wrote around 1927, 'or painting a picture, or doing embroidery; it cannot be so refined, so leisurely and gentle, so temperate, kind, courteous, restrained and magnanimous. A revolution is an insurrection, an act of violence by which one class overthrows another.'[4]

The only problem was that several people stood in Mao's way, namely the new leader of the KMT, Chiang Kai-shek, who had taken over the reins of power after Sun Yat-sen died. Chiang disliked the Communists, found their views ran contrary to his own and was convinced they were a threat to his leadership. Consequently in early 1927 he ordered the massacre of hundreds of Communists together with militant city workers. By August, Mao, feeling hemmed in by these brutal attacks and impatient to progress his own ideas not just within the party, but within the country as a whole, led a tiny force of peasant 'soldiers' in an assault on Changsha called the 'Autumn Harvest Uprising.' Behind his ideas lay one central theme, that of confiscating and redistributing all land belonging to the bourgeoisie. The uprisings, however, were swiftly defeated and Mao, along with a handful of loyal followers, escaped to the Chingkang Mountains. Once there, he established a base camp and began training peasants in the surrounding area to 'fight the good fight.'

In May 1928 Mao was elected secretary of the local party as well as party representative of the Fourth Red Army – a battalion in excess of 10,000 men. Mao was determined his troops should serve the people, otherwise, he argued, the army would only serve the feudal landlords, an idea he despised.

For the next few years there were both successes and failures, with unions forming, being smashed, then reforming, student demonstrations, reprisals, then more demonstrations. It was a period of great flux, but although progress was slow, it allowed Mao to consolidate his theories (which in essence were both Leninist and Stalinist, adapted to suit the Chinese situation) and build up a strong, organized army.

Mao's army faced further setbacks in the winter of 1930 when Chiang Kai-shek launched several massive attacks on the Communists, beginning with 'Encirclement Campaigns' which were meant to flush out the Red Army. Between 1930-1934 five of these 'sieges' occurred, four of which failed but the last, in Jianxa province, was an overwhelming success. By October 1934, seeing no alternative, approximately 86,000 communist soldiers and 15,000 cadres including Mao set out from Jianxa in a circuitous march of almost 8,000 miles (they crossed no less than twelve provinces, 18 mountain ranges and 24 rivers) towards the north. Mao travelled lightly, carrying with him little more than two blankets, a sheet, an overcoat, a few books and an oilcloth. It took the convoy 370 days to reach their destination, during which time not only did they engage in daily skirmishes and several pitched battles, they also suffered from diseases such as malaria, typhoid, influenza and dysentery. Many men lost huge amounts of weight and became anemic whilst others began suffering from nervous conditions. During the ordeal it is said that Mao married his third wife, Ho Tzu'chen, a schoolteacher, although the story has never been officially confirmed. What can be taken as gospel, however, is that the journey, which later became known as the 'Long March', was the making of Mao. By the time he and his forces (whose numbers were hugely depleted – in the first three weeks of the march over 25,000 soldiers died) had reached Shanxi province, he had been elected Chairman of the entire Communist organization. 'Without the Long March,' he later wrote, 'how could the broad masses have learned so quickly about the existence of the great truth which the Red Army embodies?'[5] For Mao, the Red Army and the Long March acted as the greatest propaganda coup ever known. During their journey they had announced to millions of Chinese citizens what the Communists stood for and they had awakened the nation's political consciousness. The Long March created a legend around the Red Army that spoke of indestructibility, bravery and limitless endurance.

At last the tide seemed to be turning. From 1937–1945 Chiang had to occupy himself fighting Japanese invaders as well as ensuring the Communists didn't overthrow his government. Meanwhile Mao married his fourth wife, a stage and film actress called Jiang Ching with whom he was to spend the rest of his life. The two shared common ideals, but in particular that art should serve both the people and the revolutionary cause.

By the end of World War II, Japan having been defeated, Chiang and Mao tried to settle their differences. Sadly it wasn't to be, and in 1946 full-scale civil war broke out in China. Initially, it seemed Chiang would win, but he hadn't counted on Mao's determination, or on the Red Army's prowess. In 1949 Peking fell and on 1 October, whilst Chiang fled to Formosa, Mao stood on Tienanmen, the gateway to the old imperial palace of Peking and proclaimed the founding of the People's Republic of China. Behind him flew the new red flag with its five gold stars. In front him stood in excess of 300,000 men, women and children. At age fifty-six, Mao was now one of the most powerful political leaders in the world.

Mao's aim was to create a united China led first and foremost by the Communist Party together with the working class and, hopefully, with the backing and aid of the Soviet Union. To this end he promoted the growth of trade unions, educational societies and cultural groups, but while on the one hand his reforms seemed

During 'The Long March' in 1934, Mao led his Communist army on a desperate, year-long, 8,000-mile trek across China, and was able to spread the word among the populace about Communist ideology in the greatest propaganda coup of all time.

progressive, it is estimated that in the first year of his coming to power (despite sharing eminence with several others including Chou En-lai, Lin Piao and Liu Shao-chi), over three million people were executed for voicing their opinions on the new Communist regime. Mao, like Stalin, knew that in order to remain in power, he had to stamp his authority on the people swiftly and without prevarication. Indeed the Soviet Union was to be the model for a great deal of Mao's thinking because, although he didn't believe that such an agrarian society as China could be modelled on Russia's new industrialized state, the latter would nonetheless be used by Mao as a constant point of reference for what China could and should achieve.

Land reform was high on Mao's agenda. After all, China's agricultural output was only seventy-six percent of what it had been in 1936 and famine loomed on the horizon. To pull the country back from disaster, Mao instigated the Agrarian Reform Law (1950). A social scientist of the period, Chen Han-seng, wrote:

'First, remnant armed bands of reactionaries are rounded up, rural despots removed and local peace ensured by the security organs of the state. Then the peasants are organized through a preliminary movement to reduce rents and reclaim deposits, during which the Peasant Associations grow in strength as a first step in re-organising village administrations. In this stage, large groups of oppressed village people gain their first experience in successfully enforcing their will on their former oppressors. Thirdly,

Mao (right) in 1938 with Chang Kuo-tao, as powerful a force in the Chinese Communist movement as Mao until he suddenly defected to the Nationalists and, after the Communist takeover, was exiled to Hong Kong.

many thousands of land reform workers, mobilised from the cities as well as the countryside, are trained to an understanding of their tasks and sent to the basic points to obtain practical experience.'6

It all sounded very organized, some might say even simple, but what lay behind the words was little short of murder as thousands of landlords whose main crime was to be richer than those they employed, were thrown off their land and often executed. At the same time, investigations began into all those people who had opposed Mao and the 'peoples' coming to power. Huge numbers were denounced and put to death without trial, whilst those lucky enough to escape with their lives were either sent to labor camps or 're-educated'.

By 1955, dissatisfied with the rate of progress the country and in particular the agricultural community was making, Mao ordered the collectivisation of farming. Families were forced into joining 'producer co-ops' where everything, tools, animals, labour, etc had to be pooled and then shared. Worse than this, there then came a period when Mao attempted to control not just the *actions* of his people, but also their *minds*.

In 1956 the Soviet leader, Krushchev, whilst addressing the Twentieth Congress of the Communist Party of the Soviet Union, criticized Stalin and some of his more repressive laws. In response, Mao decided to address all Chinese intellectuals and encourage them to express their opinions without fear of reprisal or persecution. On 2 May 1956 Mao announced, 'Let a hundred flowers bloom, let all the schools of thought contend.' However, the 'Hundred Flowers Campaign', as it was called, was a short-lived affair, for shortly afterwards Mao was to witness an uprising in Hungary, due mostly to a relaxation of censorship. Had it not been for the intervention of Russia, the revolt would have almost certainly overthrown the Communists. Suddenly, Mao had to revise his opinions. He did so swiftly, by declaring that only those arguments that strengthened the Communist Party, not those in opposition, were acceptable. In spite of his declaration, a huge amount of criticism, both of Mao and the Party flowed from all quarters of China, leading Mao to terminate the Hundred Flowers Campaign a little less than six weeks after it had begun. Worse, he then ordered the arrest of over one million men and women who had dared to criticize him and had them either executed or sent to work camps for re-education.

At this point, relations with the Soviet Union began rapidly to crumble. In 1960 Krushchev accused Mao of straying from the path of true Marxism. In July of that year Krushchev then withdrew all Soviet aid from the several industrial programmes that were being undertaken in China, and hundreds of contracts between the two countries were declared null and void.

Despite this spat, Mao still harboured ambitions to emulate the Soviet Union's industrialization model, but where Stalin had taken almost forty years to succeed in his dream, Mao wanted to complete his in less than ten. The Great Leap Forward was put into operation in 1957 and used as its slogan 'Overtake Britain in Fifteen Years'. By the end of 1958 Mao had driven almost the entire population into communes, large organized groups of between 5,000-10,000 households. 'In these rural units, the peasant, or commune member as he is called, is paid according to his work, while each household's sideline occupations, such as the rearing of a pig or chickens or growing vegetables on his private plot, provide supplements to the family income.'[7] It sounded ideal, but this was far from the case as families were forced into near military lifestyles. The hours were long; meal breaks and recreation time practically unheard of, and the agricultural yield fell far below what was required. In fact, the confusion that resulted from the reorganization of the populace resulted in the death of approximately twenty million people. Mao, never one to admit defeat even in the face of overwhelming evidence, was proud of his achievement and in 1958 toured the countryside inspecting progress. Everywhere he went, signs were posted with slogans painted upon them such as 'Communism is Good', 'Leap Forward, Still Leap Forward', 'All for Each, Each for All.' This pleased Mao, but he ignored the hardships of those peasants who had to endure the new regime. Indeed, the programme was so harsh and yields so diminished that after three short years the 'commune' system was abandoned and by 1960 most farmers had returned to collectivism, which was seen by most as the lesser of two evils.

It was at this point that Mao 'retired' (some people say he was demoted) from the Chairmanship of the Party to be replaced as head of state by Liu Shao-chi.

Mao's withdrawal did not, however, stop him having an influence over the party. He still continued to work vigorously for what he saw as the common good of the country and in 1964 a book of Chairman Mao's quotes (compiled by Army Marshal Lin Piao) was published. Better known as *The Little Red Book*, it contained hundreds of sound-bites taken from Mao's longer works and speeches and covered nearly all aspects of his Communist philosophy. It was a huge success. People would recite the quotations at all times of the day, believing them to be akin to 'life lessons', little sayings which would explain how to make everyday existence better. Teachers and parents used them to encourage their wards to behave in a positive manner, i.e. in a manner commensurate with Communist Party policies, and the text was also drummed into children while they worked in the fields. *The Little Red Book* quickly turned into a cultural icon and was also taken up by thousands of students, huge numbers of which left their studies to join the Red Guard, a political organization that was opposed to any type of revisionism or bureaucracy and in particular to any and every transgression against Marxist/Leninist theory.

Perhaps it was the success of *The Little Red Book* that finally prompted Mao to re-establish his leadership of the party. Whatever the cause, by the time *The Little Red Book* was published, Mao had decided that Liu Shao-chi was unsuitable as Communist Party chairman (in Mao's opinion he was taking China down the 'capitalist road') and that he had to be replaced.

Initially, Mao ordered the Red Guard (who were loyal only to Mao) to test party officials and intellectuals by publicly criticizing them, in particular for their 'bourgeois values'. Leaders of the party, but most especially Liu Shao-chi, were denounced, schools closed down, what little industry there was fell into decline and the resulting anarchy and terror paralysed China's entire economy. It was a period of great upheaval but one that optimistically became known as the Great Proletarian Cultural Revolution.

Many books have been written about this period and people's personal experiences during this time, including the most famous account of them all, *Wild Swans* by Jung Chang, but there were others. For instance, below is an extract by a woman called Nien Cheng who was in her fifties when the Cultural Revolution began. Attending a meeting, she sat and listened while a party official spouted out the following:

> "'Comrades!" he said, "our Great Leader Chairman Mao has initiated and is now personally directing the Great Proletarian Cultural Revolution. With our Great Helmsman to guide us, we shall proceed to victory without hindrance. The situation is excellent for us, the proletariat!
>
> "The Great Proletarian Cultural Revolution is an opportunity for all of us to study the Thought of Mao Tse-Tung more thoroughly and diligently...The enemies of socialism are cunning. Some of them raise the red flag to oppose the red flag, while others present us with smiling faces to cover up their dirty scheme. They cooperate with the imperialists abroad and the capitalist class within to try to sabotage socialism and lead the Chinese people backwards to the misery and suffering of the old days...'"[8]

Of course, the irony was that the misery and suffering the Chinese people were now to endure was brought about by the Cultural Revolution itself. Those landlords who were still left were persecuted even further, as were intellectuals, rich peasants, counter-revolutionaries, rightists, bad elements and foreign agents.

Nien Cheng was accused and arrested for being one of the latter (a British spy), and had to suffer six-and-a-half years in solitary confinement. Her treatment was brutal, but she was only one among thousands who suffered the same type of punishment, or, worse still, were executed. Jung Chang also recalls how, during this latest of revolutions, the majority of books were burned, not just in the libraries but in people's homes and how she, alongside her classmates, was ordered to get rid of all the grass and flowers from around their school, as Mao had declared all forms of greenery both 'feudal' and 'bourgeois'.

And yet, though the Cultural Revolution was, as far as Mao was concerned, effective, the Red Guard soon began to split into factions, each of which believed they were the more 'Maoist'. The result threw the country into disarray, but despite some party officials' attempts to call a halt to the revolution, Mao prevailed and the movement escalated.

On 18 August 1966 a series of Red Army rallies was held in Peking with Mao dressed in army uniform surveying his 'troops'. From a rostrum in Tienanmen Square, (the same rostrum from where he had delivered his 1 October 1949 speech founding the People's Republic), he now delivered a polemic condemning huge sections of the Communist Party. Lin Piao stood beside him, but significantly Liu Shao-chi was

They were the two most powerful leaders in the Communist world when Mao met Stalin at Stalin's birthday celebrations in 1950.

Mao's relationship with the USSR had deteriorated somewhat by the time he met with Soviet Premier Nikita Krushchev in 1957.

In an attempt to establish more friendly relations with the Chinese, US President Nixon visited Mao in 1972.

positioned standing at some distance from Mao. Out of six such rallies Liu was only pictured at the first two, after which he vanished from the scene.

Again Mao ordered that the public at large begin criticizing Liu for his 'capitalist' policies and posters denouncing him began to appear all over the country. 'Mao said that Liu should be criticized 'until he stinks', but he did not want to vilify Liu as a person. It was Liu's ideas that should be repudiated. Mao described this campaign as 'a phenomenon affecting the destiny of China and the world.'9

It was now that Liu Shao-chi, under increasing pressure from all quarters of the party, confessed to 'crimes' against the Marxist/Leninist doctrines, as a consequence of which he quickly became a figure not only of ridicule, but also of hate, especially amongst the power-hungry Red Guard. It was the ideal opportunity for Mao to step back into his old shoes of Party Chairman, an opportunity Mao seized with both hands, whilst at the same time naming Lin Piao as his successor.

But Lin was shortly to become a huge thorn in Mao's side as he frequently questioned Mao's policies and authority. Lin, himself an army man, wanted the military to assume the position of the main political force within China, as opposed to a secondary role favoured by Mao. He also decided that many of Mao's policies had actually damaged China. Soon Lin became labelled a 'revisionist', a dangerous individual and an enemy of the state. Mysteriously, Lin died in a plane crash in Mongolia in 1971. His death, however, wasn't reported within China until 1972, at the same time as which it was stated that he had attempted to overthrow the government in a failed coup shortly before he had died. In her book, *The White-Haired Girl*, Jaia Sun-Childers recalls how, after his death was announced, she was told by her classroom teacher that Lin had been a traitor and that all books whose introductions had been written by him were to be removed from their possession. The children were then handed knives and ordered to remove Lin's face from every photograph in which he appeared in their textbooks.

In the last years of his life, Chairman Mao tried to keep an iron grip over the country, but even before his death, the cult that he and others had assiduously built up began to disintegrate. Publication of *The Little Red Book* ground to a halt. Mao's picture, which had once adorned millions of posters, was less frequently printed and new statues were hardly, if ever, erected. But the Cultural Revolution continued and Mao, in an attempt to consolidate his position, declared that several new policies were to be employed. The first was the practice of having 'barefoot' or amateur doctors to work in the countryside, the second was that a large percentage of educated young men and women from the cities were to be sent to live in the countryside, and a third was that peasants and workers should attend university. If nothing else, these new policies show just how far Mao liked to interfere in the lives of China's citizens. In Mao's world, nothing was to be left up to the individual, let alone to be left to chance. A good picture of him during this period would be as a god, one whose every whim had to be obeyed. Mao was, of course, only human and all mortals have to die. At ten minutes past midnight on 9 September 1976, Mao passed away. He was eighty-two years old and had been in ill health for several years.

Immediately his death was announced, the Chinese people began wearing black armbands and gathering opposite a huge portrait of Mao that hung outside the main entrance to the Forbidden City. His body was then laid in state at the Great Hall of the People after which a memorial service was held on 18 September.

After Mao's death, the new Chinese government began reversing a good deal of his policies, in particular those which relied heavily on the cult of Mao's personality. But

perhaps most significant of all was that they began turning to the outside world –
Europe, America and Japan – for help in trying to modernize not only China's
industrial base, but also its agriculture, scientific institutions and the armed forces.
These changes were something that would never have been countenanced in Mao's
lifetime but, almost like an echo of one of his own proclamations, the reforms were
announced as the Four Modernizations.

When Mao Tse-tung died in 1976, China was, politically speaking, in a state of near
breakdown. If the Communist Party was to continue its stranglehold over the country
it knew that it had to change its policies. The Chinese people were barely managing to
feed themselves; they were disillusioned, downtrodden and weary. The Communist
Party, and by association Mao Tse-tung, had promised them a paradise, instead they
were fed a never-ending supply of fruitless slogans. To change the situation and
enthuse the people, the Party now appeals to the pride they have in their country.
Citizens are encouraged to work hard and modernize China so that once again the
country can compete on the world stage and call itself a great nation. In return, the
Chinese have been promised a stable economy and, in a direct reference to the Mao
Tse-tung era, no more political posturing or warfare.

Nevertheless, Mao has not been forgotten. His portrait still hangs in Tienanmen
Square and his corpse is, in the words of Jung Chang, still 'an object of worship' within
the Communist Party. China's current leadership continues to revere its old leader
and, as if to prove this point, perseveres with its total ban on the publication of *Wild
Swans* or any mention of the author and her work in the Chinese media. Some things
never change.

1   *Mao Tse-tung And The Chinese People*, by Roger Howard,
        Monthly Review Press, 1977.
2   *Red Star over China*, by Edgar Snow, Harmondsworth, Penguin, 1972.
3   *Mao*, by Jerome Ch'en, Englewood Cliffs, N.J., Prentice-Hall, 1969.
4   *Mao Tse-tung and the Chinese People*, by Roger Howard,
        Monthly Review Press 1977.
5   *On Tactics against Japanese Imperialism*, Mao Tse-tung
6   *China Reconstructs*, by Chen Han-seng, May 1952.
7   *Mao Tse-tung and the Chinese People*, by Roger Howard, Monthly Review Press, 1977.
8   *Prisoner of Mao: Life and Death in Shanghai*, by Nien Cheng, Grafton Books, 1986.
9   *Mao-Tse-tung and the Chinese People*, by Roger Howard,
        Monthly Review Press, 1977.

ANASTASIO GARCÍA SOMOZA

'Our Son of a Bitch'

I hope you will take this calmly and realise that what I have done
is a duty that any Nicaraguan who loves his fatherland should
have carried out long ago.
This is not a sacrifice, but a duty I hope I have been able to fulfil.
Letter written by Rigoberto López Pérez, September 1956

On 21 September 1956 in Léon, Nicaragua, a young poet and journalist by the name of Rigoberto López Pérez mingled with a crowd that had gathered to watch the country's President attend his fifth official nomination ceremony. Pérez drew closer and closer to his target until he was within striking distance, then drew out a revolver and fired four times at point-blank range. Within seconds of the shots being fired, Pérez was gunned down by the president's bodyguards. The president was immediately flown by helicopter to Managua and from there to the Gorgas Hospital in the Panama Canal Zone. Eight days later, on 29 September, the people of Nicaragua woke to the news that Anastasio García Somoza was dead. For twenty years he had terrorized the country, at the same time amassing for himself a monumental personal fortune. If the Nicaraguans thought they had rid themselves of a despotic dictator, however, then they were shortly to be disillusioned. No sooner had Anastasio Somoza died then his eldest son, Luis, stepped into his shoes.

Born in San Marcos in 1896, Anastasio García Somoza was the son of an undistinguished coffee planter. There was nothing remarkable about Anastasio's early childhood save for the fact that he was a descendent of the famous Nicaraguan bandit-cum-revolutionary of the 1840s, Siete Pañuelos. Very little is known about Somoza's early life except that he attended the Instituto Nacional del Orente after which he was packed off to the United States where he was enrolled in the Pierce School of Business Administration in Philadelphia. Having graduated, Somoza then turned his hand to a series of mundane jobs. He drifted around the US working as, amongst other things, an automobile salesman, a toilet inspector and (some people say) a counterfeiter. It was also during this period that he married Salvadora Debayle, a member of one of Nicaragua's most important aristocratic families.

In 1926, at the age of twenty, Somoza returned to Nicaragua where he soon became involved in the political scene. Back in 1912, the then president of Nicaragua, Adolfo Díaz, had called for American troops to help him fight against rebel Liberal forces and, on his return from America, Somoza joined the Liberals who at that time were headed by Juan Bautista Sacasa and José María Moncada. Several battles and skirmishes subsequently took place between the Liberals and the US and eventually the Americans decided the best course of action would be a negotiated peace settlement. The Americans wanted Diaz to continue as President but, contrary to their wishes, the Liberals set up Sacasa and several others as a rival government. More fighting followed until a second peace plan was put into operation. This time it was proposed that Diaz would remain as president until a general election could be held – in the meantime several Liberals would be incorporated into his government. Both sides would also have to disarm, after which a new, bipartisan *Guardia Nacional* under the command of the US would be established. The Liberals complied with these proposals and when the US began withdrawing its troops around 1933, were delighted that one of their number was chosen to head the Guardia: Anastasio Somoza.

Once the Americans had departed, Somoza – always with an eye to the main chance – immediately set about a plan to overthrow the present government (now headed by Sacasa) and to rid Nicaragua of another political thorn, the revolutionary guerrilla crusader, Augusto C. Sandino, who, when the US proposed its second peace plan, had opposed the idea vehemently. Sandino, however, controlled a huge portion of Nicaragua as well as some 3,000 fully trained, well-armed soldiers. The situation would have to be handled carefully, especially as Sacasa had begun peace talks with the young rebel. Somoza, unhappy with the way events were unfolding, began building up the Guardia to record levels. He also brought into play his formidable powers of persuasion and won over a number of political appointees to the Guardia who had been placed there by Sacasa to spy on Somoza. It all seemed to be going so well that Somoza had even begun persuading Sacasa that the only way to deal with Sandino was by force, but then everything changed when Sandino suddenly announced he was willing to travel to Managua and attend peace talks. Without hesitation, Sacasa sent a plane to bring Sandino to the capital. A peace treaty was agreed, one which gave Sandino's men a general amnesty providing that they handed over their weapons to the Guardia. Furthermore, Sandino was given control over a small area of land in the north of the country on the River Coco and was allowed to employ an emergency force of one hundred men.

Initially, the peace treaty seemed to work, but when it came to handing over their weapons, Somoza was infuriated to discover that barely enough guns and ammunition were surrendered to equip fifty men let alone three thousand. Sacasa let Sandino get away with this in the hope that it would encourage a peaceful future for both himself and for Nicaragua. Somoza, on the other hand, mounted a full-scale surveillance operation on everyone involved with Sandino and covertly began tapping phones and intercepting mail. In addition, hoping to provoke an outbreak of violence, he also organized for the *Sandinistas* (those one hundred men who were protected under the peace treaty) to be harassed and put in prison on as many trumped-up charges as he and his men could manufacture. In reply, Sandino sent telegrams to Sacasa, not only informing him of what the Guardia were doing, but also warning him that it was only a matter of time before Somoza attempted to overthrow the government.

Less than eight months after Sacasa had taken over the presidency, a series of explosions occurred in Managua, which shook the government to its core. No one claimed responsibility but, not wishing to risk further attacks, Sacasa imposed a state of siege and began imprisoning hundreds of Conservative army officers. Somoza couldn't have been more delighted for, aside from Sandino, Conservative operatives were (especially within the Guardia) his main opposition. With a state of siege in place the Guardia were, to all intents and purposes, in control of the entire country. Rather than take full advantage of this moment and overthrow the government, Somoza decided to play it safe and instead began implying that Sandino was planning a coup. To back up this theory the Guardia searched for and found all the weapons that Sandino had failed to hand over when the initial peace treaty was signed. In retaliation, Sandino denounced the Guardia, pointing out that it had been set up by a foreign nation, i.e. America, and that it was unconstitutional. For weeks on end the bickering continued and accusation after accusation flew from both camps, but finally Sacasa decided on a solution. Political and military control of Nicaragua's northern departments would be given to General Horace Portocarrero who was a 'Sandino man'. This was enough to soothe the *Sandinistas*, but the solution enraged Somoza who cautioned Sacasa that the Guardia would be furious at his decision. Furthermore, Somoza warned he would not be able to control his men who now felt insulted by their president. But Somoza's warning fell on deaf ears and on 21 February 1934, having attended a dinner hosted by Sacasa, Sandino (along with four other men) was assassinated.

'It was almost ten o'clock when Salvatierra drove the President's guests away from the Palace towards his own house, which lay beyond the Campo de Marte in central Managua. As they drew up to the barracks, they found the road blocked by a Guardia patrol. All five occupants were forced out of the car at gunpoint; Minister Salvatierra [the Agricultural Minister] and Don Gregorio Sandino [Sandino's father] were led away into the military compound, and the other three were bundled into a truck and driven off into the night. A few minutes later the vehicle stopped. Sandino, Umanzor and Estrada were pushed out, unceremoniously lined up and shot. Their bodies were buried nearby, under the runway of Managua's airport.'[1]

Not satisfied with murdering Sandino, Somoza further ordered that those members of the Guardia who had been stationed around Sandino's base camp in the north massacre its occupants. Only a few men managed to escape the bloodbath. Somoza had, in one fell swoop, eliminated his number one enemy.

In the aftermath of the assassination, Sacasa forced all his military officers to vow an oath of allegiance to himself as President and vowed to bring to justice Sandino's killers. Somoza played along with this, even mounting an investigation himself, but covertly he also began spreading rumours that Washington had approved the killing and that he, Somoza, acting in Nicaragua's best interests, had carried it out. Somoza also began lobbying several Liberal congressmen to begin blocking the Sacasa Administration's legislative proposals which, in effect, considerably weakened the President's political standing. Nor did Somoza stop there for, once he felt his position to be unassailable, he publicly admitted that it was indeed he who had ordered Sandino's assassination and that all those who had carried it out ought not only to be applauded but also granted an amnesty. It was a risky move, but one that paid off, for Congress immediately agreed and passed the motion. Sacasa, meanwhile, vetoed the bill only to see Congress pass it again. Strengthened by this show of support, Somoza began announcing that he intended to run for the Presidency in 1936. Sacasa was immediately advised to dismiss Somoza as head of the Guardia, but rather than do this he preferred to focus his attention on building up political support within Congress.

On September 12, Managua was once again the target for a bombing campaign. This time both Sacasa and Somoza believed the culprits were attempting a coup, but in reality it turned out to be the work of a lieutenant called Juan López who had blown up the Campo de Marte in a personal vendetta against its quartermaster. Somoza had López sentenced to death, but in order to show the people that he was still their President, Sacasa commuted the sentence to one of life imprisonment. Once again, Somoza felt he had been slighted and undermined by Sacasa, but he turned his anger to good use by campaigning even more strongly for the support of the Liberal Congressmen. It was a tit-for-tat struggle that turned increasingly vicious, in particular when Sacasa decided to grant an amnesty to López, an act which Somoza took as a direct threat to his authority. As a show of strength, Somoza ordered his troops to equip themselves with all their weaponry and parade in front of the Palacio Nacional. This was enough of a warning to Congress to repeal the amnesty, but no sooner was this done than another equally sticky situation transpired as Sacasa announced the creation of a police force, one that would be entirely distinct from the Guardia, coming under his command alone. Naturally, Somoza was furious and threatened Sacasa with a mutiny if he didn't withdraw the proposal. Sacasa backed down, but if he was seen to be weak, his wife María was anything but, and on behalf of her husband she began plotting Somoza's downfall.

At first she approached Washington for assistance. It had been the Americans, after all, who had initially set up the Guardia and given Somoza his position of authority. But the Señora was to be disappointed as the US pointed out it was no longer responsible for either Somoza or the Guardia. Undaunted by the US refusal to help, Sacasa's wife turned to her friends in Honduras and El Salvador and had them guarantee military support in her attempt to oust Somoza. Once again, however, the US scuppered her plans and made it clear to both countries that they would not sanction any such intervention. It all looked to be going Somoza's way, but in a swift about turn, Washington's next action was to talk Somoza into withdrawing from the presidential race. As a reward, Somoza would be guaranteed his position at the head of the Guardia. But no sooner was the agreement signed than Somoza roused his supporters into demonstrating their displeasure at what had occurred. At almost the same time, Managua was hit by a petrol shortage which resulted in a chauffeurs' strike and several anti-government protests. Sacasa ordered the Guardia to put an end to the

Anastasio Somoza became Director of Nicaragua's Guardia National in 1933 but, in line with the country's constitution, he had to resign his post in 1936 in order to run for the presidency. Once he was President, he also reinstated himself as Director of the Guardia.

a personal fortune of over five million dollars.

Nonetheless, Somoza was not without his enemies, or at least people who wished to oppose him politically. Somoza's spies, of whom there were many, began to warn him that Opposition groups (in particular one headed by a man called Carlos Pasos) were planning to cause civil unrest in the form of general strikes in order to stir up trouble for the government. Somoza moved quickly and quietly. On the day the action had been planned to take place, he sent Guardia troops to put the rebel leaders under house arrest. Somoza had Congress pass a bill amending the ban on re-election. But his bully-boy tactics led to angry demonstrations by the general public that in turn fuelled Carlos Pasos's determination to go it alone and set up his own political party, the Partido Liberal Independiente. Pasos then began a bitter campaign against Somoza, the worst the latter had had to face in over six years as President. Riots broke out all over Nicaragua, and citizens, in particular businessmen and their employees, were encouraged to join in the fight. Without hesitation, Somoza sent in troops to arrest anyone found demonstrating or otherwise engaged in subversive activities. At the same time he stage-managed a massive 4th of July parade to illustrate that he was still America's man and therefore had their full backing. Somoza also forced his members of Congress into passing progressive labour laws, which took the wind out of the Opposition's sails whilst at the same time allowing him space to organize the workers into government-run unions.

As far as the US was concerned, however, Somoza was becoming an increasing

liability and though it had backed him in the past, the US State Department was now none too happy to be seen supporting either him or his political objectives. Somoza, on the other hand, needed America, most particularly for financial and military support. He began wooing the American military commanders who had always looked upon him as an old friend and ally. Besides, it was more than clear that even should Somoza be ousted from power, his family would take over control. Over the years Somoza had

Somoza planted informants throughout the country and used his Guardia troops ruthlessly to quash any signs of political insurrection.

placed various relatives in key Guardia positions. Somoza's brother-in-law, Luis Manuel Debayle was a Colonel in the Guardia, while one of Somoza's bastard sons was in the officer corps. His real son, Luis, was a Captain in the Guardia and another son, Anastasio, who was already a First Lieutenant, was now attending West Point Military Academy in the US.

Nevertheless, in order to appease the American diplomats, on 29 November 1945 Somoza signed a written pledge that not only would he disallow his candidacy for a third term, he would reinstate all those civil liberties he had banned and free all political prisoners. And he was true to his word. Political detainees *were* released and anti-Somoza rallies *were* allowed. But while all this was happening in one place, no one noticed what Somoza was up to in another. Behind the scenes Somoza began to methodically change the constitution so that when he stood down as President, most of the power he enjoyed went with him. He placed loyal officers of the Guardia in key positions around the country and when his younger son, Anastasio, graduated from West Point he appointed him General of the First Battalion. Somoza also tried to plot and scheme his way round the US embargo of arms sales to Nicaragua.

But Somoza hadn't relinquished all interest in the political side of life. When his party decided to nominate Enoc Aguado as their preferred candidate for the forthcoming election, Somoza vetoed the nomination and instead forwarded Leonardo Argüello as his man. Argüello, who had been a serving minister in the Sacasa administration, was by now an old man. Naturally, this was the reason that Somoza forwarded him for the presidency. Old men were easily manipulated and this old man would be no exception.

On 2 February 1947 Nicaraguans went to the ballot box. Soon queues were forming outside polling stations, but if the Opposition had thought the day would run smoothly, they were mistaken. It was common practice in Nicaragua to line up in separate columns depending upon for whom you were going to vote, but early on it became obvious that the Opposition queues weren't moving as quickly as those for Argüello. In fact, all sorts of bureaucratic difficulties were encountered by everyone wishing to vote for the Opposition and by the end of the day, when Guardia officers closed the polling stations, it was apparent that thousands of Opposition supporters had yet to cast their vote.

It came as no surprise to most, therefore, when Leonardo Argüello was announced the victor, having been elected to the presidency with a landslide majority. Far from being a puppet president who would allow himself to be manipulated by Somoza, it turned out that Argüello was his own man who had no intention of kowtowing to his predecessor.

From the outset Argüello met with the American Ambassador to inform him of the new government's intention of removing Somoza from any position of authority. In the weeks following the election Argüello also worked tirelessly to begin undermining Somoza's authority within the Guardia. Without a moment's notice, Argüello removed Somoza's men from their key positions of authority and moved them to less important posts. He also purged the public services of Somoza stalwarts and chose a new cabinet of men who were more often than not anti the previous president. Somoza found his power base under attack from all angles.

Having accomplished all this in such a short space of time, the Americans were convinced that Argüello was about to provide Somoza with his come-uppance. The only sign of resistance that Somoza could muster was to parade three battered tanks in front of the Presidential Palace. It was hardly a show of great military strength, but Somoza was quickly to regain the upper hand. When Congress began nominating individuals who would succeed Argüello should he die, Somoza made certain he picked out the designates. Somoza also sent out orders to all the regional military centers instructing commanders not to obey any orders that didn't come directly from him. Then he moved in for the kill. Barely three weeks after Argüello had been sworn in as President, he came under attack. All the telephone lines to the Presidential Palace were cut after which, in a dawn raid, all those military officers loyal to Argüello were placed under house arrest. Leonardo Argüello himself managed to escape to the Mexican embassy which was fortunate for, less than twenty-four hours after the coup had begun, Somoza was announcing to a shocked congress that their ex-President had been plotting nothing less than a dictatorship. The irony was not lost on any of those in attendance and yet they didn't dare oppose Somoza who promptly appointed Benjamín Lacayo Sacasa as interim president.

On hearing the news in Washington, US President Truman ordered all American troops out of Nicaragua and withdrew all remaining military aid, but none of this fazed Somoza who, foreseeing a Cold War looming on the horizon, invited the US to set up military bases on Nicaraguan land. It was an offer too good to refuse and by 1948 not only was Nicaragua enjoying good diplomatic relations with most South American countries, it was also a close ally of the US as well.

Somoza's next move was one guaranteed to further his own political career. Shortly after he had appointed Benjamin Sacasa as stand-in President, he had him replaced by his own Uncle, Victor Román y Reyes. Somoza then rewrote the Constitution so that he could run for another term as President. As luck would have it, Somoza didn't even have to wait for election-time to gain the presidency as Román y Reyes died suddenly of a heart attack and Congress, never keen to cross Somoza, duly appointed him President for the completion of his uncle's term of office. When elections were finally held, Somoza won a landslide victory as the Opposition had already been bribed into accepting defeat in return for a say in all political decisions.

But not everything was going Somoza's way, for at this point he received information that yet another assassination plot was under way, led by an ex-Conservative member of parliament, Emiliano Chamorro and backed by the Costa Rican leader Colonel 'Pepe' Figueres. In a plan similar to that implemented for the Sandino killing, they had plotted to kidnap Somoza after he had left a late meeting at the American Embassy. Instead, Somoza got in first, arresting everyone thought to be involved in the plot and hunting down anyone who tried to escape. Afterwards the

At a press conference in 1955, Somoza challenged Costa Rican President Jose Figueres to a duel to settle their countries' differences, saying, 'If he hates me so much let him come out and fight like a man without trying to involve the innocent people of the two countries.'

prisoners were executed without even the benefit of a show trial. Almost the only people to escape were the initiators of the plot, Chamorro and Figueres who both fled back to Costa Rica.

Incandescent with rage, Somoza then began what he thought would be a swift war against Costa Rica. On 11 January 1954 he sent his troops across the border into Costa Rican territory, but Figueres fought back for all he was worth and persuaded the US to come to his aid. No sooner had the war begun than it was over, Somoza's troops quickly retreating back towards Nicaragua. Defeated in one war, Somoza then had to face another, only this time it was economic. Having dragged the country from near-poverty to become one of the most successful in the whole of Latin America, Somoza was now faced with volatile international markets and decided to decrease the value of the *córdoba*. Suddenly, whole sections of middle-class and working-class Nicaraguans were hit in the pocket. Those men and women who had built up small businesses were most badly hit, but in an act of complete defiance, instead of admitting his mistake,

Somoza announced that he was going to run for a fifth term as President. For some, this was all too much to bear and for one man in particular it spelt the beginning of the end.

'My dear Mother,

Though you have never known, I have always been involved in everything concerned with attacking the dismal regime which rules over our fatherland. In view of the fact that all attempts at making Nicaragua once again (or for the first time) a free country, without stain or dishonor, have failed, and even though my comrades disagree with me, I have decided to try to be the person who will begin the end of this tyranny.'[3]

Rigoberto López Pérez, a Nicaraguan exile in San Salvador, a poet and journalist who had watched his country's years of suffering at the hands of Somoza, had decided enough was enough. He spent weeks practicing with a revolver so that he could assure himself that he wouldn't fail in his attempt and he plotted down to the last second the exact time and place he would gun down the President, even going so far as to follow Somoza around the country, studying his habits and mapping out his day-to-day itinerary. Despite his preparations, Pérez's first attempt failed for, on 14 September 1956, while the President was celebrating the centenary of the battle in which a nineteenth-century North American adventurer by the name of William Walker, who had usurped the Nicaraguan government, was defeated, Pérez couldn't get close enough to his target and so called off the killing. Instead he waited six days until Somoza was in León announcing his decision to run for a fifth term in office. Somoza's staff had organized an open reception for the President at the Casa del Obrero. The day was hot and Somoza's bodyguards, having grown sluggish in the heat, weren't at their most responsive. It wasn't difficult for Pérez to approach his target and, within seconds of so doing, he had shot Somoza four times at point-blank range.

Anastasio Garcia Somoza was, on the orders of US President Dwight D. Eisenhower, immediately rushed by helicopter to the Gorgas Hospital in the Panama Canal Zone, but later died of his injuries. By the time his death was announced to the public on 29 September 1956, Luis Somoza Debayle, Anastasio's eldest son, had taken over the reins of power and so began the Somoza family's long dynastic control over Nicaragua.

[1] *Dictators Never Die: A Portrait of Nicaragua and the Somozas*, by Eduardo Crawley,
       C. Hurst & Company, London, 1979.
[2] Ibid.
[3] Ibid.

FRANÇOIS 'PAPA DOC' DUVALIER

The Quiet Country Doctor

'The Tontons Macoute,' the purser broke in with wicked glee. 'The
President's bogey-men. They wear dark glasses and they call on
their victims after dark.'

Graham Greene, *The Comedians*

In the Caribbean sits a small tropical island dotted with palm trees, exotic flowers, succulent fruits. There are green mountain regions which stretch down to fertile pasturelands separated from the sea by sandy white beaches. Indeed this tiny island looks much like any other tropical paradise that you might find while gliding through the azure waters of the Caribbean. But there is one significant difference. Look closely and you will discover no high-rise hotels, no pleasure beaches nor restaurants tempting you with exotic local dishes, for this is Haiti, a land that over the centuries has been torn apart by civil unrest, a land that during the late 1950s and into the 60s suffered under one of the most vile dictatorships in world history, that of François 'Papa Doc' Duvalier.

Haiti was first discovered, leastways by westerners, in 1492 by Christopher Columbus, who named it *La Isla Espanola* which was later shortened to *Hispanola*. At the time the island was populated by Arawak Indians who themselves referred to the place as 'Hayti' (which in translation means mountainous land). Sadly, as was often the way in cases of colonization, the natives were soon being abused by the newcomers who, realizing that the island was rich in natural resources, put the Arawaks to work in the sugar cane and cocoa fields.

But the Spanish couldn't keep Haiti all to themselves for long and Britain and France soon began demanding parts of the island for themselves. Finally, in the middle of the seventeenth century, after much warring, the island became a French colony. As well as being a rich source of sugar and cocoa, the island also yielded huge amounts of coffee and cotton, but the more Haiti produced, the more was wanted and, in the end, desperate to keep up with demand, the French looked to Africa to supply them with labour. Suddenly the island was swamped with slaves. Importing slaves may have seemed like the answer to the problem of having too few workers but it soon caused several headaches all of its own. The slaves brought with them their own religion in the form of voodoo. Voodoo was (and still is) a very powerful force for all those who adhere to its rites. Amongst other things, voodoo involves animal sacrifice, magic rituals, and the worship of dozens of spirit deities who are believed to 'possess' believers during voodoo ceremonies. Clearly, this was far removed from the Christian beliefs of the French, and served to reinforce their bigoted attitude towards the African slaves. The French treated the slaves with utter brutality (it is reputed that over 500,000 were either flogged, starved or buried alive) showing them far less regard than they would common livestock. Inevitably, this caused enormous resentment within an already volatile community. The introduction of the Africans also created a third class of people, the 'mulattos' (light-skinned black people), who were the result of relations between slave owners and their slaves. In later years these mulattos would form a new strata in an already complicated class system on the island, looking down upon their darker-skinned compatriots and treating them with contempt.

By 1791, the slave community had had enough of their lords and masters and a successful revolt was initiated which saw the French overthrown. So successful was the uprising that in 1804 Haiti became the first black independent nation. But the bloodshed and internecine warfare did not stop there. A man by the name of General Dessalines declared himself emperor but when it came to abusing the people he was little better than the French and, as a result, he was assassinated. Next came Henri Christophe, an illiterate ex-slave, who took over the north of Haiti, while a mulatto, Alexandre Pétion, ruled in the south. When Christophe died (he committed suicide by shooting himself with a silver bullet), the north and the south united and for a brief time things looked peaceful but by 1844 the island was once again ripped apart. This time two new countries emerged, with Haiti at one end of the island and the Dominican Republic at the other. Suddenly Haiti was thrown into a state of anarchy and between 1843-1915 it suffered under twenty-two heads of state, most of whom met with violent ends. President Guillaume Sam was the last of their number and when he was dismembered, the Americans decided it was time to invade Haiti and bring some kind of stability to the region. The US remained in the country for over fourteen years and, with all their resources, managed to re-build much of Haiti's infrastructure. New roads were constructed along with schools, hospitals and sewerage systems, but the Haitians didn't look kindly upon the Americans, whom they regarded as interlopers. Finally, in 1934, America (at the instigation of US President Franklin D. Roosevelt) withdrew, but politically Haiti was still in a state of constant flux. It wasn't until 1957, when François Duvalier appeared on the scene, that any kind of stability looked possible. But if the Haitians thought they had found a saviour in their new leader, sadly they couldn't have been more mistaken.

Born a short distance from the National Palace during the military dictatorship of one Nord Alexis on 14 April 1907 in Port-au-Prince, François Duvalier was the son of Duval Duvalier who worked over a period of years as a primary schoolteacher, a journalist and a justice of the peace. His mother was Uritia Abraham, a bakery employee.

During François' early years, Haiti was in a state of almost perpetual turmoil.

'When he was one year old General Antoine Simon overthrew Alexis. He was four when a revolution ousted Simon and five when an explosion reduced the old wooden Palais National, and President Cincinnatus Leconte along with it, to splinters. Duvalier was six when President Tancrède Auguste was poisoned; his funeral was interrupted when two generals began fighting over his succession…One Michel Oreste got the job, but he was overthrown the following year by a man named Zamor, who in turn fell a year later to Davilmar.'[1]

Political upheavals aside, the young François' childhood was unremarkable save for the fact that in a country where 90% of the population went uneducated, he at least received a good schooling. As a boy he is known first to have attended the Lycée Pétion and, after leaving school, to have received a short apprenticeship on a newspaper called *Action Nationale* where he used the pen name Abcerrahman, which is a phonetic spelling of Abd-al-Rahman – the first caliph who established a medical school in Cordova. Later, Duvalier attended the faculty of medicine at the University of Haiti and worked for part of his doctor's internship at the Hospice Saint François-de-Sales. It was as a physician that Duvalier came by his favoured nickname of 'Papa Doc'.

On 27 December 1939, Duvalier married Simone Ovide Faine, a nurse's aide whom he had met while the two worked together in the Hospice. Simone came from very humble beginnings; born the illegitimate daughter of a mulatto merchant called Jules Faine and one of the maids in his household, she spent much of her early life in an orphanage in the hills above Port-au-Prince. Ordinarily, a young doctor would not marry beneath his class, but Simone grew into a very beautiful young woman (with a very pale skin) and the couple were united in the St Pierre Church of Pétionville. 'It wasn't an idyllic marriage' said Bernard Diederich, joint author of a biography on Duvalier, but nonetheless the couple produced four children: Marie Denise, Simone, Nicole and last but not least Jean-Claude (who would later become better known as 'Baby Doc' Duvalier).

From 1934 to 1946 Papa Doc worked in a series of different hospitals and clinics researching, with the aid of a US-sponsored campaign, various tropical diseases including yaws, which is a highly infectious bacterial complaint manifesting itself as bumps on the skin of the face, hands, feet and elsewhere. As a result of all his hard work in this area, Papa Doc began to gain a reputation as a humanitarian, someone who cared about the parlous state of the poorer elements of Haitian society. This reputation stood him in very good stead when, between 1946 and 1950, he took over as director-general of the National Public Health Service as well as Secretary of Labour. Around this time he is also believed to have become a member of *Le Groupe des Griots*, a party of writers and activists committed to Black Nationalism and voodoo. No one could fault Papa Doc and with all his good work amongst the sick and the needy, his very name seemed synonymous with everything that was charitable in the world. He was a father figure, a benign patriarch, a doctor who would make his country 'better'.

On 22 September 1957, this innocuous-looking, soft spoken black man, Papa Doc Duvalier (with the military's backing), was elected President of the country triumphing over Louis Déjoie, an educated, middle-class mulatto. In fact, four candidates had entered the race to be elected: François Duvalier, Louis Déjoie, Clément Jumelle and Daniel Fignolé, but before the voting had begun Fignolé was sent into exile in the US, having been accused of trying to 'buy' the army and Jumelle withdrew from the race due to his (correct) belief that the military were arranging for Duvalier to win. Duvalier's victory was so overwhelming (Duvalier: 18,841 votes; Déjoie: 463) that many charges of corruption followed though, unsurprisingly, none were proved.

Initially Duvalier promised to establish a 'noirist' regime, the type of rule that would bring to an end the political stranglehold that the Haitian upper classes (those who were predominately pale-skinned, wealthy, French-speaking and Catholic) had over the country. In their place he would establish a voodoo culture more suited to the masses. Papa Doc himself was a follower and practitioner of voodoo and was rumoured to be a *houngan* - a voodoo sorcerer who can mediate between humans and spirits while in a trance-like state. His wife Simone was also a believer. Instead of restoring order and bringing prosperity to Haiti, however, Papa Doc plunged the country into fourteen dark, terrible years of fear and violence.

Worried that the military might threaten the security of his presidency, Papa Doc sacked the head of the armed forces, replacing him with an officer who was more sympathetic to his policies. He also, after an unsuccessful attempt to overthrow him in June 1958, reduced the overall size of the army and closed down the military academy.

Papa Doc then formed a 'Palace Guard', a group of men that was to be his own private army but, perhaps most sinister of all, Duvalier further snubbed tradition by forming, along with his chief aide, Clément Barbot, a rural militia estimated to number in the region of 9,000-15,000 men. These militiamen were called the Volunteers for National Security (*Volontaires de la Sécurité Nationale* or VSN) but were commonly referred to as the Tontons Macoute (derived from the Creole term for a mythological bogeyman who grabs people in the middle of the night and makes them disappear forever). According to various studies, barely two years after Papa Doc came to power the Tontons Macoute had twice the power of the army and were feared throughout the country not only for their murderous ways, but also because many of their number were practitioners of voodoo and therefore had the 'dark forces' working in their favour. In fact, the Tontons Macoute were mainly recruited from the capital city's vast slum areas and were only equipped with antiquated firearms. The fact that they didn't receive a state salary meant that they had to rely on extortion, bribery and corruption in order to make a living, which in turn led them to commit countless acts of violence.

Nor did the extortion stop at the Tontons Macoute; it was prevalent in every echelon of the new government, right up to Papa Doc himself. Far from being a timid, passive country doctor as he had at first portrayed himself, on being elected Papa Doc showed his true colors, establishing huge government rake-offs from Haiti's main industrial interests and using bribery as a means of fleecing hundreds of domestic businesses. Worse still, eager to control any opposition to his power base, he saw to it that his 'enemies' were sent to the notorious Fort Dimanche where, in most cases, they were tortured to death. Fort Dimanche, or Fort Mort as it was nicknamed, was built during the US occupation of Haiti. Initially it was used as a shooting range for training the military, but when Duvalier came to power the building was turned into a

*Although he had traded on his image as a doctor and scientist when campaigning for
election, President François 'Papa Doc' Duvalier was a follower of voodoo and rumoured to
be a hougan, or voodoo sorcerer.*

headquarters for training the Tontons Macoute before becoming a center for the detention, torture and/or execution of anyone whom Duvalier deemed a threat. Suddenly, newspaper editors from publications such as the *Miroir* and *L'Indépendent*, radio station owners and journalists were jailed on specious charges of sedition, and Duvalier's henchman, Barbot, set about bombing their offices. In this way all forms of opposition were either extinguished or driven underground, for politicians and media men alike were too frightened to express their views openly.

But if François 'Papa Doc' Duvalier was a terrifying figure to the educated upper and middle classes in Haiti, he was nothing short of a demon to the uneducated peasantry. Having studied voodoo and aligned himself behind this religion, Papa Doc milked it to the last by posing as Baron Samedi, a particularly evil voodoo deity who could put the living in touch with the dead. Uncannily, Duvalier did look remarkably like Samedi, especially when he dressed up in similar attire to the voodoo god, who is most often depicted wearing a black top hat, black coat tails and sunglasses. Taking this one stage further, Duvalier also had posters printed that unashamedly suggested he was at one with the voodoo spirits, Jesus Christ and God himself. Most famously there is an image of Duvalier standing alongside Jesus Christ, who has his right hand resting on Duvalier's shoulder, with a caption underneath reading, 'I HAVE CHOSEN HIM'. That these images, along with Duvalier's constant bombardment of the radio stations with his ranting and raving, served to cow the illiterate under-classes, is undeniable. 'François Duvalier,' writes David Hawkes in an essay written in 1997, 'was able to secure his political power by exploiting the credulity and superstition of the Haitian peasantry. He represents a phenomenon of pre-enlightenment societies: the tyrant who does not base his legitimacy on reason or democracy, but on mystical and supernatural foundations. Visiting Haiti is probably the closest one can come to visiting medieval Europe.'[2]

That Papa Doc was a highly manipulative individual who knew just how to keep his subjects at bay goes without saying, but he treated his friends in much the same manner; no one ever knew quite where they stood with this man, as was proved two years after he came to power.

On 24 May 1959 Duvalier suffered a massive heart attack and fell into a coma. The best doctors were flown in from the US to look after the president, but while he was incapacitated, Clément Barbot, the man who had helped Duvalier set up the Tontons Macoute and who now headed that organization, took over as interim leader. Barbot stepped in to his master's shoes very easily and seemed to enjoy presiding over cabinet meetings and making political decisions. But it was a bad decision for, later, when Duvalier had fully recuperated, the dictator didn't forget quite how effectively his number one hatchet man had managed to replace him. On 14 July 1960, Barbot was arrested by his own Tontons Macoute and later taken to Fort Dimanche on charges of corruption. Barbot was imprisoned and tortured for a period of eighteen months, then Duvalier ordered his release. Now it was Barbot's turn to feel hatred towards his former ally and on 26 April 1963, in an attempt to kidnap Duvalier's children and force the President to resign, he had the children's chauffeur and two bodyguards ambushed and killed. Naturally Duvalier was overcome by rage and immediately ordered reprisals. A bloodbath ensued.

'Tontons Macoutes patrolled the streets, sirens wailing. Road blocks were everywhere. It took hours to cross town or travel up the hill to Pétionville, where the road checks were both tedious and rough. Some former army officers, having no idea of the danger they were in, drove to pick up their children at school and on their return home were arrested at road blocks and never seen again.'[3]

But Barbot himself evaded capture and for several weeks those loyal to Duvalier and those to Barbot played a deadly game of cat and mouse throughout Haiti. Every night after dark the Tontons Macoute would be on the prowl for their victim until on 14 July, Barbot, having regrouped and decided on a second assassination attempt, was cornered in a sugarcane field by the Duvalierists who then set the field alight and shot the insurgents down as they ran to escape the flames.

Unsurprisingly, Barbot's attempt to remove Duvalier wasn't the only challenge to his leadership for, previously, in what must surely be one of the most bizarre attempts to overthrow any government, three Haitian men together with two Florida deputy sheriffs and three adventurers landed on Haitian soil with the sole intention of assassinating Papa Doc. Their mission was doomed to failure from the start and all eight men were shot during the attempt. But the carnage didn't stop there, for this attempted coup had devastating consequences for another of Duvalier's opponents, his former rival for the presidency, Clément Jumelle. Believing (or concocting the belief) that Clément Jumelle's two brothers were somehow involved in this latest plot, Duvalier sent Barbot and his Tontons Macoute to kill Ducasse and Charles Jumelle. They were hunted down to a small house in Bois Verna where they were both shot. Photographs were taken of the corpses holding pistols.

'Last night,' a statement by the Minister of the Interior, Frédéric Duvigneaud read, 'in the interval of exactly one month from 29 July, the Forces of Order once again were faced with the old revolutionary demon and again triumphed. Charles and Ducasse Jumelle who, with their brother Clément Jumelle, were the co-authors of the Mahotières[4] and Pétionville bomb plots and the tragic events of 29 July, were killed last night...'

Subsequently, the owner of the house in which the two brothers were found, Jean-Jacques Monfiston, was arrested and taken to Fort Dimanche where he was slowly tortured to death in an effort to extract information from him as to the whereabouts of Clément. But Monfiston remained silent to the end and Clément Jumelle eventually died of natural causes.

Nobody, or so it appeared, could oust Papa Doc Duvalier and on 30 April 1961, as if to prove this point, elections were held and duly rigged in order that he could win 100% of the votes. An article in the *New York Times* ran as follows: 'Latin America has witnessed many fraudulent elections throughout its history but none has been more outrageous than the one which has just taken place in Haiti.'

Unperturbed by this and other comments from abroad, Duvalier declared that his party was the only legitimate and legal one in Haiti and duly appointed Duvalierists to all fifty-eight congressional seats.

It was at this juncture that the US, who had up until then supported the Duvalier regime[5], ceased its economic aid programme owing to John F. Kennedy's increasing concern that Duvalier was misappropriating the money, siphoning it off into his own private bank accounts. Kennedy was also concerned that Duvalier wished to employ

In 1939, Duvalier married Simone Ovide Faine, a nurse's aide he met while the two were working in the Hospice Saint Francois-de-Sales. They had four children – Marie Denise, Simone, Nicole and Jean-Claude, who would later become known as 'Baby Doc'.

the US Marine Corps to strengthen the Tontons Macoute. But the US's reluctance to support Papa Doc only served to strengthen his image at home, for it gave Duvalier the perfect excuse to portray himself as a principled opponent of a thuggish, uncaring America. Further attempts were then made at ousting Duvalier, supposedly with the covert backing of America's Central Intelligence Agency, but coup after coup came to nothing, and far from growing weaker in the face of opposition, Duvalier went from strength to strength.

By 1964 the annual per capita income in Haiti was at an all-time low (in fact it was the lowest in the whole of the western hemisphere) standing at $80, added to which the illiteracy rate (despite a 'Duvalierist' campaign to eradicate it) still stood at 90%. Haiti's population suffered food and fuel shortages, the latter causing blackouts all over the country. But none of the above concerned Duvalier; quite the contrary, for in April of that year he changed the Haitian constitution and had himself appointed President for life. On 4 March The *Haiti Journal* declared:

'Duvalier is the professor of energy. Like Napoleon Bonaparte, Duvalier is an electrifier of souls, a powerful multiplier of energy…Duvalier is one of the greatest leaders of contemporary times…because the Renovator of the Haitian Fatherland synthesizes all there is of courage, bravery, genius, diplomacy, patriotism, and tact in the titans of ancient and modern times.'

Of course, as with all dictators, there were hundreds of uncorroborated horror stories (the majority of which came from those fleeing Haiti) which might, or might not, be true, but it is safe to say that even if one tenth were accurate then Duvalier's regime was one of the worst in world history. It was reported that while victims were being tortured by the Tontons Macoute, Duvalier would watch from behind peepholes in the walls. There is also a story concerning six teenagers who, in an attempt at free expression, spray-painted a wall with the words, 'DOWN WITH DUVALIER'. Each of the teenagers was hunted down and murdered. Duvalier then declared that all youth groups from that point on would be illegal, adding that membership would also be punishable by death. Another story involves a political opponent of Duvalier's, Yvan D. Laraque, who was tracked down and killed in the north of the country. His body was shipped back to Port-au-Prince where it was dressed in underwear and propped up at an intersection between Grand Rue and Somoza Avenue, under a Coke sign that read, 'WELCOME TO HAITI'. There it rotted in the sun for days on end. Laraque had been involved in yet another attempt to end Duvalier's reign of terror (this time near Jérémie airport) and afterwards the Tontons Macoute were ordered to kill the families of all those who had fought alongside him. According to several accounts, men, women and children were tortured and executed and one family in particular was singled out for reprisals, the Sansaricqs who were made to walk naked through the streets of Jérémie before they were shot dead. It was also reported that the Tontons Macoute initiated the practice of shooting women and children first to further enrage and upset the male members of their families, and that often children were hacked to death while still being carried in their mothers' arms.

The insanity continued, with yet another bizarre, though less blood curdling, with a project to build a utopian city. The populace, together with any foreigners who had a financial interest in Haiti, were fleeced of their money, all of which went into building Duvalierville (now known as Cabaret) which was erected in honour of Papa Doc and which was filled not only with statues and monuments of the President, but also with enormous neon signs proclaiming amongst other things, 'I HAVE NO ENEMIES SAVE THE ENEMIES OF HAITI' or 'I AM THE BEST THING THAT HAS EVER HAPPENED TO YOU.'

But perhaps the most extraordinary piece of self-promotion came when the government printed a booklet called *Le Catéchisme de la revolution* which, amongst other things, contained a revised Lord's Prayer:

'Our Doc who art in the National Palace for life, hallowed be Thy name by present and future generations. Thy will be done at Port-au-Prince and in the provinces. Give us this day our new Haiti and never forgive the trespasses of the anti-patriots who spit every day on our country; let them succumb to temptation, and under the weight of their venom, deliver them not from any evil...'

Two of these 'anti-patriots', Marcel Numa and Louis Drouin, having been involved, along with eleven others, in yet another attempted overthrow of Duvalier, were subsequently caught and on 12 November 1964 tied to pine poles and set before a nine-man firing squad. Crowds were encouraged to attend the execution – men, women and children – and leaflets were handed out in support of Papa Doc whom it was said would always protect the people of Haiti from such renegades. The whole event was then televised and broadcast to the entire nation as if it were some kind of game show.

Added to this there were also rumours of black magic ceremonies being held in the presidential palace. Several former associates of Duvalier reported that Papa Doc studied goat's entrails for political guidance, that one night a year he would sleep on the gravestone of General Dessalines with whom he claimed he was in spiritual contact, that he was constantly summoning sorcerers (*bocors*) to the palace to help him see into the future, that he buried people alive and had his voodoo associates sacrifice babies in his honor.

All of this served only to create misery and fear throughout the populace and the appallingly low average national wage meant that intellectuals, teachers, doctors, college-educated professionals, all began leaving Haiti in droves. It was too dangerous for them to stay, and they could barely scrape together a living. This created a serious lack of medical supplies, and malnutrition bordering on famine swept the island. The majority of the population were living a borderline existence in huts without sanitation or clean running water. Even when, after John F. Kennedy's untimely death in 1963, the US relaxed its stance on Haiti (once again because of its strategic location near Cuba) and began sending in aid, the people received no help because, true to form, Duvalier misappropriated the funds and transferred them into his own secret bank accounts.

When Papa Doc died in 1971, the people of Haiti might have expected their circumstances to improve but Duvalier had changed the country's constitution to ensure that his son would succeed him as President. When Baby Doc took over, things went from bad to worse with huge amounts of the national revenue being siphoned off into Swiss bank accounts.

By 1967 attempts to oust Papa Doc from power had intensified. Several bombs exploded near the presidential palace, after which nineteen of Duvalier's presidential guards (including Major José Borges who had been in charge of the Radio 'Voice of the Duvalierist Revolution') were arrested, executed and buried at Fort Dimanche.

'I am an arm of steel,' said Duvalier after this latest blood was spilled, 'hitting inexorably…hitting inexorably…hitting inexorably. I have shot these…officers in order to project the revolution and those serving it…I align…myself with the great leaders of peoples as Kemal Ataturk, Lenin, Kwame Nkrumah, Patrice Lumumba, Azikwe, Mao Tse-tung.'

Other coups followed, including several begun overseas by disenfranchised exiles. In fact it wasn't until 1971 that Haiti saw an end to their dictator's rule. Having suffered months of ill health, on 22 April François 'Papa Doc' Duvalier died (doctors diagnosed myocardial infarcts) and for a brief moment the entire country, save for his family and a few loyal followers, heaved a sigh of relief. His funeral, which was held two days later, lasted six hours during which 101 cannon rounds were fired, while a Haitian musician sang a composition entitled, 'François, we thank you for loving us. Your star will be shining in the night.'

But the mild euphoria that the populace experienced at Papa Doc's departure was short-lived, for back in the early sixties, when Duvalier rigged the election in his favor, he had also changed the constitution so that his son, Jean-Claude, could take over the reins of power on his death. Much like another, later dictator, Saddam Hussein, François Duvalier was all set to establish a tyrannical dynasty, only he hadn't counted on 'Baby' Doc's complete inadequacy.

Initially it looked as if Baby Doc might be different from his father, a kinder, more lenient leader. On coming to power, he introduced several economic and judicial reforms, reopened the same military academy that his father had closed, whilst also releasing several political prisoners. But the words 'like father, like son' couldn't be better applied when talking about the Duvaliers, for while Baby Doc declared an amnesty for all exiles, he simultaneously excluded all Communists and trouble makers from returning. In effect, this meant that the majority of exiles still had to remain outside the country. Baby Doc also refused to allow any opposition to his presidency and insisted on retaining ultimate control over who to appoint within government. In addition, US agents reported that huge amounts (in the region of 64%) of Haiti's revenues were being skimmed off and misappropriated together with tens of millions of dollars from public funds which all ended up in Baby Doc's Swiss bank accounts.

The Baby Doc years were just as turbulent and unpleasant as had been his father's, for the majority of Haitians suffered under further years of misrule. Finally, on 7 February 1986, with the military pressing for his abdication, Baby Doc and his wife accepted an offer of assistance from the US government and fled into self-imposed exile in France.

With the Duvaliers gone, it might have been hoped that their hold over Haiti would soon be forgotten, but for a country where the majority of people still believe in and practice voodoo, the influence of the dead over the living is so entrenched that, no doubt, somewhere, someone is still praising their 'Papa', still fearful of what his spirit might come back and do.

[1] From *Papa Doc: Haiti and its Dictator* by Bernard Diederich & Al Burt, Penguin Books, 1969.

[2] From 'Tyranny and Enlightenment in Haiti and Britain' by David Hawkes, published in *Bad Subjects*, Issue 30, February 1997.

[3] From *Papa Doc: Haiti and its Dictator* by Bernard Diederich & Al Burt, Penguin Books, 1969.

[3] The Mahotières bomb (30 April 1958) was originally alleged to have been instigated by Louis Dejoie, who in order to escape Duvalier and his thugs requested asylum in the Mexican Embassy. The Pétionville bomb (29 June 1958) was the work of an iron-worker called Kelly Thompson who later implicated the Jumelles.

[4] This support was due for the most part to America's long-term obsession with anti-Communism for they believed that if they helped Haiti economically the government would not sway to the left as in nearby Cuba.

KIM IL SUNG
North Korea's Stalin

In this land of stark contradictions, the military can boast
advanced military hardware, while thousands still till the land by
hand...At nightfall, Pyongyang and other cities shiver, while the
brightest lights are the headlamps of the occasional passing
vehicle. North Korea has the look of the former German
Democratic Republic 50 years ago, and gives the impression that
a version of the Chinese Cultural Revolution is still in full swing.
This is a country traumatised by Japanese occupation during the
Second World War, American bombing and a belief in secular
leaders, alive and dead, that verges on the divine.

'The Land that Time Forgot' by Mark Seddon,
The *Guardian*, 11 March 2003

Kim Il Sung governed North Korea for forty-nine years, longer than any other twentieth century Korean leader. To his supporters he was like a demigod, he was their supreme champion, a man who gallantly took up arms against Korea's Japanese oppressors, a staunch Communist and brilliant philosopher. Statues and monuments erected in his honor include a triumphal arch (*chuch'et'ap*) bigger than the one that graces Paris, a tower which represents his political ideas, and countless museums. But to his detractors Kim Il Sung was little more than an evil potentate, a man who fabricated huge parts of his life, a man who kowtowed to the USSR, who instigated a brutal civil war and who thought nothing of killing those who opposed him.

As far as any records show, Kim Il Sung was born Kim Sŏng-ju on 15 April 1912 in Mangyondae, in Japan-controlled Korea. His parents moved to Manchuria and consequently the young Kim received a Chinese education. His parents, who came from very ordinary backgrounds, died when Kim was relatively young. His father, Kim Hyŏng-jik, a shopkeeper, died in 1930 and his mother, Kang Pan Sok, two years later in 1932. Kim's education came to a halt abruptly in 1929 when the teenager was expelled from school for participating in several illegal student activities. At the age of seventeen, Kim had become a member of the Communist Youth Association, but although several Korean historians would have us believe that it was during this time that Kim began to read Marx and Lenin, it is far more likely his indoctrination came from associating with various anti-Japanese Korean Nationalists.

In the nineteenth century, Korea, much like its neighbor, China, had been forced by combined European and Japanese powers to sign treaties allowing trade and other commercial contact with the outside world. Around 1910 Japan then annexed Korea, bringing the country and its people under Japanese rule. Much blood was shed during this period and thousands of Koreans were jailed for rebelling against those they saw as invaders. Japan managed to maintain its stranglehold over Korea, although various sections of Korean society began forming guerrilla groups in an attempt to fight back.

On 10 May 1929, having been expelled from school, Kim was jailed for a little under a year after which, on his release from prison, he joined a Korean Independence Army unit under the command of Yang Se Bong. Not long afterwards, Kim left this

Kim Il Sung trained with the Red Army in the Soviet Union until 1948 when Stalin appointed him leader of the Democratic People's Republic of Korea. The Democratic People's Republic was separated from the Republic of Korea to the south along the 38th parallel with the North a Soviet satellite state and the South dominated by the USA.

unit and formed his own small guerrilla fighting force within Manchuria. His activities during this period have no doubt been exaggerated in order to embellish the myth behind the man, yet there must be some kernel of truth to the stories of his bravery and prowess.

Despite huge efforts on the part of the guerrilla forces, Japan continued to dominate Korea throughout the 1930s and early 40s, and in a concerted effort to stamp out all dissent, attempted to wipe out Korean culture. Koreans were forced to change their names to Japanese ones, learn the Japanese language and adopt a Japanese lifestyle.

Not until the end of World War II, with Japan defeated and in ruins, did a light begin to shine at the end of the tunnel for those fighting for independence in Korea.

A little earlier, in March 1941, Kim Il Sung had fled Manchuria for the Soviet Far East where he had received military training from the Red Army. A US intelligence report states, 'Faced with the threat of extinction by the Japanese, a few hundred under the leadership of Kim Il Sung, long-time Communist, made their way North and into the Soviet Maritime Province. After verifying their political and military backgrounds, the Soviets established these people in a training camp at YASHKI Station, in the general area of KHAMAROVSK. Here and later at RARARASH, near the junction of the USSR-Korea and Manchurian frontiers these Koreans were trained in espionage, radio communications, sabotage and general military subjects.'[1]

It was also while Kim Il Sung was in the USSR that he met and fell in love with his first wife, Kim Chŏng-suk. The two were married and a little less than a year later their first child was born, a boy who would later go on to rule over North Korea with as heavy a hand as his father's. Meanwhile, Kim Il Sung continued to train with the Red Guard and ingratiate himself with the Soviet authorities so that, by 1945, when Korea was liberated by US and Soviet forces, he could return to his homeland safe in the knowledge that he would be welcomed.

By 1948, with the USSR occupying the north of Korea and the USA occupying the south, the country was divided along the 38th parallel into the Democratic People's Republic of Korea under the leadership of Kim Il Sung (elected by Stalin), and the Republic of Korea under Syngman Rhee. Both administrations claimed that they were the only legitimate government on the peninsula thus leading, over the next few years, to further conflict.

With Kim Il Sung's takeover came many accusations that he was nothing more than a puppet of the Soviet Union, placed in command to turn the country into a Communist satellite state, one that would be controlled by the USSR. The Soviets did little help to improve Kim's image, for instead of letting him forge his own way, they insisted on promoting and popularising him themselves within the country. The USSR, together with Kim, then implemented six 'democratic reforms' that included the redistribution of land, the introduction of the eight-hour working day and the nationalization of heavy industry. Further to this, the USSR also helped Kim to create the Korean People's Army, which incorporated Kim's old guerrilla comrades into its ranks. Kim's partisans came to occupy key positions in every security organization within the country, thereby enabling Kim to keep tight control over every aspect of North Korea and of his government.

But Kim was not without his detractors, several of whom tried to oust him from power. Using all his guile as a guerrilla fighter, and relying on the Soviet authorities for their full support, he managed to quell any unrest. Then, in 1950, having built up the Korean People's Army to full strength and with the full backing of Stalin (some commentators go as far as to say that Stalin was in fact the sole instigator), Kim decided to invade 'traitorous' South Korea in an attempt to unify the two countries by military force.

The Korean War (also known as the Forgotten War by certain Americans, as it fell between the far more pervasive World War II and the Vietnam War) began on 25 June 1950. The United Nations immediately condemned the invasion, calling it an outright act of aggression, but Kim Il Sung chose to ignore their demands that he and his troops withdraw. Instead US President Harry Truman, in what he saw as a fight against Communism, decided to send land, sea and air forces in to South Korea. General Douglas MacArthur was appointed as supreme commander not just of the US forces, but also of the fifteen other nations who joined in the fight on the side of the South.

Before the escalation of the conflict, on 17 July 1950 in an interview given to the French newspaper *L'Humanité*, Kim Il Sung said that he didn't foresee a long war. His timetable was such that he hoped to have 'liberated' the South by 15 August of that same year. It was an ambitious plan and one that, as history later testified, was destined to go horribly wrong. Although in the first few weeks of Kim's campaign North Korean soldiers met with little resistance, when UN forces launched a dare-devil amphibious landing at Inchon on the west coast, the advantage swung from the North to the South. By 19 October 1950 General MacArthur had pushed into North Korea and taken the capital of Pyongyang. Had it not been for the subsequent involvement of the Chinese, this might have spelled the end of Kim Il Sung, but the Chinese, incensed by what they saw as a capitalist plot against a Communist state, sent a massive number of troops into the area and the center of conflict was pushed back to the 38th parallel. The fighting was bitter, and heavy casualties were sustained on both sides. Yet if American losses were high, they were nothing compared to those suffered by the Chinese. By the end of the war, US losses stood at 54,000 dead and 103,000 wounded while Chinese and Korean casualties ran into the millions.

But while the Korean War was being fought on both sides of the border, there were additional political problems on the North Korean side that put Kim Il Sung's position as party leader in jeopardy. After the US invasion of Pyongyang, Kim had publicly criticized several key government officials, including loyal partisans and Soviet Koreans, a number of whom were consequently relieved of their jobs and expelled from the party. Kim also made a speech in which he said a distinction should be made between those loyal to the party and those who had shown disloyalty. The latter group should be punished irrespective of their rank. The job of seeking out those who had criticized the party fell to the head of the Inspection Committee, a man by the name of Hŏ Ka-i. Hŏ went about his business and between December 1950 and November 1951 he expelled and punished 450,000 out of 600,000 Communist Party officials. Ironically, Hŏ's actions appear to have infuriated Kim, who saw the purge as a direct threat to his own authority, for while Kim had instigated the investigation, Hŏ had, in an attempt to remodel the party along his own lines, taken it to an extreme. Kim now openly criticized Hŏ and accused him of sundry crimes against the party and, therefore, the country. Hŏ was in dangerous position and pressure on him was mounting when suddenly, on 4 August 1953 at a meeting of the Central Committee, it was announced that Hŏ had committed suicide. Whether this was true, or whether Hŏ had been executed, is unclear but the outcome was the same: Hŏ was dead and Kim's power base was, in the short term, safe.

Hŏ wasn't the only one intent on overthrowing Kim Il Sung. In September 1951 another party official by the name of Yi Sung-yŏp was reported as planning a military coup. Although the facts are somewhat shady, it is believed that Li's attempted overthrow was put into action in early 1953 but failed, after which Kim had all twelve conspirators arrested. Three days after the conclusion of the Korean War, the men went on trial for high treason. Their defence was practically non-existent and subsequently ten out of the twelve were put to death, while the remaining two were incarcerated for between twelve to fifteen years.

By the end of the Korean War it was evident that neither the North nor the South had achieved what it had set out to accomplish. The South, and by association the USA and its allies, had not rid itself of the Communist North, while the North had not been able to overrun the South and unite the two countries. In fact, it was the Chinese rather than Kim Il Sung who brought about a conclusion to the war and negotiated a settlement between themselves and the Americans. Despite this, Kim Il Sung, who had mobilized Koreans to fight against Koreans, who had been responsible for the death of millions of citizens on both sides of the border, took all the honors for bringing about a ceasefire and stated that he alone was victorious.

Of course, in reality Kim was in no position to gloat, for North Korea had been devastated by the Americans' constant bombing of its cities and vast tracts of countryside. (North Korea was far more heavily bombed than either Japan or Germany had been during the Second World War.) It was necessary, therefore, to re-energize the economy, and to do so Kim visited the Soviet Union in search of an extended loan. By this time, Stalin was dead and the Soviet government was in a state of turmoil. Nonetheless, Kim managed to secure a new deal with the Motherland and on returning to Korea began reforming both agriculture and industry. Just like his Soviet and Chinese ideological role models, Kim confiscated most of the privately owned land from its legal owners and began turning all farms into co-operatives with the profits being shared out according to the amount of work contributed by each member. In industry he ordered that, instead of producing essential goods that were required by his own people, the factories were to start making consumer goods that could be sold overseas.

Kim Il Sung begins the evacuation of Chinese troops from North Korea in 1958. Within the next three years he would also have distanced himself from the Soviet Union and built himself into a cult personality, about whom it was said that the sun rose because he rose.

As paranoid as any other dictator, Kim also began purging the party of all those he felt even slightly disapproved of either him or his policies. Significantly, the group that suffered most during this period were the Soviet-Koreans.

After Stalin died, the Soviet Union had begun to 'de-Stalinize' the country and the new Soviet leaders began to advocate a peaceful co-existence with the West. This ran contrary to everything Kim Il Sung believed, for at that time he was attempting to establish a Stalinist Korea, besides which the idea of peaceful co-existence with the West, and in particular South Korea, was unthinkable. As a consequence, all Soviet-Koreans were treated as if they were traitors and Kim then implemented what became known as the Juche (literally 'self-reliance') Idea which, in essence, was a creative application of Marxism and Leninism specifically tailored to North Korea's unique conditions. The Juche Idea was thereafter used as a weapon to justify Kim's dictatorship and keep at bay any thought of joining the Soviets in their de-Stalinization program. The Juche system also sought to indoctrinate the people with the idea that without the Party the entire country would fall to rack and ruin. In other words, Juche philosophy was nothing more than a theory of dictatorship, one which conveniently built Kim Il Sung into a cult personality (every North Korean household had to display a photograph of Kim Il Sung; every man, woman and child had to pin Kim's photograph over their hearts) whose absolute power was not to be questioned. The sun was said to rise because Kim Il Sung had risen and to set because he had commanded it to do so. By the time of the Fourth Party Conference in September 1961, Kim had consolidated his position to such an extent that he alone was regarded as North Korea's Supreme Commander.

Labor camps or gulags were now established and, according to Hwang Jang Yop, a leading defector from North Korea to the South, were split into two types: the first were reserved for the 'upper echelons' of the Party and were mainly labor camps, while the second kind of camp was for ordinary citizens who had in one way or another incurred the wrath of the Party. The latter were sent into isolated, non-arable districts where they were left to starve to death. Hwang estimated that there were ten of these 'no-go' areas with approximately 30,000 individuals scraping together a living in each.

The 'upper echelon' labor camps were equally as harsh. The prisoners were sent to work on local farms, in local factories or down local coal mines; the chances were that they would die of exhaustion due to lack of food or succumb to the vicious beatings meted out by the guards. Kim Il Sung was ruthless in this respect and issued a directive that if someone was found guilty of crimes against the state then three generations of his or her family should be wiped out in order to cleanse his 'socialist paradise'.

One first-hand account of these gulags by former political prisoner Chul-Hwan-Kang, runs as follows:

'...Because of my grandfather [who was accused of espionage], the whole family was sent to Yodok political prisoner camp. This happened when I was nine. I was born in North Korea and until then I had truly believed that Kim Il-Sung was the great leader and the benevolent father. However, this changed because of my experiences at the political prisoner camp. The realities of the prison camp were totally beyond my imagination... I witnessed public executions, forced labor, and other inhumane atrocities. A new prisoner in the North Korean political prison camps is taught not to consider themselves as human beings. The prisoners cannot complain of beatings or even murders. Even the children are subject to forced labor, and about one third of them die of malnutrition and heavy labor. I also suffered from malnutrition three months after being imprisoned, lacking even the strength to walk. Because we were not given any source of protein, we would catch and eat snakes, frogs, or even worms in order to survive...'[2]

Chul then goes on to describe how he was also witness to many public executions where the victim would be blindfolded and tied to a post before being shot. Afterwards the crowd were encouraged to pelt the corpse with stones, the bigger the better. 'The reason why these executions are held in public,' he said, 'is to instill fear in the prisoners and to prevent disobedience or escapes.'[3]

That such places existed (and tragically still exist to this day) in North Korea only reinforced the dubious nature of Kim's regime. It was as evil as any of the other more prominent Eastern bloc countries including that of Stalinist Russia, or Maoist China, but whereas both of these countries were to some extent open books as far as the West was concerned, North Korea continued to remain a secret society, a personal kingdom answering to the whims of one man.

By 1967 Kim Il Sung had isolated North Korea even further from the world by falling out with the Chinese who, during the Cultural Revolution, looked very unkindly upon anyone whom they considered pro-Russian. The Chinese Red Guard began denouncing Kim; they plastered walls with posters reproving his leadership and began spreading ugly rumors concerning his domestic policies.

But more important to Kim than these somewhat ludicrous insults was the dispute between himself and China over their shared border, which measured approximately 880 miles and encompassed the sacred mountain (sacred to the Koreans, that is) of Paektusan. This border dispute could have become very difficult for Kim Il Sung had it not been for the gradual relaxation of the Cultural Revolution and thereafter the resumption of increasingly cordial relations between the two nations.

Conflict may have been averted on the foreign policy front but the same could not be said for internal affairs within Korea. Immediately following the Korean War, Kim's tough industrialization programme had reaped many rewards. Production was far higher than in South Korea. However, it was a short-lived period of success for in the mid 1960s Kim Il Sung made the fatal mistake of biting the hand that fed him and alienated the Soviet Union. He announced that the USSR had used its economic aid programme to interfere one time too many in Korean affairs, and the Soviet Union withdrew its finances and technical assistance from the country. If this wasn't worrying enough, South Korea then formed a new anti-Communist government (after a successful military coup). The South Koreans also resumed relations with Japan and proceeded to make a huge economic recovery, one that spurred them on to expand their military capacity. It was a threat Kim Il Sung couldn't, or wouldn't, ignore and it subsequently became policy to strengthen the military at the expense of any economic development.

'…the partisan generals revealed the four basic military policies of the party: to arm the entire populace, to fortify the entire country, to train every soldier to become cadre, and to modernize military weapons and equipment. When he broke his silence on North Korean relations with fraternal socialist countries in October 1966…Kim elaborated on the four military policies. Kim said that the policy of arming the entire populace meant building a flawless defense system both in the front and in the rear by arming not only the soldiers but also the workers, the peasants, and the entire people.'[4]

Every worker within the factories and on the cooperative farms was forced to undertake military training. The elderly, together with children as young as seven or eight years old, were also indoctrinated and taught to use guns. Thousands upon thousands of underground shelters were dug out, and huge underground storage

The 76-feet-high gilded statue of Kim Il Sung at the Masudae Grand Monument was erected in 1972 to celebrate the 60th birthday of the 'Great Leader'.

government. The death penalty is normally reserved either for those convicted of murder or for those convicted of 'colluding with imperialists'. There are several cases in which people have been executed for much lesser misdemeanors. Amnesty cites the case of a woman who was found guilty of embezzlement and was executed in the Sama Dong district of the capital, Pyongyang, in 1988, as well as the case of two brothers who were found guilty of stealing rice and executed in Hamhung City in 1982-3. The very fact that North Koreans are having to steal rice in order to survive only backs up what the United Nations has feared for many years. 'At least 42% of their children are stunted from chronic malnutrition, a recent United Nations survey showed. In 44 out of North Korea's 206 counties, however, no foreign aid worker has ever been allowed to set foot. Conditions in these "closed counties" – home to troublesome citizens and secret military facilities – are feared to be far worse.'[8]

As far as international relations, the stability of the region and even world safety are concerned, Kim Jong-il has proved even more troublesome than his father. Under his regime, North Korea has produced a nuclear arsenal that has prompted US President George Bush to name the country as one of a handful of nations (Iran, Iraq and Syria being three others) which make up an 'axis of evil'.

Kim Il Sung died on 8 July 1994, plunging North Korea into a three-year period of mourning. It was the end of an ignominious reign, one which had started, to all intents and purposes, with Kim Il Sung seemingly committed to serving his people and thereby his country. It ended, however, with the people serving Kim Il Sung, downtrodden, uneducated, starving; their only legacy an economically unviable country isolated from the industrialized nations of the rest of the world and ruled by a man determined to perpetuate his father's legacy.

[1] *Kim Il Sung: The North Korean Leader* by Dae-Sook Suh, A Study of the
      East Asian Institute, Columbia University, 1988.
[2] www.nkhumanrights.org
[3] Ibid
[4] *Kim Il Sung: The North Korean Leader* by Dae-Sook Suh, A Study of the
      East Asian Institute, Columbia University, 1988.
[5] Ibid
[6] Portion of a speech made by Kim Il Sung at the eighteenth plenum of the
      Central Committee on 16 November 1968.
[7] From speech by Kim Il Sung, *The Youth Must Take Over the Revolution and
      Carry it Forward*, Foreign Languages House, 1976.
[8] 'Women Trade Sex for Food in Hungry Korea', Michael Sheridan,
      The *Sunday Times*, 27 July 2003.

AUGUSTO UGARTE PINOCHET

General of Death

> Our position on the problems of human rights violations is basically legal, ethical and preventative. No healthy, solid stable democracy can build itself upon a foundation of forgetting the most serious crimes against the right to life, integrity and freedom committed in Chilean history and within a policy of state terrorism that unleashed maximum political violence against society. We reaffirm that there is no ethical nor judicial reason why crimes of human rights violations should remain in impunity. We are asking that crimes against humanity be punished in the same way that common ones are.
>
> From the Statement by the Group of Families of the Detained and Disappeared, 23 July 1995.

On Thursday 2 March 2000 at RAF Waddington in Lincolnshire, Great Britain, a Chilean Air Force jet took off at just after midday carrying with it an eighty-four-year old man whose sixteen-month 'stay' in Britain had been the subject of newspaper headlines throughout the world. The man's name was General Augusto Pinochet and his extended sojourn had been brought about by extradition proceedings filed by Spain, Switzerland, Belgium and France, all seeking to put him on trial for human rights abuses allegedly committed during Pinochet's terror-driven, seventeen-year rule of Chile.

Born on 26 November 1915 in the coastal port of Valparaíso, Augusto Pinochet was (like another dictator included in this book – Adolf Hitler) the son of a customs official and therefore came from a fairly affluent, middle-class family. As a child he attended the San Rafael Seminary as well as the French Father's School of Valparaíso, graduating at the age of seventeen. It was his mother who encouraged him towards a military career and with her backing he applied to, and was accepted by, the Chilean *Escuela Militar* (military college). After a four-year officer-training course he graduated in 1936 having achieved the rank of sub-lieutenant. Initially he joined the *Chacabuco* Regiment in Concepción before moving to the *Maipo* Regiment back in Valparaíso. His rise within the army was swift; by 1939 he had become a second lieutenant and by 1941 he had become a full lieutenant. All in all, these were happy years for Pinochet. The army was like his second home; he loved its rules and regulations, the strict discipline and the fact that he was good at his job. It was also during this period that he met and later, in January 1943, married Lucia Hiriart Rodriguez with whom he was to have five children: two sons and three daughters.

At the end of 1945 Pinochet once more changed regiments, this time joining the *Carampangue* Regiment in Iquique after which he went to work for Chile's War Academy where, in 1951, he achieved the title of Officer Chief-of-Staff. Afterwards he spent two years in Africa and then in 1956 he was sent to Quito in Ecuador to establish a War Academy there. Pinochet stayed in Quito for three-and-a-half years, during which time he studied military geography and army intelligence.

In his early years, Augusto Pinochet had not displayed any particular interest in politics although, as a high-ranking official, he was involved during the 1950s in the clampdown of the Chilean Communist Party. Paradoxically, as several scholars have pointed out, it was his lack of political ambition that saw him advance in 1973 to the title of Commander-in-Chief of the Army under the then left-wing government led by Salvador Allende. Allende was a Socialist who, in 1970, had become the world's first democratically elected Marxist President. Blaming Chile's previous capitalist system for his country's economic decline, Allende began an extensive programme of nationalization, which included the country's US-controlled copper mines as well as other foreign industries and banks. Allende also ordered that those in high managerial positions, particularly in factories, hand over the reins of power to the workers. Initially this programme was very popular, the working classes seeing a rapid improvement in their living conditions, but it all came at a price. By 1972 the country was in serious economic difficulty. Furthermore, Allende had upset his North American cousins (namely US President Richard Nixon) by championing such Communist regimes as those found in Cuba, North Korea, China and North Vietnam, as well as by cultivating very strong links with the Soviet Union. Consequently, the US began withdrawing all loans to Chile but, on the orders of Nixon, the CIA began pumping money into the Chilean army so that it might in the future stage a military coup.

By 1972, in the hope of averting the worst economic disaster in Chile's history, the government attempted to spend its way out of decline, but the result was hyperinflation and complete economic paralysis. Towns and cities ground to a halt, many goods were in short supply and factories closed. In 1973, parliamentary elections were called but this only served to deepen the crisis as the results were inconclusive. Suddenly people, both left-wing and right-wing, were taking to the streets to demonstrate their discontent while in the background the CIA upped the ante and began financing strikes and acts of sabotage. It was under these conditions, on 23 August 1973, that President Allende, believing Augusto Pinochet to be a loyal military officer, promoted him to Commander-in-Chief of the army. Never was a man so wrong in his judgement of character, for less than one month later, on 11 September, the military, led by Pinochet, staged a violent, bloody coup d'état. According to documents produced almost two decades later by the US State Department, Pinochet was being backed by massive amounts of US military aid which increased dramatically to US $10.9 million in 1972 as the coup plans were being drawn up and put into operation.

Allende was killed defending the Presidential Palace, and seventy-two of his closest aides and advisers were either captured or surrendered. They were taken to a military base and executed. Once this was accomplished, the Commanders-in-Chief of the army, air force, navy and police formed a junta (a government created by a small group of people following a coup d'état) with Augusto Pinochet as its leader. The next day Chileans woke up to hear the news that their new government had declared a state of martial law. They were informed that Parliament would remain closed for the foreseeable future. Over the following few months, in an attempt to rid the country of Allende's Socialist policies, all political and trade union activity was banned. Pinochet defended these actions by saying that they were the only way in which to rescue Chile from the chaos the Socialists had caused and from further Communist threat. Nor was there much resistance to this militaristic style of leadership, for in truth many Chileans supported Pinochet's actions and were relieved when, in 1974, he appointed himself President.

Tragically, however, the violence of the coup was far from over. Part and parcel of Pinochet's crack-down on all forms of opposition included the formation of a new secret police force called the National Intelligence Directorate (Dirección Nacional de Inteligencia – or DINA) which began organizing the 'disappearance' or outright murder of thousands of Allende supporters, as well as anyone who spoke out against the new regime. DINA (who reported directly to Pinochet) also created secret detention centres in which they tortured detainees, particularly supporters of Allende's old party. The man in charge of this unit, Colonel Manuel Contreras set in motion 'Operation Condor', a conspiracy involving several South American countries in the murder of political opponents. 'Foreign armies and security services cooperated in dealing with political opponents from one country who crossed into another, and assigned their own men to out-of-country operations to avoid the identification of local agents.'[1] More than two decades later, these covert assassinations then became part of the basis for Spanish Judge Baltazar Garzón's attempt to extradite Augusto Pinochet to Spain on charges of genocide, torture and terrorism. Colonel Contreras was also responsible for ordering the assassination of General Carlos Prats Gonzalález (defence minister under Allende) and his wife, Soffia Cuthbert, by car bomb in Buenos Aires, Argentina on 29 September 1974.

During the early Pinochet years, DINA also made it their job to infiltrate schools, churches, trade unions and the media. Naturally, the junta justified their actions by insisting it was necessary if they were to stamp out Chile's Marxist past and restore order to the country, but the extent of the arrests in the first few months of Pinochet coming to power meant that the prisons could no longer house all those who had been detained. Sports stadia, naval vessels and military compounds were pressed into service to incarcerate the prisoners. 'According to figures given by the military regime and registered by the *Vicaria de la Solidaridad*, between 1973 and 1975 there were 42,486 political detentions. Also, according to the *Vicaria* between 1976 to 1988,

A professional soldier, Augosto Ugarte Pinochet graduated as a sub-lieutenant from Chile's
Escuela Militar military college in 1936 and rose to become Commander-in-Chief of the
army before taking control of the country in a military coup in 1972.

12,134 people were individually arrested for political reasons and 26,431 collective
arrests took place. Between 1977 to 1988 4,134 persons were threatened or harassed,
1,008 were victims of forced disappearance and 2,100 people died for political
reasons.'[2]

But if the statistics were horrifying, then the personal experiences were far worse.
It seemed Pinochet sanctioned all types of torture including locking victims two at a
time in two-foot square cells, electrocution with steel rods, mock executions, near-
drownings, beatings and sexual torture. Those who survived were both physically and

mentally scarred for life. They could never forget their ordeals and some even went so far as to say that they wished they hadn't lived, but had been executed, so great was their suffering. One such testimony, given by Alberto Enriqué Neumann Lagos, a medical doctor who was detained at the Pisagua concentration camp, outlines the atrocities. On 1 June 1990 he told a Chilean court how, when he arrived at Pisagua he was immediately witness to the execution of three men by firing squad. He was ordered to certify that they were dead but only two of them were, so the third was shot in the head. Another testimony, cited in an Amnesty International report, ran as follows:

'About 12 people in civilian clothes broke into his home in the first quarter of 1982. No arrest-warrant was shown. They searched the premises for two hours and arrested him, his father and another relative. They hooded and handcuffed him, then drove him to the CNI centre.

'For the first five days he was interrogated several times a day, and simultaneously tortured, mainly physically. He was slapped and struck on the head, mouth, body and genitals, and his buttocks and extremities were kicked. He was also electrically tortured on two occasions, each lasting five minutes. He was made to sit on a chair and electric current was applied to his back via a cable conducting current from a machine he thought was hand-driven.

'The interrogations continued for the next 14 days he spent at the CNI centre. They included threats, including threats of execution (a pistol was aimed at his temple) and threats to his family.'[3]

This account was only one of hundreds collected by Amnesty International, and by no means describes the worst excesses of the Pinochet torture machine. No wonder civil unrest ground to a halt. By 1975 Pinochet had the upper hand over almost all his opponents and had laid down the foundations of a police state that was strong enough to withstand any opposition to his regime.

Now he turned his attention to the economy and, with the help of group of men called the 'Chicago boys' (so named because they had all studied economics at the University of Chicago), he began introducing free-market policies and radically reducing welfare payouts. The results were, for a small band of relatively well-off Chileans, miraculous. Suddenly inflation was curbed and property began to be handed back to its original owners. Those companies that Salvador Allende had been at pains to nationalize were returned to private ownership. Production rates increased, economic growth accelerated, but for those lower down the scale, unemployment rose and poverty once again grew closer and closer to home. In fact the disparity between the upper and lower classes was so huge it almost beggared belief. In 1989, the majority of workers earned less than they had in 1973, while employers found their salaries skyrocketing. Nor were the workers' poor earnings the only consequence of Pinochet's economic reforms, for while encouraging foreign businesses to invest in the country, he did nothing to implement environmental regulations, resulting in Chile becoming one of the most polluted countries in the world.

In 1976 Jimmy Carter became US President. As a democrat and champion of several civil rights movements, his inauguration led to a general cooling off of relations between Chile and the US. Pinochet was also implicated in the assassination in Washington DC of Orlando Letelier on 21 September 1976. Letelier had been a former Chilean ambassador to the US as well as being Foreign Minister and afterwards Defense Minister under Salvador Allende. After Allende's death, Letelier was arrested, tortured and eventually ended up as a political prisoner in Tierra del Fuego. On his release he managed to escape the country and set up home in Washington DC where he began working towards restoring democracy in Chile. He was killed by a car bomb along with his assistant Ronni Moffit. Later, several people were prosecuted for his death which was commonly believed to be part and parcel of 'Operation Condor'. Michael Townley was one of those to stand trial; a US expatriate, he had close links with DINA as well as with Manuel Contreras. Townley also implicated Pinochet in the murders but nothing was done to bring the Chilean President to justice.

Perhaps spurred on by his apparent immunity to prosecution, in 1977 Pinochet announced that there would be no return to democracy in the foreseeable future. Instead, he continued to rule the country with an iron grip and ensured that only his cronies were placed in key positions. It was also during 1977 that the United Nations Human Rights Commission first condemned the Pinochet regime for 'the continued and inadmissible violation of human rights'. Pinochet paid no heed, instead implementing an amnesty law which protected all his military officers who might have committed human rights abuses since the 1973 coup. Arrogant, brutal and ruthless, Pinochet then launched a referendum in 1978, asking the people to endorse his regime, afterwards claiming that seventy-eight percent of the vote had gone in his favour. Despite his apparent indifference to the protestations of the United Nations, however, in 1978 Pinochet ordered that evidence of Chile's human rights abuses be hidden. As a result, hundreds of corpses were exhumed and dumped in the Pacific Ocean.

By 1980 it was obvious to everyone that Pinochet had no intentions of relinquishing control and returning Chile to civilian rule. Instead, he introduced a new constitution that allowed him to remain as President until 1989. The new constitution further allowed the government to restrict freedom of speech and to arrest or exile any citizen it so wished without the right to appeal. These were draconian measures meant to intimidate the population and yet it was during the 1980s that things began to go seriously wrong for the President.

In 1982, the economy, which had been buoyant, took a turn for the worse and plunged to an all-time low. Ten years before, unemployment had stood at around four per cent but by 1982 it had rocketed to twenty-two per cent, resulting in misery for millions. The economic chaos had a knock-on effect, for it ignited civil unrest. Demonstrators began to take to the streets and, to the growing alarm of Pinochet and his cohorts, opposition groups, instead of disappearing, started to grow in strength and popularity.

By 1985 these groups decided that the best course of action would be to unite against the regime. They joined forces to form the 'National Accord for Transition to Full Democracy' and demanded Pinochet hear their case. It can only be imagined how Pinochet reacted in private, but in public he rejected their request outright, a move guaranteed to further infuriate opposition groups and citizens alike. On 7 September 1986 the Manuel Rodríguez Patriotic Front (FPMR), which was thought to be an armed wing of the Communist Party, attempted to assassinate Pinochet by ambushing his car. Pinochet was returning to Santiago having spent the weekend at his country residence. Suddenly a van carrying a mobile home swung across the road in front of the presidential cavalcade. Guns were fired and hand grenades thrown. It was a miracle that Pinochet wasn't killed but the assassination attempt left five dead and many more injured. Pinochet was now even more determined to crack down on left-wing opposition groups. Hundreds of people were arrested and jailed but his attempts to cow the people and carry on in office met with an ignominious end. A year after the attempted assassination, a plebiscite to determine if Pinochet should stay in office was

When Pinochet visited Britain in 1998 for medical treatment and was held pending a legal ruling on extradition, this French woman was one of many who protested about 'disparus', those who 'disappeared' during Pinochet's rule in Chile, holding up a poster featuring four who disappeared from the same family in 1976.

instigated. The plebiscite was held on 5 October 1988 and, much to his everlasting fury, on 6 October Pinochet had to admit defeat. Almost fifty-five percent of the population had voted against him, preferring the far more moderate veteran lawyer Patricio Aylwin, who belonged to the Christian Democratic Party. Despite his terrible loss, Pinochet did not relinquish his military position, but stayed on as army chief.

In the aftermath of the Pinochet dictatorship, the new government set up a National Commission on Truth and Reconciliation whose main job it was to investigate human rights abuses during the Pinochet regime. Its report made for depressing reading, for not only did it find that the security forces were responsible for 2,115 deaths (this number later rose dramatically), but that they were also responsible for the detention and torture of hundreds of people without trial. The secret police were immediately disbanded, but no one who had been on the receiving end of Pinochet's rule of terror could forgive or forget what they had had to live through and in 1992 the National Corporation for Reconciliation and Reparation was formed to take over from the National Commission. By 1996 the Corporation had found the Pinochet regime guilty of the deaths of 3,197 people between September 1973 and March 1980. 600 military personnel (mainly officers) were named as having taken part in human rights abuses. To add insult to injury, however, Pinochet was made a senator-for-life and, as a former President, remained immune from prosecution, despite the fact that in 1996 Spain had announced that it wanted to try him for international terrorism as well as genocide. The Spanish case was being brought by the families of some of Pinochet's victims who claimed that agents under the direct instruction of Pinochet had attempted to murder men and women in Argentina, Italy, the US and various other sovereign states. Meanwhile, stepping down as Commander-in-Chief of the army in 1998, Pinochet seemed perfectly safe tucked up in Chile with every assurance that he couldn't be touched. That was all to change when he fell ill and decided to go to Great Britain in search of medical treatment.

Travelling on a diplomatic passport, Augusto Pinochet arrived in Great Britain on 22 September 1998 and underwent minor surgery for back problems at the London Bridge Hospital on 9 October. But it wasn't long before the Spanish judges, Baltazar Garzón and Manuel García Castellon, who had been investigating cases of human rights' violations committed against Spanish citizens during Pinochet's seventeen-year reign of terror, issued a request for his detention. Pinochet was arrested by Scotland Yard officers on a priority 'red warrant', causing uproar amongst the diplomatic community, but great rejoicing among Britain's hundreds of Chilean exiles, one of whom was the former personal doctor of President Salvador Allende, Osar Soto. Soto was quoted as saying, 'It is a great triumph of justice. Pinochet must now give account for more than 3,000 deaths, exiles and tortures in the seventeen years of his dictatorship.'4

But what brought joy to one group of people brought dismay to another. The British government was flung headfirst into a diplomatic storm out of all proportion to Spain's initial request. The United States was less than happy about the pending extradition and was thought to be bringing pressure to bear on Britain's Foreign Office to release Pinochet, for fear that any investigation by Spain into charges of genocide and torture would uncover unsavoury facts about the US role in the coup that had brought Salvador Allende's government tumbling down.

Over the next few weeks the legal wrangling grew more and more complicated. General Pinochet, through the legal firm of Kingsley Napley, issued a statement to the effect that: 'General Pinochet entered the United Kingdom with the full prior knowledge of Her Majesty's Government and with the approval of the Foreign Office…Any attempt to extradite him from the UK will be resolutely opposed. Both he and his family are confident of success.'[5] But at the same time as this statement was being issued, a British-based Chilean human rights group was also indicating that it was in the process of bringing a private prosecution against Pinochet so that he would have to be detained indefinitely in Britain.

Initially, however, the British High Court ruled in Pinochet's favor stating that as a former head of state he could not be prosecuted, although the British Crown Prosecution Service was given leave to appeal, which it did very swiftly. On 25 November the House of Lords then upheld that appeal and consequently the extradition request. This time it was Pinochet's legal team that had to act in haste. Once again the defendant's lawyers went to the High Court to appeal against the previous decision but on 24 March 1999, by a 6-1 majority, the law lords again refused the request and said that Pinochet was not immune to extradition.

At this stage the former British Prime Minister, Lady Margaret Thatcher, stepped into the fray making her first speech in the House of Lords for over three years. Lady Thatcher was a close political ally of General Pinochet, mainly because, during the 1982 Falklands War, Pinochet had tacitly supported Britain in its fight against the Argentineans by allowing SAS forces to set up bases on Chilean soil. Thatcher argued that, should the Spanish successfully extradite Pinochet, then no former leader of any country would be able to operate as they saw fit for fear of later reprisals.

'Those still in government,' she said, 'will be inhibited from taking the right action in a crisis, because they may later appear before a foreign court to answer for it. And – in a final ironic twist – those who do wield absolute power in their countries are highly unlikely now to relinquish it, for fear of ending their days in a Spanish prison.'[6]

Despite Thatcher's interference, however, the government continued to insist that Pinochet's case would be judged entirely on its legal merits, not on extraneous factors such as former diplomatic relations. And so the appeals and counter-appeals dragged on. On 15 April 1999 Jack Straw stated that there were no compassionate grounds to halt the legal proceedings and the next day a new arrest warrant was issued but on 6 October, having suffered from two minor strokes, Pinochet was excused from attending a hearing at Bow Street Magistrates Court. Indeed, according to several reports, Pinochet's health was beginning significantly to decline. In March 2000, the Chilean foreign minister, Juan Gabriel Valdes, petitioned Jack Straw to send Pinochet home on the grounds of ill health. Perhaps because the British government didn't want to be witness to the Chilean military guard escorting home the flag-draped coffin of

During the May Day demonstrations in Caracas, Venezuela, in 1978, these protestors displayed posters of those believed to have been kidnapped by Pinochet's henchmen.

the ex-dictator, or perhaps because they had come under mounting pressure from both home and abroad to release him, Jack Straw bowed to the inevitable and ordered a series of medical tests be run on the detainee.

Four doctors examined Pinochet, including one neurologist and two geriatric specialists, declaring that they thought him medically unfit to stand trial. The doctors stated that the former dictator was suffering from a long list of ailments that included diabetes, heart problems, a history of gout, deafness, memory defects, spinal problems and Parkinson-like features. In conclusion, they also stated that there was clinical evidence of brain damage which would make it highly unlikely that Pinochet could 'meaningfully participate' in any trial. The government's Chief Medical Officer, Professor Liam Donaldson, further stated that he had found the medical assessments 'extremely thorough' and that he didn't expect Pinochet's health to improve.

It appeared as if the battle was over. Pinochet had won, and the hopes of those men and women who had wanted to see Pinochet stand trial in Spain were sorely dashed. In the aftermath of the doctors' reports Jack Straw halted extradition proceedings against the General, but in a bizarre statement given the outcome of the 'non-trial', stated that the Pinochet case had been the most important legal proceedings since the Nuremberg trials.

After seventeen months of house arrest, Augusto Pinochet was now a free man. But neither he nor his legal team waited long to bask in their glory. In fact, the Chilean airforce jet which was to carry him back to his homeland had been preparing for this day from the moment Pinochet was placed under arrest.

Baltazar Garzón, the Spanish judge, was unimpressed but despite orchestrating a last-ditch attempt to bring Pinochet to justice, Spain's foreign minister, Abel Matutes, declined to fight Jack Straw's decision and stated that he would not authorize a legal challenge.

Returning to Chile on 2 March 2000, who knows what was going through General Pinochet's mind, but on landing at Santiago airport, his supporters gave him a hero's welcome, complete with military band and a guard of honor. There were, however, also massive anti-Pinochet demonstrations in Santiago with protestors demanding that he be jailed. Later that evening a candlelit vigil was held outside the Presidential Palace in remembrance of the human rights abuses that Pinochet had committed.

A little less than four months later the Chilean Supreme Court ruled an end to their former President's immunity.

Pinochet was charged with eighteen kidnappings, fifty-seven executions, torture, illegal burial and illicit association – all of which were carried out subsequent to the 1973 coup. The judge at the head of the investigation, Juan Guzman Tapia had not only examined the various charges of torture and unlawful killing that had taken place during Pinochet's regime, but he had also looked into the demise of more than seventy individuals in the so-called 'Caravan of Death'. This was a special mission that had been organized by the then high-ranking General Sergio Arellano Starck. On the direct orders of Pinochet, the General, travelling by Puma helicopter with a hand-picked band of trusted henchmen armed with grenades, machine guns and knives, visited several provincial cities and towns in northern and southern Chile (La Serena, Copiapo, Calama, to name but a few). There he had systematically executed union leaders and political functionaries previously associated with the Allende government. In effect, this action terrorized citizens and crushed Chile's long-held tradition of civil (as opposed to military) institutions and respect for the law.

Naturally, human rights groups were once again overjoyed at the news of Pinochet's 'Chilean' arrest. Carlos Reyes of the London-based organization, Chile Democratico, who was subjected to a series of abuses at the hands of Pinochet's men, announced that many Chileans would be dancing in the streets. But Reyes, along with countless other former torture victims, was once again to be sorely disappointed for, as in Britain, Pinochet's ill health was presented as adequate reason to drop all charges. On 1 July 2002 the Chilean Supreme Court reaffirmed that the former President would not stand trial because of ill health (in particular his mental ill health) and three days later Pinochet resigned as a 'senator for life'. According to his son, this dramatic decision was made 'as a contribution to social peace in Chile' but Pinochet had not attended the Senate for several years.

Like so many former dictators, General Pinochet now enjoys a quiet retirement without the worry of further court cases or the humiliation of being sent to prison. That his wasn't the most brutal regime when compared to several others that appear in this book is no defense for what occurred during his time in office. Nor is the excuse that the deaths for which he was responsible were a necessary evil in order to bring law and order back to the country. Pinochet wasn't fighting a war; those who were executed or tortured weren't soldiers; they were innocent civilians who simply opposed his regime. For them there will never be an amnesty, there will never be an easy retirement. Those who survived will carry their sentences with them for the rest of their lives.

[1] From 'Operation Condor and Pinochet', *Los Angeles Times*, 1 November 1998.
[2] *Estado, Poder, Persona*, Vol.II, CODEPU, 1995.
[3] From *Chile: Evidence of torture: an Amnesty International report*, London (Amnesty Publications), 1983.
[4] 'Pinochet Arrested in London' by David Connett, John Hooper and Peter Beaumont, 18 October, 1998.
[5] 'Diplomatic Crises Over Pinochet' by Duncan Campbell, Nick Hopkins, Ian Black and Ewen MacAskill, The *Guardian*, 20 October 1998.
[6] From 'Pinochet arrest damages Britain, says Thatcher', by Michael White, The *Guardian*, 7 July 1999.

NICOLAE CEAUSESCU

Visionary Architect of the Nation's Future

'Because of the crimes they committed against the people, I plead,
on behalf of the victims of these two tyrants, for the death sentence
for the two defendants. The bill of indictment contains the following
points: Genocide, in accordance with Article 256 of the penal code.
Two: Armed attack on the people and the state power, in accordance
with Article 163 of the penal code. The destruction of buildings and
state institutions, undermining of the national economy, in
accordance with Articles 165 and 145 of the penal code.'
Taken from the Transcript of the Closed Trial of Nicolae and Elena
Ceausescu, 25 December 1989.

Eastern European history is raddled with countries whose internal politics are a melting pot of scandalously corrupt royalty, absentee landlords, foreign invasions, occupying forces, assassinations, bloodshed and general warring and, sadly, the history of Romania is no exception. After World War I numerous political parties emerged in Romania, including the fascist Iron Guard led by Corneliu Codreanu which by 1935 had come to dominate the political scene. In 1938 it was then the turn of King Carol II to lay down his cards and announce a royal dictatorship, but despite ordering the assassination of Codreanu, King Carol's rule was not without its setbacks, namely the occupation of vast tracts of land by, amongst others, the USSR, Hungary and Bulgaria. In turn this led to widespread demonstrations across Romania, forcing Carol to abdicate in favour of his teenage son, Michael, who was then shortly ousted from power by Marshal Ion Antonescu who declared a fascist dictatorship. By 1941 Antonescu had joined in Hitler's anti-Soviet war although when he realized that Germany was losing, he switched allegiances and joined the Allied forces. Subsequently, when the World War II drew to a close, Soviet-backed Communists won Romania's 1946 elections and a Romanian People's Republic was established. King Michael was forced to abdicate and Marshall Ion Antonescu was executed after which Romania, under the rule of Petru Groza, entered the huge network of Soviet-dominated satellite countries. It wasn't until the 1960s, under the leadership of first, Gheorghe Gheorghiu-Dej and afterwards, Nicolae Ceausescu that the Communist Party of Romania began to sever links with the Soviet Union and become increasingly independent. Indeed so sever was the break between Romania and the USSR that in 1968, Ceausescu felt strong enough to condemn the Soviet invasion of Czechoslovakia, a move that earned him much praise, in addition to economic aid from the West. But, what augured so well for democratic Europe sadly began to spell disaster for the Romanian people as Nicolae Ceausescu soon resorted to a dictatorial style of leadership, one that over a short period of time brought misery to the entire country.

Nicolae Andruta Ceausescu was born on 26 January 1918 to parents of peasant stock in the tiny village of Scornicesti, in south-western Romania. At the age of eleven his family moved to Bucharest and Nicolae was put to work as a shoemaker's apprentice. In 1932 Ceausescu joined the Romanian Communist Youth Party and a year later had so impressed his superiors that he was chosen to represent the group at an anti-fascist conference held in Bucharest. At the tender age of fifteen, Nicolae was then arrested for inciting a strike and distributing leaflets which were contrary to government policies. In fact this was the first of several such 'crimes' for which he was imprisoned, the next being in June 1934, this time for collecting signatures protesting the trial of a group of Grivita railroad workers (whose leader was the soon-to-be-President of Romania, Gheorghe Gheorghiu-Dej), and thereafter he was twice imprisoned towards the end of that year for distributing Communist literature. At this point his police record stated that he was a dangerous Communist agitator and subsequently he was exiled from Bucharest and sent back to his birth village of Scornicesti. But the authorities couldn't keep a track of Ceausescu for long, and shortly after his return he went 'underground', returning to Bucharest some time later in order to continue his political activism. Over the next few years Ceausescu spent his time being arrested, jailed, released and re-arrested until 1940 when he was sent to Jilava prison near Bucharest. Shortly afterwards the prison was attacked by members of the Iron Guard who killed sixty-four prisoners. Ceausescu escaped with his life only to be transferred to a concentration camp at Tirgu Jiu where he was jailed alongside such Communist luminaries as Chivu Stoica, Ion Georghe Maurer and, most important of all, Gheorghe Gheorghiu-Dej, to whom he had already lent support during Dej's 1933 trial. After his release from Tirgu Jiu in 1944, Ceausescu was immediately appointed

Nicolae Andruta Ceausescu became First Secretary of the Romanian Communist Party and the country's leader in 1965 on the death of his predecessor, Gheorghe Gheorghiu-Dej.

head of the Union of Communist Youth for which he worked tirelessly.

In 1946 Nicolae Ceausescu decided to marry. Back in 1939 he had met a young woman by the name of Elena Petrescu. Although uneducated, she shared his enthusiasm for politics and during the 1930s had joined the Young Communist League. It appeared to be the ideal match and the two subsequently enjoyed a long (if somewhat notorious) partnership. In fact one of their first acts as man and wife was to adopt a young boy by the name of Valentin for, at that time, the Romanian Workers' Party was encouraging members to adopt war orphans.

By 1947 the Communists were in the ascendant and when Gheorghe Gheorghiu-Dej became premier in 1952, Ceausescu, as Gheorghiu-Dej's protégé, was made deputy head of the country's Ministry of Agriculture. In fact Ceausescu's rise within the Party ranks was relatively swift and soon he was swapping Agriculture for the Ministry of Armed Forces. In between times, Ceausescu's family was also growing, with Elena giving birth first to a daughter Zoia, in March 1950 and then to a son, Nicu, in 1951. Shortly afterwards Ceausescu was promoted to being a full member of the Party's (now renamed the Romanian Workers' Party or RWP) Central Committee after which he became a member of the Politburo (effectively the most powerful organ of the Communist Party's executive). This was a great honor and sealed his future success as a leading politician, particularly when, in 1965, Gheorghe Gheorghiu-Dej died. Three days later Ceausescu took over as the country's First Secretary and alongside drawing up a new constitution, changed the name of the country from the Peoples' Republic of Romania to the Socialist Republic of Romania, thus signalling his government's Socialist leanings.

To begin with, Nicolae Ceausescu was a relatively popular leader, due for the most part to his independent stance when it came to all matters Russian. Pre-Ceausescu, Romania had slavishly followed the USSR and aligned itself behind Stalin, almost to the point where it lost its own national identity. But when the Soviet Union entered Czechoslovakia on 22 August 1968, Ceausescu, who was by then Head of State, spoke to a huge crowd of Romanians who had gathered in the Pieta Republicii, stating:

'Let us be ready, comrades, to defend at any moment our Socialist homeland, Romania. It is inconceivable in the world today when the people are rising to struggle in defence of their national independence and for equal rights, that a Socialist state, that Socialist states, should transgress the freedom and independence of another state…We have decided to start from today forming armed patriotic detachments of workers, peasants and intellectuals, defenders of the independence of the country…The entire Romanian people will not allow anybody to violate the territory of our homeland.'[1]

This played well with the crowd and although Ceausescu softened his stance later, for a long time afterwards Romanians felt their leader had only the country's best interests at heart. The truth of the matter, however, was far less savory, for while championing a more independent foreign policy at home Ceausescu was being anything but liberal. In fact he was establishing a highly Stalinist type of government, one that on the whole championed a strict centralized administration. A prime example of this was the organization of the Secret Police (the *Securitate*) who began spying on citizens, denying them the right of free speech, in addition to censoring the press. The *Securitate* had the power to arrest anyone on suspicion of being a class enemy or, worse still, a foreign spy and furthermore they could detain them without trial for as long as they wished.

One of the worst atrocities the *Securitate* committed during Ceausescu's reign was the setting up and running of work camps which were used to house prisoners who were then set to cut a 37-mile-long canal (soon to be dubbed the Death Canal) between the Danube and the Black Sea. This was a monumental project that involved hundreds of thousands of prisoners toiling in the most appalling conditions. Most of them would die during the canal's construction, but work wasn't suspended, quite the opposite, for Ceausescu saw this as an ideal opportunity to rid Romania of 'undesirable minority groups'. To this end huge numbers of Transylvanian and Moldavian Hungarians were deported to the Dobruja labor camp charged with the most inoffensive of crimes, such as talking in their mother tongue. The work they had to do was nothing short of slave labor such as digging out trenches, cutting out rock and carting soil by wheel-barrow, but when foreign delegations were shown round, the prisoners were hidden out of sight so that no one could see the hideous conditions they were living and working in. The camps didn't have adequate sanitation, food or medical supplies, as a consequence of which many died of TB and dysentery having already been weakened by lack of food and constant beatings. In short the prisoners were treated worse than animals, but when the project was completed (in 1984), Ceausescu deemed it one of his greatest achievements, an indication, if any were by then needed, of the mindless cruelty of his regime.

In 1966 Ceausescu upped the ante by passing new laws banning contraception and abortion. Ostensibly this was to 'boost' the population, but in effect it was simply another means of intimidating citizens. All women in the factories were subjected to monthly gynaecological examinations to ensure that the new laws were being obeyed. 'They were taken to clinics where they would be subjected to a full medical and internal examination often in the presence of government agents who some Romanians nicknamed 'the menstrual police'. 'The Foetus,' Ceausescu claimed in one of his more infamous speeches, 'is the property of the entire society. Anyone who avoids having children is a deserter who abandons the laws of national continuity.'[2] Despite this, however, many women resorted to dangerous, back-street abortions, often doing irreversible damage to themselves or to their unborn foetuses. As if to add insult to injury, Ceausescu then further ordered that all women under the age of forty produce a minimum of four children (a number that was later increased to five). Childless women were subsequently singled out and forced to pay higher taxes. Unfortunately the new abortion laws also ran concurrently with a time in Romania's history where food was in short supply, which meant that newborn children were often underweight. Indeed those babies that weighed 1,500 grams or less were often declared 'miscarriages' and denied further treatment. Doctors began cooking their books and forging statistics. ' "If a child died in our district, we lost 10 to 25 percent of our salary," said Dr. Geta Stanescu of Bucharest. "But it wasn't our fault: we had no medicine or milk, and the families were poor."[3]

But if the above was a brutal attack against women's rights, Ceausescu's next move was nothing short of dragging his people to the brink of starvation. In 1971 Ceausescu

While much of his country languished in poverty and faced crippling food and energy shortages, Ceausescu, posing here by the lily pond at his villa near Bucharest, lived in luxury and wore imported suits.

visited China and Northern Korea meeting both Mao Tse-tung and Kim Il Sung, both of whose regimes suitably impressed him. On his return to Romania, Ceausescu therefore determined to re-industrialize his country along the same lines as his comrades had done and to this end borrowed vast amounts of money from western credit institutions. The money was then used to aid a massive depopulation of rural areas, relocating the inhabitants in the cities where they were set to work manufacturing luxury goods which could be exported. But Ceausescu had over-extended himself; leastways by the 1980s he had accumulated approximately $10 billion dollars-worth of debt. Subsequently he made the fatal decision to start exporting everything his country could produce, including its most important natural resource, food. Having depopulated the countryside and virtually run agriculture into the ground there wasn't a lot of grain or farm produce to go round, but by shipping out stocks of meat, vegetables, fruit, etc, suddenly Romania began suffering terrible food shortages. Ceausescu no longer had the means to buy in medical supplies, nor had he enough money to run his already uneconomic oil refineries, which even at this stage were only functioning at 10 per cent of their capacity. By the 1980s austerity measures were put in place and bread rationing introduced. Queues formed outside shops and people often had to wait hours only to be told that what they had come for had already run out. Suddenly people were being told that due to the fuel shortages they could only use 40 watt bulbs to light their homes, and at night only one in every three street lamps were switched on. The fuel shortages also led to a crisis in the hospitals as power cuts disrupted operations and life-support machines flickered on and off. Because petrol was in such short supply, ambulances were ordered not to go out on calls to patients over the age of seventy.

But if the Romanian people were suffering during this period, Nicolae Ceausescu and his family were living the high life. In fact the disparity between the two was nothing short of obscene. For instance, the Ceausescus enjoyed the privilege of owning over forty luxury palaces, although the jewel in the crown was, without doubt, the Primaverii Palace in Bucharest. After the Ceausescus' demise, whole rooms were discovered filled with the trappings of wealth. For instance one room was devoted to Elena's vast collection of fur coats, while another housed hundreds of dresses and even more pairs of shoes. A third room was devoted to Nicolae's bespoke suits and hunting outfits (many of which were never worn). The palaces were no less well dressed either, but were filled to the brim with exquisite silverware, priceless carpets, chandeliers, porcelain and marble. And the opulence found inside the palaces was equalled by that found outside, i.e. the vast collection of cars which included a Buick Electra which had been a gift from US President Richard Nixon, together with several Mercedes. Then there were the luxury yachts, the *Snagov I*, the *Snagov II* and Nicolae's large collection of 'Rocket' speedboats. In 1984 Ceausescu ordered the demolition of 10,000 hectares of prime real estate in the Uranus Hills residential area of Bucharest in order to make way for yet another palace. This time he wanted an entire boulevard built (at least as long and as impressive as Paris's Champs-Elysees) ending with the 'Casa Poporului' or House of the People. When it was completed, the building was 277 feet tall and had a surface area of over 220,000 square yards, making it the second largest building in the world after The Pentagon.

Anyone might have identified the owner of this and of all the other trappings of wealth as a western playboy, not a stalwart of the communist party, let alone Romania's President.

Nonetheless Nicolae Ceausescu continued to spend Romania's money (money borrowed from the west) on his own luxury lifestyle, while Romanian citizens were left to reap the effects of his disastrous policies, which, tragically for them, didn't stop short of food or fuel shortages. Orphanages began springing up all over the country due for the most part to a population boom after Ceausescu's law had been passed forbidding abortion and contraception. Because of the food shortages, families could no longer feed themselves and unplanned children were therefore the last thing that they needed. Needless to say, conditions inside the orphanages were appalling. Food, blankets, clothing and, in particular, medicine were all in short supply, if not totally non-existent. Children were often kept naked for want of clothes to dress them in, and because of the unsanitary conditions in which they were kept many suffered from chronic diarrhoea, lice infestation, worms and scabies. But, sadly, even these conditions weren't the worst of the situation, for doctors, who for years had been prevented from keeping up with western medical advances owing to Ceausescu's draconian laws, began giving the children blood transfusions in the hope of aiding their nutritional needs. Instead, what occurred was an HIV/AIDS epidemic of gargantuan proportions, as the blood had never been tested, Ceausescu believing that only decadent westerners carried the disease. By the end of Ceausescu's regime there were more than 150,000 children living in the Romanian orphanages, thousands of which, at the age of two or three, still hadn't learnt to walk, and thousands more of which were infected with the HIV virus.

Since Ceausescu had taken over the party in 1965, he had brought nothing but misery to his people and yet, despite this, on 28 March 1974, he was made President for Life of the Republic by the Grand National Assembly. Nothing short of a revolution could remove Ceausescu and his cronies from power, but it was to be well over a decade later before such a miracle occurred. In the meantime Nicolae Ceausescu turned his attention on one of his strongest pet hates: the minority Hungarian population within Romania. After the Communists took over the country those Hungarians who lived in Romania (in particular those in Transylvania) found themselves suffering not only the edicts of Communism but also the increasingly nationalistic Ceausescu dream. For instance, under Ceausescu's guidance, the Communist authorities insisted on redistributing eighty per cent of Hungarian-owned land to Romanians, added to which Hungarian schools were closed and all school textbooks (which were without exception written by Romanians) had a definite anti-Hungarian bias. Hungarians were banned from speaking their mother tongue in public areas and if caught so doing could be arrested, beaten and/or imprisoned. In the 1980s, as part of Ceausescu's massive industrialization programme, many Hungarian villages

Elena Ceausescu, seen here at the closing ceremony of the Romanian Communist Party's 14th congress in Bucharest in 1989, became the second most powerful person in the country next to her husband, although her claimed academic qualifications were farcical.

were bulldozed to the ground and the villagers forcibly resettled in other parts of the country. But if Nicolae Ceausescu was a despot, his wife Elena was, perhaps, even more of a tyrant.

In 1975 Elena 'persuaded' several eminent scientists to write papers, which she then appropriated and published under her own name. In addition, Elena – though never having completed her elementary education – somehow managed to acquire a PhD in chemistry and later became a Director of the Institute of Chemistry. Most people realized her qualifications were fake, but nobody dared speak up to point out the lies. Nor did her ambition stop with academia. By 1979 she had had herself appointed an ex-officio member of Nicolae's cabinet and by 1980 she became First Deputy Premier, i.e. the second most powerful person in the country after her husband. Indeed, many people believed she was behind some of Nicolae's less savory policies. Despite this, however, both Nicolae and his wife managed to build up what later become known as a 'personality cult' around their two figures.

When Nicolae had visited China and North Korea, he had been impressed by the image of authority that both Mao Tse-tung and Kim Il Sung had created, and wanted to set up much the same system in Romania. In practice this meant nurturing the idea (through the press and through television) that Ceausescu was akin to a father figure to

Romania. More than that, he was a portrayed as a creative Communist whose ideas were the source of all Romanian accomplishments. He and his cronies named the period of his rule a 'golden age' thus implying that the arts and the sciences were flourishing under his guidance, and he encouraged the media to refer to him in reverential terms using phrases such as 'visionary architect of the nation's future', or 'guarantor of the nation's progress and independence'. All over the cities, the towns, in government buildings and classrooms, large pictures and photographs of Nicolae and Elena appeared on the walls. Indeed Elena Ceausescu enjoyed much the same recognition as her husband, being referred to by the press variously as 'Mother of the Fatherland', 'Leading Fighter of the Party for the Glorious Destiny of Romania' the 'Party's Torch' and other such ludicrous soubriquets. Both Elena and Nicolae Ceausescu's birthdays were celebrated as national holidays. Their son, Nicu, was treated with much the same honor and it soon became known that should Ceausescu die then either Elena or Nicu were to succeed him as President. Indeed nepotism seemed to be the order of the day as two of Ceausescu's brothers were promoted to key positions within the Romanian army and the *Securitate* and at one point over twenty-seven of Ceausescu's close relatives also held powerful positions within the party itself.

By the time of the Thirteenth Party Congress held in November 1984, despite a rapidly crumbling economy and a population on the brink of starvation, Nicolae seemed to be in an unassailable position. He announced that there would be no change to his forced industrialization policy and made no mention of the food rationing that was occurring nationwide, nor of the electricity cuts and fuel shortages. In fact with all the arrogance of a man whose living standards had risen while his whole country's had plummeted, he predicted that by 1995 Romania would be a totally energy self-sufficient nation. Naturally however, no such turnabout occurred and by 1989 the country was on the brink of total collapse. Only then did public discontent gather so much momentum that on 16 December, in the city of Timisoara, a public riot broke out.

Ostensibly the riot had begun as a peaceful protest in support of a dissident Hungarian minister named the Reverend Laszlo Tokes. Tokes was facing deportation for speaking out against the Ceausescu regime, in particular condemning it for its persecution of Hungarians. But, though the gathering began peacefully enough, it soon turned into a massive demonstration against the government and riot police stepped in to break up the crowds. The police were then joined by members of the *Securitate* and afterwards by the army. Suddenly events took on a life of their own and, on the command of General Victor Stanculescu, troops opened fire on the crowd. Several hundred citizens were killed and, in the aftermath of the bloodshed, most people turned their anger on Ceausescu whom they felt was responsible for giving Stanculescu his orders to fire.

The following night 50,000 citizens took to the streets of Timisoara only this time they were openly criticizing the government in general and Ceausescu in particular. Unfazed by the civil unrest, Ceausescu (some say on the advice of Elena) decided to hold a public rally himself and to this end, on 21 December, he ordered a mass gathering in Bucharest's central square – then known as the Pieta Republica (but now known as the Pieta Revolutiei). On the night over 80,000 citizens turned out to hear what their President would say, but Ceausescu, no doubt because he was totally out of touch with the people, misjudged their mood and when he began to spout Party rhetoric and rant on about socio-economic policies, the crowd began to heckle. Standing on the balcony of the Central Committee building, it was obvious that Ceausescu was taken off guard. The crowd shouted out, 'Down with the Dictators!' and 'Timisoara! Timisoara!' and Ceausescu stood as if in a daze.

Nor was that the worst of it for the President because not only were the crowds privy to this momentous occasion, but the whole event was being broadcast to the nation and although shortly afterwards the plug was pulled on the programme by the censors who then replaced it with patriotic songs, by that time it was too late, everyone in the country had witnessed the Ceausescus' humiliation.

Moments later Nicolae and Elena were hustled back inside the Central Committee Building where they made the second mistake of the day and, instead of escaping the city that night, they decided to wait until the following morning. Why they did this, no one can say for certain, but some people have laid the blame on Elena, saying that she thought the whole event was nothing more than a storm in a teacup and would soon blow over. But for the Ceausescus the storm had only just begun.

By morning, protestors had broken into the Central Committee Building and had begun hunting their prey, but aware finally of the danger they were in, Nicolae and Elena had arranged for a helicopter to pick them up from the building's roof. Sadly for them, that's where their plan ended, for they had nowhere to run to or hide and when the helicopter eventually landed, both Ceausescus were arrested and taken to a military base at Tirgoviste, which lies approximately fifty kilometres north of Bucharest. No sooner had they arrived than they were put on trial before a military tribunal, which was made up of three civilians, five judges, two prosecutors, two defence lawyers and a cameraman who was to record the proceedings. At the beginning of the trial one of the prosecutors, General Dan Voinea, outlined the charges against them which included 'crimes against the people' and acts which were 'incompatible with human dignity'.

But from the very beginning Nicolae refused to co-operate with the proceedings, saying that he would only recognize the Grand National Assembly. 'I will only speak in front of it,' he said. Despite his (and Elena's) non-co-operation, however, the prosecution went ahead with its case, the following being a typical example of the type of charge laid against the accused:

'In the same way he [Ceausescu] refused to hold a dialogue with the people, now he also refuses to speak with us. He always claimed to act and speak on behalf of the people, to be a beloved son of the people, but he only tyrannized the people all the time. You are faced with charges that you held really sumptuous celebrations on all holidays at your house. The details are known. These two defendants procured the most luxurious foodstuffs and clothes from abroad. The people only received 200 grams [seven ounces] per day, against an identity card. These two defendants have robbed the people, and not even today do they want to talk. They are cowards.'[4]

Time and again Nicolae was asked to respond, but his answer was always the same, that he would only speak in front of the Grand National Assembly. Even when the prosecutor informed him that this body had been dissolved, his reaction was one of incredulity, not of repentance. 'No one can dissolve the National Assembly,' he said, to which the prosecutor replied that it had been replaced by the National Salvation Front. 'No one recognizes that,' Nicolae responded. 'That is why the people are fighting all over the country. This gang will be destroyed.'

And so the trial continued with a constant tit-for-tat repartee between the two accused and their prosecutors. Elena, even more than her husband, obviously regarded the trial as beneath her contempt and even when the judge mocked her for being nothing more than an uneducated boor, she didn't rise to the bait. Instead the two remained emotionless throughout the trial and according to their defense counsel, Tico Teodorescu, refused point blank to take his advice and plead insanity. 'They felt deeply insulted,' he said, 'unable or unwilling to grasp their only lifeline. They rejected my help after that.'[5] Another list of crimes was then read out to the court, including the genocide of over 60,000 citizens, the destruction of hundreds of Romanian villages, a policy of starving the people and of causing unnecessary suffering to thousands of children. Finally the prosecutor stated that, although he was against the death penalty, in this case he would like to make an exception because 'we are not talking about people'. The judge and even the Ceausescus' defense counsel agreed and subsequently death sentences were passed on both of the accused. Thereafter justice was swift. The two were led out of the room and into a small courtyard where they were told to stand near the back. The prosecutor, General Dan Voinea, who had stepped out for a cigarette, witnessed the whole scene and later recalled that Nicolae Ceausescu stopped when he saw a group of soldiers waiting in the courtyard. 'It was then that he realized he would be executed, I believe' said Voinea.[6] Afterwards they took Nicolae and put him against the back wall and shot him and then they did the same to Elena. The date was 25 December 1989. The Romanian people had just received their best Christmas present in over a quarter of a century. Subsequently photographs were taken of the dead couple and the pictures sent all round the world where they appeared on nearly every newspaper's front page. The couple looked like nothing more than two old-age pensioners lying crumpled in the snow, but on closer inspection you could see that the right-hand side of Nicolae Ceausescu's head was smeared with blood, as was that of Elena's.

Nicolae Ceausescu ruled Romania for just under twenty-four years and, although he had started his career with the best of intentions, during his period in office he had brought the entire country to its knees and ordered the deaths of thousands of citizens. He had made peoples' lives miserable by denying them basic human rights such as heating, food, medical care and education. Romania had been living in the Dark Ages and when foreign reporters eventually gained entry to the country to see for themselves what had occurred, nothing struck them more forcibly than the sub-human conditions within Romania's orphanages. These, more than anything else, spelt out just how terrible the Ceausescu era had been and caused the world to sit up and take note.

In the aftermath of the revolution, Ion Iliescu was called upon to lead the first post-Communist government until a general election could be held. Iliescu immediately declared in public broadcasts on both television and radio that his duty lay in destroying the previous Communist totalitarian system, in removing one-party rule, but most importantly in restoring human dignity and respecting human rights. He also guaranteed the people freedom of expression and a complete overhaul of the economic system to ensure growth and prosperity. Subsequently on 20 May 1990 Iliescu was elected President of Romania and although he later said that he regretted the hasty trial of the Ceausescus, insisted that it had been done to prevent the revolution turning into a civil war. 'It would have been good to secure the two and to hold a trial under normal conditions, but the tension in Bucharest rose and the danger of a generalized civil war existed,' he said.[7] Ilescu's last term in office will expire in December 2004, for unlike his predecessor, he changed the constitution so that no leader could hold office for longer than two terms.

After their deaths, Nicolae and Elena's bodies were transferred to the Ghencea cemetery in Bucharest where they were buried in separate plots. Nobody tends their graves, both of which are overgrown with weeds, but it is unlikely that the Romanian people will ever forget the Ceausescu years.

[1] *Ceausescu's Romania,* by Julian Hale, George G. Harrap & Co. Ltd, 1971.
[2] *Overplanned Parenthood: Ceausescu's Cruel Law*, Karen Breslau, *Newsweek*,
     22 January 1990.
[3] Ibid
[4] From *Transcript of the Closed Trial of Nicolae and Elena Ceausescu,*
     25 December, 1989. The text is available on several websites,
     including http://www.timisoara.com/timisoara/rev/trialscript.html.
[5] Ibid.
[6] United Press International, 25 January 1990.
[7] Reuters Information Service, 1995

POL POT

Brother Number One

We children love Angka limitlessly,
Because of you we have better lives and live quite happily.
Before the revolution, children were poor and lived like animals,
We were cold and suffered,
But the enemy didn't care about us.
Only skin covered our bones, so thin we were worried
All night we slept on the ground,
We begged and looked for food in trash cans during the day,
Now Angka brings us good health, strength.
And now we live in the commune.
The light of revolution, equality and freedom shines gloriously.
Oh, Angka, we deeply love you.
We resolve to follow your red way...

'Angka Dar Qotdam' (The Great Angka)
Children's song learnt under the Khmer Rouge.

On 17 April 1975 the Khmer Rouge took over Phnom Penh, thus ending five years of bloody civil war in Cambodia. But little did the citizens realize that their troubles had in reality only just begun for, by the end of their new leader Pol Pot's rule in 1979, the country had been transformed into a land of killing fields where scores of skeletons lay scattered in ditches and bones littered the mud. In fact between one and two million Cambodians had been murdered, that is to say over thirty per cent of the country's entire population.

The youngest of seven children, Pol Pot was born on 19 May 1928 in Prek Sbauv in what was then French Indochina. His given name at birth was Saloth Sar (he only adopted the name Pol Pot in 1976 as a *nom de guerre*). Pol Pot's father was a prosperous rice farmer, but despite this, the young boy never worked in the fields because, aged six, he was sent to Phnom Penh to live with one of his elder brothers to study Buddhism. This he did for a number of years although, eventually, he was to receive his formal education through a series of French language schools and later at a Catholic college. Despite being a relatively bright student, Pol Pot failed to gain his school-leaving certificate although this didn't stop him from winning a government scholarship to Paris to study Radio Electronics. Whilst in France he met his first wife, Khieu Ponnary. She was eight years Pol Pot's senior, but despite her good influence and her obvious intelligence (she was the first woman in Cambodia to be awarded the *Baccalaureate*), he failed to gain his degree, instead becoming involved with groups of

Marxist students (including Cambodians such as Ieng Sary, Song Sen, Khieu Samphan) whose leanings were towards revolutionary socialism. Khieu Samphan in particular was a big influence on the young Pol Pot, for it was Samphan who believed that in order to achieve a true social revolution in Cambodia, it was necessary to regress the whole country back to being a peasant economy, one void of education, industry, towns or currency. While in Paris, Pol Pot also became a member of the French Communist Party and aided by his fellow left-wing Cambodians helped set up an Association of Khmer Students whose main aim was to challenge Cambodia's Prince Sihanouk and President Lon Nol.

On returning to Cambodia, Pol Pot continued with his revolutionary ideas, joining Cambodia's own Communist party (which by this point had been re-named the Kampuchean Peoples' Revolutionary Party or KPRP) for which he worked tirelessly. But by 1960 he and his fellow radicals had grown tired of the party's ineffectuality, so they overthrew the leaders and took control of the group, renaming it the Workers' Party of Kampuchea (WPK). Pol Pot was elected to the number three position in the new Party hierarchy and by early 1963 he had climbed even further up the ladder when he was chosen as the WPKs new General Secretary (the highest position of all) after the mysterious disappearance of the previous leader. Later that same year he and a small group of close allies left Phnom Penh to regroup on the Cambodian/Vietnam border where they set up an insurgency base named 'Office 100'. From here Pol Pot, in an effort to learn from his Communist Vietnamese neighbors,

walked the Ho Chi Minh Trail to Hanoi for secret consultations with the then General Secretary of the Vietnamese Communist Party, Le Duan. However, at this point, Vietnam was preoccupied with its own civil war as well as the war against the USA and was in no mind or position to help anyone but themselves. Instead they asked Pol Pot to subordinate Cambodia's interests to Vietnam's, but Pol Pot was unimpressed by the request and returned to Cambodia more determined than ever to concentrate on his own war.

Having become involved with a Marxist group while studying in Paris in the 1950s, on his return to Cambodia, Pol Pot and his fellow radicals overthrew the Cambodian Communist Party leadership.

In 1966 Pol Pot visited China where he was very impressed to see the Cultural Revolution in progress and by the time he returned to Cambodia he was determined to bring some of the same ideas to bear on his own country. For the second time in its short history the WPK changed its name, this time to the Kampuchean Communist Party (KCP), though they were more popularly known as the 'Khmer Rouge'. Politically things were growing increasingly difficult for Pol Pot, as a consequence of which, in 1967, he took refuge in north-eastern Cambodia where he lived amongst the hill tribes. These were the 'original Khmers', a self-sufficient group of people who had no use for money and to whom Buddhism was anathema. In fact their simple, communal life-style was much to Pol Pot's liking.

By the end of the year he and his political revolutionaries had begun to wage a series of vicious attacks against the government forces, and by the end of 1968 eleven out of the country's eighteen provinces had also reported civil unrest. Running concurrently with this homegrown rebellion, the USA, in an effort to defeat Vietnam, began blanket bombing not only their enemy, but also Communist-run sanctuaries and supply routes inside Cambodia's borders, with the result that over 600,000 Cambodians died. But far from stamping out Communist resistance, the Khmer Rouge, with Pol Pot at its head, suddenly increased in popularity and party membership swelled. In particular, the Khmer Rouge appealed to the peasantry because, like most Maoist regimes, it appeared to lionize ignorance over education, the countryside over the city and, most important of all, the poor over the rich.

In 1970 desperate to solicit either Chinese or Russian aid to prevent North Vietnam from further encroachments on Cambodian territory (the USA was pushing the North Vietnamese further and further across the border), Prince Sihanouk travelled abroad. It was a bad calculation for, as soon as he was out of the country, government opponents seized the opportunity to exile him and installed Lon Nol in his place as Premier. Back in China meanwhile Prince Sihanouk formed a 'government in exile', in addition to which he made a concerted effort to build an alliance between his Party and that of the Khmer Rouge, both of whom were desperate to rid Cambodia of Lon Nol. The Khmer Rouge began to receive a certain amount of financial support from China, which allowed them to train and equip their soldiers to a far greater degree. Suddenly what had been nothing more than an unruly guerrilla rabble of less than 5,000 grew into a well-trained, effective fighting force of over 100,000. The scene was set for a bitter civil war and one duly followed. By 1973 the Khmer Rouge had successfully taken control of almost sixty per cent of Cambodia's territory and in March 1974 they captured the old capital city of Odongk. In a nasty foretaste of what was to come, however, the Khmer Rouge decimated the city, driving over 20,000 inhabitants from their homes into the countryside. Hundreds of teachers, intellectuals and public servants were taken out and executed simply for being more educated than the average citizen. Afterwards, the Khmer Rouge swept on towards Phnom Penh, surrounding it during early 1975. By 1 April, President Lom Nol had resigned, but rather than surrender to the Khmer

Pol Pot leads a column of Kampuchean Communist Party guerilla fighters, popularly known as the Khmer Rouge, through a forest clearing in June 1979.

Rouge, he fled the country to seek refuge abroad.

After his departure it didn't take long for Phnom Penh to fall for, on 17 April, the Cambodian New Year, troops entered the capital victorious. Naturally the public knew of the Khmer Rouge, who they were and in general what they stood for, but no one had heard of their leader, Pol Pot. Indeed even members of his own family (in particular his brother, Saloth Nhep) were left in the dark, for it wasn't until years later when pictures of him began appearing on the walls of communal dining halls etc, that they realized who he was.

Pol Pot had achieved his ultimate goal: his troops had overtaken the country and he was supreme leader. Now it was time to put his revolutionary ideas into practice.

To begin with Pol Pot declared that the year was no longer 1975, it was 'Year Zero' a term meant to indicate new beginnings for the country, a purification of everything that was wrong with Cambodia, in particular the amount of western influence over cultural life, religion etc. In effect, Year Zero was nothing more than an excuse for four years of murder and mayhem, as Pol Pot systematically ripped Cambodia apart, cut all ties with the outside world, destroyed the country's entire economic structure, demolished foreign banks and destroyed churches Worse still, Pol Pot made his people suffer unimaginable torments.

Within two days of entering Phnom Penh, the Khmer Rouge had 'evacuated' the entire population, driving them into the countryside at gunpoint, giving the excuse that there wouldn't be enough food in the city to support everyone. In reality the truth was far less charitable, for the Khmer Rouge realized it couldn't combat dissent in the cities and towns as easily as it had done in rural areas which were mainly populated by uneducated peasants. Urban districts on the other hand were full of intellectuals, not to mention foreign nationals whose ideas ran contrary to everything the Khmer Rouge believed. Teachers, doctors, nurses, lawyers, shop owners, sewage workers – it didn't matter who you were or what you did, everyone had to leave on pain of death and relocate to rural areas in order to work in the fields, build dams, roads or bridges. But the mass evacuations themselves (for it wasn't only Phnom Penh which was hit) caused hundreds of thousands of people to die, mostly due to lack of food and water, but also from heat stroke (the elderly and young were particularly badly affected). As the long lines of people wound through the countryside, they passed the bloated corpses of fellow evacuees on the roadsides. Dysentery, malnutrition, exposure and dehydration were rampant.

Meanwhile in Phnom Penh, Pol Pot was quickly unravelling the very fabric of the entire nation, for not only had he separated families from their homes and their places of work, he also closed down each and every economic institution. Foreign embassies were boarded up, schools and newspapers ransacked and closed down. Members of the old Lon Nol government together with police, Christian clergymen, military officers, Muslim leaders, teachers and public servants were arrested and executed without trial. Smaller crimes were dealt with no less brutally. Those caught hiding personal possessions, for instance, could be detained and tortured. Everything belonged to the State, *including* the people. Anyone who had been unfortunate enough to live and work in the cities was to be purified through hard labor and no one, not even pregnant women, the very young or the very old were exempt. Suddenly the rice fields (soon to be known as the 'killing fields') were full to the brim with people working in every type of weather, in every condition imaginable for if you didn't put in a day's work, you didn't get fed. Not that the rations that people had to live on were enough to keep them from starvation. It was a battle for survival, which was further underlined by a Khmer Rouge slogan of that time which said, 'To keep you is no gain and to destroy you is no loss.' If you didn't work, you either died of hunger or were shot for insurrection.

Worse still the family unit was deemed bourgeois and therefore unlawful. Wives were separated from husbands, mothers from sons and children were actively encouraged to spy on adults and report them for any misdemeanors, however insignificant.

Pol Pot, always a stickler for detail, further decided that in order for his revolution to be fully effective he would need to eradicate all forms of individualism. With this in mind he divided the population into three separate categories. The first were the *Penh sith*; they had full rights which meant that they could claim full food rations and in addition were free to join the Party or the army if they so wished. This group consisted almost wholly of the uneducated peasantry, people whom Pol Pot felt to be no threat. The second group were the *Triems* who, in effect, were candidates for the *Penh sith* and as such were second in line for food rations. The *Triems* were also allowed to hold minor political positions, but first had to prove themselves worthy of the honor. Finally the third group were the *Bannheu* who enjoyed no rights at all, but in particular any right to food or fresh drinking water. To be a *Bannheu* meant you were the lowest of the low and most people belonging to this group were those men and women the government either wanted to liquidate or to punish. You had to work from dawn until dusk if you were a *Bannheu*, you had no accommodation and you only survived if you could find enough scraps of food that no one else wanted. Sadly, however, all three groups were subject to sundry other laws, the breaking of which could all be punishable by death. These included engaging in sexual relations, complaining about living conditions, wearing jewellery, keeping family photographs, grieving the death of a relative or expressing religious beliefs. A huge number of those found guilty of any of the above found themselves transported to a former school house turned detention centre, Tuol Sleng in Phnom Penh (often referred to as S-21), where over 14,000 men, women and children were either tortured or executed between 1974 – 1978. On arrival prisoners would be photographed and a detailed account of their lives (including their childhoods) would be recorded. The prisoners were then led to tiny cells where they would be shackled to the walls, two or three to a unit. On the walls were pinned the rules and regulations.

> You must answer accordingly to my questions.
> Do not turn them away.
> Do not try to hide the facts by making pretexts of this or that.
> You are strictly prohibited to contest me.
> Do not be a fool for you are a person who dares to thwart the revolution.
> You must immediately answer my questions without wasting time to reflect.
> Do not tell me either about your immoralities or the revolution.
> While getting lashes or electrification you must not cry at all.
> Do nothing. Sit still and wait for my orders. If there is no order, keep quiet. When I ask you to do something you must do it right away without protesting.
> Do not make pretexts about Kampuchea.
> If you do not follow all the above rules, you shall get many lashes of electric wire.
> If you disobey any point of my regulations you shall get either ten lashes or five shocks of electric discharge.[1]

Prisoners were required to follow every last order to the letter. To do anything, even to urinate without permission or to alter their positions while trying to sleep, met with a severe beating. The conditions were also highly unsanitary and many prisoners caught infectious diseases. In fact there was little to no hope of surviving this institution (out of thousands, only seven people left Tuol Sleng alive), the ethos being that those who had been arrested were guilty and therefore had to be punished. The man in charge was called Kaing Khek Iev, but was better known by his revolutionary name 'Deuch'. Deuch had, in a small notebook, written down the various types of torture practiced by both him and his men. One entry describes how four young girls were stabbed in the throat, then timed to see how long it took for them to die. Another entry in a similarly brutal vein talks of slashing open a girl's stomach then placing her in a tub of water to see how long it took her to drown.

'Sometimes while the prisoners were sleeping on the bamboo floor, the Khmer Rouge bayoneted them from below, injuring some in the back or in the feet, causing very painful wounds.'[2] Indeed the torturers had everything on hand including a cemetery, Cheung Ek, where in recent times, over 8,000 human skulls have been discovered.

Tuol Sleng was not the only detention centre in existence; at least twenty others were dotted all over Cambodia and if no detention centre was close enough, any abandoned building would be deemed adequate as the following testimony proves.

'From the time they took my father out of our hut, he was kicked, dragged and beaten all the way to the killing site. Before he was executed he was cuffed in chains along with three other men and was confined in a basement inside an abandoned temple. He went without food for several days because Khmer Rouge cadres knew that he was going to be killed anyway before they finally decided to take him to the grave…The beating was so severe that it paralysed his speech and consciousness. By this time, he was just lying on the floor unable to move or ask for mercy.'[3]

On 5 January 1976 the Khmer Rouge renamed Cambodia, calling it Democratic Kampuchea. At the same time Pol Pot was made Prime Minister, however unlike most heads of state, he remained a shadowy figure both at home and abroad and was better known by the name of Brother Number One. Other members of his cabinet were called Brother Number Two, Brother Number Three, etc. This type of anonymous labelling was pursued throughout the country. The government (which was better known as *Angka*) announced that it was now the true parents of all Cambodian children. Subsequently, teenagers were separated from their families and sent to 're-education' camps where they were taught how to kill, torture and maim.

Children under the age of six were also taken from their parents and looked after by chosen 'grandmothers' who instilled in them the importance of Party loyalty, and children between the ages of six and twelve were mostly herded into mobile troops who roamed the countryside rooting out anyone who wasn't towing the party line.

This last group were the most terrifying of all. Wearing red bandanas, uneducated, but brain-washed to the point of hysteria, they could be found wreaking havoc all over Cambodia, shooting down citizens indiscriminately without any provocation, let alone any legal justification or recourse to any judicial system. There was no real law save that which these children chose to impose, and many of them simply enjoyed making adults cower at their feet and beg for their lives.

However, when it came to stripping Cambodia of every last vestige of humanity and of its past traditions and institutions, Pol Pot did not stop at the family unit. He was also intent on destroying Cambodia's oldest religion, that of Buddhism, which he saw as a direct threat to his authority. Traditionally, at some point in almost every Cambodian boy's life, he would spend some time in a Buddhist monastery either training to be a monk or simply learning about the religion. All this was to stop under Pol Pot who, on coming to power, forbade the practice of Buddhism. The Khmer Rouge executed hundreds of the most prominent monks, defrocked others and destroyed temples. It became forbidden to follow the teachings of Buddhism (which in many ways were an integral part of a Cambodian's life) because Pol Pot realized that they contradicted his revolutionary theories. For instance, the Buddhist practice of receiving merit through the act of giving ran contrary to everything Pol Pot was attempting to achieve.

The intelligentsia was also a target, as anyone seen to have an education and therefore the ability to question the Khmer Rouge and by association Pol Pot were deemed unsafe. Schools and libraries were closed down and some were burnt to the ground. To own a book was a crime and, on occasion, those people who wore spectacles were singled out and executed because they 'looked' intellectual. Further suffering was also experienced due to the complete stoppage of foreign medical aid. This came as a huge blow to everyone in the country (excepting its rulers) for it meant that if you fell ill, not only were there no properly trained doctors or nurses to help you, now there was no medicine either. Instead, the government instructed people to use herbal medicines and, although disease began to run rife, Pol Pot ignored his peoples' suffering. This was all part and parcel of his plan to encourage self-reliance. The country had to be able to function in isolation from the rest of the world, but in particular from the West. In fact, the West hardly knew what was happening inside Kampuchea for, having closed down all the newspapers and TV stations, having thrown out all the foreign diplomats and destroyed the postal service, little or no news of the atrocities was escaping to the outside world. Only occasionally did someone cross Cambodia's borders, but on telling of the genocide that was occurring, of the beatings and cannibalism, they weren't taken seriously. Quite the opposite, for the UN continued to seek Cambodia's attendance at its summits. Finally, in 1978, two journalists, Elizabeth Becker from the *New York Times* and Richard Dudman, who were also accompanied by the British academic Malcolm Caldwell, sought and were granted an audience with Pol Pot. Writing of the encounter almost two decades later, Elizabeth Becker recalled the following:

'He [Pol Pot] was actually elegant – with a pleasing smile and delicate, alert eyes….In the softest voice, without a script or piece of paper, Pol Pot went on to lecture us for over an hour.

'He ranted and raved about the impending Vietnamese invasion – always in the quietest of tones – saying he was sure that American and European troops of NATO would intervene on his behalf and fight the Vietnamese and their Soviet allies in the rice paddies and highways of Cambodia.

'There was no interrupting. There were no questions about the condition of the Cambodian people, about the executions and killing fields. Pol Pot's vision had no room for anything but enemies and justification of his behaviour.'[4]

After the interview the three foreigners were whisked away to a hotel where later that night, on hearing gunfire, Elizabeth Becker ran upstairs to Malcolm Caldwell's bedroom only to find his body slumped across the floor. He was riddled with bullet holes. To this day Elizabeth Becker still cannot understand why the Khmer Rouge found it necessary to execute him, nor why they hadn't killed her and Richard Dudman as well.

By the end of 1976 the Khmer Rouge had put in place a four-year agricultural plan, one that was supposed to treble output in under twelve months. Pol Pot also introduced a rigid timetable for the planting and harvesting of crops; however he didn't take into account the different weather conditions in the different parts of the country. Consequently in 1977, even with almost the entire population working in the fields or otherwise engaged in agricultural production, food shortages occurred which led to famine and more deaths. No one had any pride in their work; there were no incentives to produce more, or to work harder. The only goal in life was to stay *alive* and this led some people to cannibalism. That his citizens had to turn to such extremes in order to survive mattered little to Pol Pot, who further ordered that anyone found practicing cannibalism was to be buried up to their neck and left to die. Afterwards their heads would be removed and stuck on long poles as a warning to others.

But despite the food crisis and despite the killing of hundreds of thousands of citizens, in 1977 Pol Pot left Cambodia and travelled to China to elicit more support, notably not in terms of food aid, but for military backing, as he had begun to fear Vietnam might invade. Pol Pot had always harbored racist tendencies. In Cambodia itself he had tried to cleanse the country of both the ethnic Chams and of the Muslims. Now he turned on the Vietnamese. At first the Khmer Rouge eliminated anyone with Vietnamese relatives or Vietnamese connections over the border, but later on it became dangerous to speak the Vietnamese language or even to look slightly Vietnamese. Cambodian troops were instructed to mount guerrilla attacks over the Vietnamese border, but perhaps the most horrifying addendum to this home-grown racism was the list of instructions handed down by Pol Pot himself that anyone married to a Vietnamese woman was to kill her or face execution themselves.

There seemed to be no end to the executions, no end to the day-to-day torture of living in such a totalitarian regime. Even party officials weren't exempt from the horror, for during 1977-1978 Pol Pot began to perceive threats from within his own

It is almost impossible to say exactly how many Cambodians were murdered, tortured or starved to death under Pol Pot's regime but some estimates put the figure at around two million. At one mass burial site, Cheung Ek, over 8,000 skulls have been discovered.

government. When he seized power back in 1975 there had been twenty-two members of the Central Committee of the Communist Party. By 1978 there were only four members left, the remaining eighteen having been executed. Indeed it didn't matter who you were or where you came from – you could be a soldier, a civil servant, a street vendor, a supporter of Prince Sihanouk, a student or a member of the government and still you were killed, for in reality the whole country was turning in on itself, murdering one another in the most inhumane ways possible, beating and starving their brothers and sisters.

By 1978 the situation inside Cambodia was near total breakdown. Citizens seemed not to care whether they remained alive, and large tracts of countryside were going unfarmed. Added to this, the Vietnamese, tired of the repeated border skirmishes between their troops and those of the Khmer Rouge and hearing reports of the mass murder over the border and the slaughter and persecution of many Vietnamese citizens, deployed several divisions of its army along the Cambodian/Vietnam border. They also sponsored an anti-Pol Pot political movement, which was called the Kampuchean National United Front for National Salvation.

On 25 December 1978, 150,000 Vietnamese troops broke down Cambodia's border defenses and by 6 January were within a few miles of Phnom Penh. Pol Pot's troops were in no fit state to fight, for not only were they undernourished, they were also disorganized due to a complete breakdown of command (one that mirrored the country's breakdown as a whole). The Cambodian army didn't know which way to turn, whom to trust or whether to flee or defend their country against the invaders. On the other hand, the Cambodian citizens were in no such dilemma and welcomed the Vietnamese with open arms. Here were the liberators they had waited for, for so many years.

Phnom Penh fell on 7 January1979 at which point Pol Pot, along with a handful of top Khmer Rouge officials, fled to Cambodia's remote north-western regions and from there to Cambodia's border with Thailand. Subsequently he formed a new power base, this time calling it the Khmer People's Liberation Front. He also announced a new Party manifesto to the effect that he would guarantee complete political and religious freedom if he were to be reinstated as President. Naturally no one took his statement seriously and shortly afterwards, apart from sporadic guerrilla attacks and reports of his marrying for a second time (his first wife having gone insane), Pol disappeared from the political map. It was to be over seventeen years before he was heard from again.

In June 1997 the Cambodian government (Prime Minister Norodom Ranariddh and Second Prime Minister Hun Sen) announced that Pol Pot had, at long last, been captured by a small faction of disillusioned Khmer Rouge soldiers near Anlong Veng in northern Cambodia. The man responsible for his arrest was Ta Mok, Brother Number Five in the chain of command, who had been outraged at Pol Pot's execution of another leading Khmer Rouge minister, Song Seng, along with his wife and children. However, although news of Pol Pot's arrest brought joy to many, and although the government said that it hoped to put him on trial before an international court, in the event this wasn't to be.

Responsible for the deaths of between one and two million people, guilty of starving an entire population and implicated in sanctioning the vicious torture of thousands of citizens, the Khmer Rouge guerrillas, and in particular Ta Mok, refused to hand Pol Pot over to the mainline Cambodian authorities. Instead they kept him under 'house' arrest deep in the Cambodian jungle, during which time he gave an interview to Nate Thayer, a journalist with the *Far Eastern Economic Review*.

'Do you think' asked Pol Pot '…am I a violent person? No. So, as far as my conscience and my mission were concerned, there was no problem. This needs to be clarified…My experience was the same as that of my movement. We were new and inexperienced and events kept occurring one after the other which we had to deal with…For the love of the nation and the people it was the right thing to do, but in the course of our actions we made mistakes.'

Finally, negotiations did begin between the government and Ta Mok for the removal of Pol Pot to Thailand where he could be arrested by US authorities and from there be brought before an international tribunal. But this wasn't to be, for on 15 April 1998, Pol Pot died. His body was put on display for a small group of Western journalists to confirm his demise. Surrounded by teenage Khmer Rouge soldiers who were armed with AK-47 rifles, a bouquet of pink and white flowers rested on the dead despot's head. According to Pol Pot's wife, he had died in his sleep although later the authorities announced his death was due to a heart attack which had been further exacerbated by a lack of adequate medical supplies.

On a per capita basis the Khmer Rouge and in particular Pol Pot were responsible for the deadliest regime in modern Asian history. Pol Pot might have wished to take the country back to year Zero and wipe out his countrymen's memories, but no one still living in Cambodia today will ever forget Brother Number One.

[1] *Tuol-Sleng as a Prison*, by Youk Chhang – Director of the Documentation Centre of Cambodia. More details can be found at: http://www.bigpond.com.kh/users/dccam.genocide.

[2] From *'The Number'* – *Quantifying Crimes Against Humanity in Cambodia*, Documentation Centre of Cambodia, Mapping Project, 1999.

[3] From a statement given by Sisowath Doung Chanto, www.cybercambodia.com

[4] *Pol Pot Remembered*, Elizabeth Becker, news.bbc.co.uk, 20 April, 1998.

IDI AMIN

Big Daddy

'Uganda is a fairy tale. You climb up a railway instead of a
beanstalk and at the top there is a wonderful new world. The
scenery is different, the climate is different and most of all, the
people are different from anything elsewhere to be seen in the
whole range of Africa.'

Winston Churchill

Situated in the heartlands of Africa and bordered by Sudan, Kenya, Tanzania and
Rwanda, Uganda is a country of outstanding beauty. Amongst other natural
splendors, it can boast the Ruwenzori Mountains (the Mountains of the
Moon), the Maramagambo forests and Lake Victoria. The first European explorer to
set eyes on this paradise was John Hannon Speke, who wrote of its people, 'I cut a poor
figure in comparison. They wore neat bark cloth cloaks resembling the best yellow
corduroy cloth, crimp and well set, as if stiffened with starch, and over that as upper
cloaks, a patchwork of small antelope skins, which I observed were sewn together as
well as any English glovers could have pierced them...'[1]

Sadly this idyllic picture was not always a peaceful one, for the history of Uganda
boasted as much bloodshed as any other African nation. However, that being said,
nothing could have prepared its people for what was to occur on 25 January 1971
when the country fell under near military dictatorship. Suddenly the entire nation was
plunged into an era of unprecedented cruelty and wanton aggression. Idi Amin Dada
had begun his eight-year reign of terror.

1 January 1928. In a small hamlet situated a short distance from Koboko on the
border of northern Uganda and southern Sudan, a woman gave birth to a baby boy,
subsequently named Idi Amin Dada. Idi's father was a Kakwa Muslim, while his
mother was a Christian Lugbara; both however belonged to the Nubians, a tribe of
people who were renowned for their strength and brutality. Idi's birth wasn't especially
propitious, after all the hamlet where he was born was nothing more than a few mud
huts surrounded by scanty vegetable patches and miles and miles of un-farmable land.
Not long after his birth, however, Idi's mother decided to take herself and her child to
Lugazi, which was a fair-sized town located on the Kampal-Jinja road. Idi's mother
(nothing is known of what became of his father) tried to keep her and her son from
starvation by practicing spells and creating potions for anyone willing to pay a few
pennies. Often they would camp near different army barracks, for at that time Uganda
was still under British rule and therefore boasted a large military presence. (Uganda
didn't gain independence from Britain until October 1962.)

The young Amin grew up in awe of the British army and in particular was impressed by the elegant uniforms worn by the King's African Rifles. In fact, it was probably this troop of men who instilled the young Amin with his desire to gain military experience and subsequently exact control over his fellow man. Having achieved only an elementary education, in 1946 Idi Amin Dada enlisted as a private in the 4th Battalion of the King's African Rifles. Intelligence, so it seemed, was low on the list of priorities, as the recruiting officers were looking for men who displayed a good physique (Amin stood at 6ft 4in tall and not only enjoyed boxing but was heavyweight champion of Uganda), who could shoot well and who were completely subservient. Amin fitted the bill down to the last letter, although it did take him an extremely long time (seven years) to reach the position of Lance Corporal. Even so Major Iain Grahame (who at the time was still a subaltern) commented:

'It was clear even in 1953 that Idi was an outstanding leader. He was brave, showed initiative, was tremendously loyal and a great athlete. He couldn't speak any English, except to say "Good Morning, Sir," but it was obvious he would get promoted fairly rapidly, despite the fact that he was terribly handicapped by his obvious lack of education.'[2]

Perhaps it was this untrained mind, coupled with the harsh regime of military life that set Amin on the path towards brutality, for it wasn't long before his military record was blotted by a particularly nasty 'incident'. While out on patrol in north west Kenya, he and a group of his men stumbled upon a group of Turkana cattle rustlers whom Amin immediately cornered and then proceeded to torture, before stabbing them and leaving them to bleed to death. Unfortunately for Amin, one of his men reported his actions to the RSM, but always one to maintain absolute respect for his superiors, Amin acquitted himself so well in front of the tribunal that he was cleared of any wrong-doing. But that wasn't the end of the affair, as Amin didn't forget the name of his accuser, Private Samuel Adaka, whom, it is said, was later shot dead by Amin while out on military maneuvers.

The above incident notwithstanding, Idi Amin relished his time in the army. It gave him influence, a home, a regular salary, food and, most important of all, respect.

In 1959, in anticipation of the forthcoming independence of the nation, Idi Amin was promoted to the position of *Effendi*, a Warrant Officer rank. Amin was sent to Kenya for further training and, on his return to Uganda, was awarded the Sword of Honor. It was a huge privilege, but one that was soon to be topped when Major Graham chose him alongside one other Ugandan, Shaban Opolot, for the commission of Lieutenant in the 4th Battalion.

In 1962 Uganda achieved independence and, shortly afterwards, Amin assumed control of one of the new Ugandan army battalions. Subsequently he was sent to Britain for further military training on a Commanding Officer's course in Wiltshire, but Amin never completed the programme and returned to Uganda in 1964. Later he was sent to Israel on a parachute course, but he failed this too, refusing (so it is said) to attempt even one jump. None the less the Israelis awarded him his wings and Amin returned to Uganda triumphant.

Major-General Idi Amin is sworn in as Uganda's Head of State under the supervision of Chief Justice Sir Desmond Sheridan. Amin would later go on to award himself the titles President for Life, His Excellency Field Marshal Idi Amin Dada VC, DSO, MC, Conqueror of the British Empire and King of Scotland.

By 1966, Uganda's political situation had grown increasingly unstable. When the country gained independence, Milton Obote had been elected Prime Minister. Uganda, like many African countries, was dominated by internal warring between the various tribes that made up the population. Obote, by profession a lawyer, came from the minority Langi tribe. Aware that to elect an entire government made up of men from his own background would be foolhardy, he appointed the ruler of the Buganda tribe, King Freddy, as President. But, for Obote, every step forward spelt two steps back and by electing King Freddy to this prestigious post Obote alienated other, smaller factions. Mindful of this potentially volatile situation, Obote tried to curb King Freddy's power, a move which upset the Buganda and that subsequently required military control. Enter the new Deputy Commander of the army, Idi Amin Dada.

Amin was swift to act. Riding on the back of a jeep that was mounted with a 122mm gun, he let off round after round of ammunition, all targeted at King Freddy's palace and while the attack didn't kill King Freddy, it did have the effect of frightening him into exile in Britain.

For the next few years Idi Amin, despite several key differences in opinion between him and Milton Obote (namely that Obote was intent on giving promotions to Langi and Acholi soldiers in the army at the expense of Amin's own tribe), could do little wrong in the eyes of the latter. Indeed so confident was Obote in Amin's loyalty that in January 1971, he didn't give a second thought to attending a Commonwealth Prime Minister's conference in Singapore. It was a rash move, one that Obote would live to regret.

On 25 January, an armed squad of Ugandan soldiers burst into the Voice of Uganda radio station. Taking over the controls, martial music suddenly replaced normal programmes after which the voice of Warrant Officer Class 2, Sam Aswa, announced:

'The Uganda Armed Forces have this day decided to take over power from Obote and hand it to our fellow soldier Major General Idi Amin Dada…and we hereby entrust him to lead this our beloved country of Uganda to peace and goodwill among all.

'We call upon everybody to continue with their work in the normal way. We warn all foreign governments not to interfere in Uganda's internal affairs. Any such interference will be crushed with great force because we are ready.'[3]

These words were no idle threat, for earlier in the day troops loyal to Amin had surrounded the Parliament building as well as the Nsamba police barracks, the police training college, which lay a few miles outside Kampala, and the Owen Falls Hydro-Electric dam. At Entebbe airport barbed wire was laid across the runways and encircled the airport buildings. Just before this was done, four Catholic priests had arrived, one of them to say good-bye to the other three who were all due to fly out to Canada. Without warning a shell burst through the airport's central waiting area, killing two of the priests outright. Later their bodies were thrown into the Nile to be eaten by crocodiles.

Foreign tourists were corralled in their hotels and mortar fire rang out over Kampala. A curfew was instigated, but no one kept to it. Instead there was jubilation on the streets. Cars appeared decorated with colored paper and trailing strings of tin cans. Small children ran along the pavements waving banana leaves, and every now and then soldiers would let off peals of gunfire. People tore down Obote posters and either shredded them or jumped on them for no one, it seemed, had liked the former Prime Minister or his government.

Meanwhile, a beleaguered Obote was flying back to Africa via Bombay. Initially his party landed at Kenya's Embakasi airport, but after a brief visit with Kenya's vice-president, Daniel Arap Moi, the Ugandans flew on to Tanzania where they were finally granted asylum.

Back in Uganda, the story could not have been more different. Idi Amin was riding high on a tide of public approval and, with this in mind, began making the first of many rash, unrealistic statements:

'For my part,' announced Amin, 'I can only wish great luck and good sailing to the Uganda Second Republic. My Government will at the right time make arrangements for honest, fair and completely free general elections...I shall then go back to the barracks and take orders from whoever is elected president. My Government firmly believes in peace and the international brotherhood of man...I will maintain good relations with all countries of the world...I don't believe in a one party system.'[4]

But contrary to this statement, after Amin staged his coup, the tyranny began almost immediately. Anyone who had sympathized with Obote was executed, and Amin issued a directive stating that his troops could detain anyone suspected of being involved in a crime. Unprecedented killing sprees began, any opposition to Amin being swiftly extinguished by his specially trained extermination squads. In Kampala, army chief-of-staff, Brigadier Hussein Suleiman who was loyal to Obote was arrested and taken to the notorious Luzira prison where he died as a result of being beaten and slashed with the butt ends of several rifles. Acholi and Langi soldiers were also targeted by Amin and his henchmen, lined up to have their skulls smashed in with sledgehammers. Further to this, two Americans were executed: Nicholas Stroh, a journalist working for the Philadelphia *Evening Bulletin* and Robert Seidle, who was a lecturer in Sociology. Both men went to investigate the Acholi and Langi killings only to be killed themselves. In fact, overnight, thousands of prominent Ugandan citizens 'disappeared' and those who did eventually materialize in Amin's jails were swiftly executed to make room for the huge influx of new prisoners. Despite all this, the people still celebrated Amin's coming to power, perhaps because they couldn't actually believe what was happening in front of their eyes. Similarly, when Amin was officially sworn in as Uganda's new Head of State, most foreign nations followed suit and recognized the new government as legitimate. Amin visited both Britain and Israel during the early days of his regime. In Britain he met not only with the then Prime Minister, Edward Heath, who promised that he would prolong Uganda's debt repayments which were in the region of approximately £30 million ($48 million), but Amin also lunched with Queen Elizabeth II at Buckingham Palace. Amin was no less well lauded when he reached Israel and by the time he returned to Uganda he was triumphant.

But all the wining and dining with foreign dignitaries couldn't hide the true state of Uganda under Amin's rule, for shortly after he came to power it was evident that the farming economy, which at that time accounted for at least ninety per cent of the country's exports, was in dire straits. In addition, though Amin had promised to hold general elections and return the country to civilian government, he indefinitely reneged on the deal. No one was going to seize power from him. Far from it, he now set about systematically terrorizing Uganda's Asian community, using them as a scapegoat for all the country's economic ills.

Seized by a kind of demonic will, Amin ordered that all Asians be thrown out of Uganda, giving them ninety days in which to leave. Radio stations started broadcasting songs with words such as 'Farewell Asians, farewell Asians, you have milked the economy for too long' and suddenly thousands of passports were deemed illegal. Amin classified his expulsion measures Uganda's 'Economic War'. After all, the Asians were rich, they had played the Ugandan economy for all it was worth and had also fully exploited it. In addition, the Asian community were racists because they discriminated against Africans, they wouldn't mix with their African neighbors and, finally, the Asians weren't Uganda's responsibility – if anyone was to blame it was Britain.

Amin's torrent of abuse encouraged the army to join in the fray and soon Asians were being physically attacked, their homes were being broken into and their businesses looted. Meanwhile, as more Asians fled from the abuse, so the Ugandan economy suffered, as one business closed down after another. Also Britain, angered by what it saw as the persecution of a legitimate minority population, cancelled a loan to Uganda said to be in the region of £12 million ($19 million). It was a sorry state of affairs; none the less Amin pressed on with his racist policies until, by the end of 1972, only a handful of Asians remained in the country (the rest having sought sanctuary in Britain, Canada,

An imposing figure at 6ft 4in (over 2 meters) tall, former Ugandan heavyweight boxing champion Amin presides as fourteen whites, including five Britons and a woman, are sworn in to the Ugandan Army in 1975, vowing to fight against South Africa.

India and the United States). More surprising, having counted this 'Economic War' a huge success, Amin went on to offer his help in resolving Britain's problems within Northern Ireland and he also claimed that the United States had asked for his help with reference to sorting out the Vietnam war. These last were significant signs of Amin's increasing megalomania (during his lifetime he awarded himself a series of honorific titles that ran from His Excellency Field Marshal Idi Amin Dada, VC, DSO, MC, Conqueror of the British Empire, to the most ludicrous of them all, King of Scotland); in other words here was a man who thought he could bully his way onto the world stage, a man who saw nothing wrong with his tyrannical, not to mention violent, methods of oppression. And the fact that Amin was not consistent in his likings or hatreds also led one to believe that here was a man capable of chilling, psychopathic behavior.

Early in 1972, having courted Israel as if she were a blushing bride, Amin suddenly, and without explanation reigned down a torrent of abuse on his old friend. He accused Israel of planning an invasion of Uganda and when, on 5 September 1972, eight Arab terrorists (who were later identified as belonging to a Palestinian group called 'Black September') gunned down 11 Israeli athletes who were competing in the Munich Olympics, Amin was so pleased that on 12 September he sent a telegram to the then UN Secretary General, Kurt Waldheim: 'Germany is the right place where, when Hitler was Prime Minister and Supreme Commander, he burnt over six million Jews. This is because Hitler and all German people knew that the Israelis are not people who are working in the interest of the people of the world and that is why they burnt the Israelis alive with gas in the soil of Germany…' And in addition to this he also stated that since no statue of Hitler had been erected in Germany, that he, Idi Amin, would erect one in Uganda.

But though Idi Amin enjoyed dabbling in foreign affairs, he was at the same time fully pre-occupied on the home front where he could practice what he preached safe in the knowledge there would be no reprisals. Nowhere is this better illustrated than when Amin had Chief Justice Kiwanuka arrested after Kiwanuka had declared that the detainment of a British-born businessman, Donald Stewart, was unlawful. The ruling infuriated Amin who immediately ordered Kiwanuka's abduction and eventual imprisonment in Makindye prison where he was later to die, some say after being hammered to death with steel rods.

At almost the same time as the Kiwanuka affair, several hundred Milton Obote supporters from over the border in Tanzania tried to stage an invasion of Uganda, but the whole affair was a disaster; one which only prompted Amin to exercise his demonic nature over former Obote associates still living in the country. These included such notable figures as the former Internal Affairs Minister, Basil Bataringaya, who was abducted, tortured and then decapitated. The former Minister of Agriculture, John Kakonge together with Frank Kalimuzo, Francis Walugembe, James Ochola, Michael Rubanga and in the region of 85 others vanished.

Other disappearances occurred, together with executions staged in public, to cow the population into obedience. The men were usually stripped naked, manacled at the hands and feet, blindfolded, then tied to trees after which a white apron would be placed around their torsos with a black cross marking where they were to be shot.

At this point an interesting insight into Amin's nature transpired in the form of a memorandum written by the exiled Minster for Education, Edward Rugumayo, who wrote amongst other things: 'He [Amin] is racist and a fascist; a murderer and a blasphemer…He possesses no moral or political standards. He sets his own "standards", writes his own "rules" and changes them as he moves along…If we take the aspect of illiteracy for a President of a modern state, the problem takes on fantastic dimensions. For instance, Amin finds it well nigh impossible to sit in an office for a day. He cannot concentrate on any serious topic for half a morning. He does not read. He cannot write…His abysmal ignorance has made him hate education, educated people and educational institutions. He brags that if he could rule the country well, then there is no need for highly educated people.'[5]

Rugumayo also went on to outline the various methods Amin and his henchmen implemented to murder their victims. These included cutting off the genitals or an arm

Having spent eight years defrauding, torturing and murdering his own people, Amin fled into exile in Libya in 1979, living in luxury for ten years before spending the last thirteen years of his life in Saudi Arabia. He died on 16 August 2003.

or leg and letting the victim bleed to death. Alternatively, victims had flesh cut away from them and then were forced to consume it. Other methods included lining men up and forcing the first man to lie down while the man standing next to him would have to smash his head in with a hammer, after which he would have to lie down and be subjected to the same death, and so on down the line.

Holes would be dug which were then filled with ice-cold water and the victims placed inside where they would slowly freeze to death. Bayonets were used to puncture victims' bodies, rhinoceros whips were used to beat victims into submission and women were systematically tortured and raped. Afterwards the bodies were, more often than not, disposed of in the river Nile where crocodiles would consume the remains.

It was a chilling portrait and one that in time would only grow worse. Indeed, even Amin's own family weren't spared his psychopathic nature. In March 1974 Amin declared his intention of divorcing three of his wives. One of these included a woman called Kay Adroa. Three months later, her body turned up in the boot of a car. Her arms, legs and head had been cut off and each was wrapped in a separate piece of cloth. A post mortem revealed that Kay had been the victim of an abortion that had gone wrong and that her body had been dismembered after her death. But who was to blame? Certainly no one was brave enough to point the finger at Idi Amin, but many people knew he was behind it. Even more alarming was what occurred after her death, when Amin ordered that her limbs be sewn on to her torso again, only attached to the wrong joints while her head was to be sewn on back to front. This aberration completed, Amin then forced Kay's young children together with Kay's parents and a group of government officials to view the body.

By the fifth anniversary of Amin's military coup there was little if any sign of a let-up to the killings that had come to mark the regime as one of the most bloody and barbaric in twentieth-century history. Occasionally small groups of students would pluck up enough courage to demonstrate their anger, shouting out slogans such as 'Save us from oppression', or they would tear down the hundreds of posters of Amin that scattered the cities, but these were drops in the ocean, minute uprisings that could be easily quashed. What couldn't be so easily ignored, however, and what perhaps signalled the beginning of the end for Amin occurred on 28 June 1976.

Air France flight 139 from Tel Aviv to Paris via Athens, which was carrying 258 passengers and aircrew, had only just departed from Athens airport when it was hijacked by four Palestinian terrorists. Initially the Palestinians wished to be flown to Libya, but instead the plane put down for fuel at Entebbe airport after which everyone on board was herded into a disused terminal wing. The hijackers were demanding the release of 53 freedom fighters imprisoned in Israel, Switzerland, Kenya, West Germany and France, and if they weren't released by the end of forty-eight hours, then the plane alongside all the passengers would be blown up. It was an extremely delicate situation, but one which Idi Amin Dada delighted in. Suddenly he was at the center of world attention. He sent his own troops in to surround the air terminal and 'guard' the passengers while the terrorists were allowed to bathe and eat, and he made no bones about the fact that he supported their cause, telling the hostages that it was in their interest to convey to their own governments the necessity of resolving the Palestinian situation.

Ominously, the hostages were separated into two groups: Jewish and non-Jewish. Approximately half of the latter group were subsequently freed. Everyone who was left behind then began praying that somehow the situation could be resolved peacefully, but a short time before the deadline was up, an elderly passenger, Dora Bloch, who held dual British-Israeli citizenship, started choking on a piece of cooked meat and was taken by ambulance to Mulago Hospital where the British High Commissioner, Peter Chandley, gave his assurance that she would be safe.

Meanwhile at the airport, negotiations continued whilst in the background Mossad, the Israeli intelligence service, busied themselves gathering as much information as they could about Entebbe airport from the engineers who had built it, as well as from the freed hostages who by this time had been flown to Paris. Shortly after midnight on 3 July a small fleet of Israeli planes accompanied by Phantom fighters began their descent of Lake Victoria towards Entebbe. In addition, a Boeing jet was sent directly to Nairobi airport carrying 23 Israeli doctors. One hour after the Israeli commandos landed at Entebbe they took off again carrying with them the rescued hostages. In total they had killed twenty of Idi Amin's own troops as well as every single Palestinian terrorist. Only one factor was missing. Dora Bloch was left behind. Having been assured safe passage out of Uganda, the elderly woman now disappeared. Amin insisted she had been returned to Entebbe before the Israelis raided the airport, but the world doubted his word. Eventually her body was discovered, dumped in the Namanve Forest. A young photographer with the Ministry of Information, Jimmy Parma, recorded the incident and was duly killed for his pains. His body, like that of Dora Bloch's, was then dumped in the same forest.

Finally, Amin admitted that Dora Bloch had been killed, but responding to Britain's inquiries on behalf of Mrs Bloch's family, Amin made one of his most bizarre statements saying, 'They [the British] are jealous because I have not married a British woman. They wanted me to be their brother-in-law or their father-in-law.'

In the aftermath of Entebbe, Amin went after anyone he thought had not acquitted himself well. This included all those who worked at the airport, who were hunted down and killed, as well as several prominent citizens who expressed no more than ambivalence towards the Israeli mission to save the hostages. Amin also heaped blame on Kenya, who had aided the Israelis in their incursion onto Ugandan soil. Left, right and centre people were executed or mysteriously disappeared. Kenyans, Amin declared, weren't Africans at all; they were a subhuman species that didn't deserve to live. The situation deteriorated further with both sides accusing each other of crimes against humanity, but Amin's vitriol was by far the more dangerous, and shortly after he'd attacked the Kenyans he began spreading his net of hatred further and further to include white-dominated countries such as Rhodesia, Namibia and South Africa. 'Kill them all,' he spluttered, 'all the Europeans in Rhodesia whether they hide in homes, trees, rivers or jungles. War is war. Zimbabweans must take over the land of those Europeans, and have 100 per cent control of their motherland.'[6] But his outbursts were not only confined to the above, for within Uganda itself Amin continued to wreak havoc on the population, maiming and killing whomever he pleased. One of the most notorious incidents was that of Archbishop Janani Luwum who was executed in Uganda's State Research Bureau. According to Ben Luwum, the Archbishop's son, Amin was personally involved in both his father's torture and execution after which, it is rumored, the Archbishop's head was severed from the rest of his body and kept in a deep freezer along with other such items.

'Waiters would be ordered to bring the heads to the dinner table, where a solitary Amin would rail at them before engaging in "normal" conversation with his unusual guests.'[7]

Ironically, however, given Amin's growing dislike of white-dominated African nations, it was a black African country, Tanzania, who finally put paid to his vile regime. In an attempt to frighten his own citizens into further submission Amin had begun accusing Tanzania of trying to mount a bloody invasion; he sent small bands of soldiers over the border to seek out and kill the 'intruders'. The Tanzanian President, Joseph Nyrere, was quite rightly incensed. For years he had had to suffer Amin's unstable nature; this was to be the last straw.

In April 1979 Nyrere ordered troops into Uganda and despite desperate pleas by Amin, one of which included invoking the help of the Pope (Nyrere was Catholic) to persuade the Tanzanian President to withdraw his troops, no such action was forthcoming. Even with the intervention of Colonel Gaddafi of Libya who sent Amin 1,500 troops, it was too little too late. Reports filtered through that many of Amin's soldiers were deserting their posts and when, on 11 April, Kampala fell to the Tanzanians, Ugandans celebrated in the street.

Overnight, army vehicles sped through the city with loudspeakers blaring out the good news. 'The fascist dictator is finished.' 'A return to sanity.' 'Long live Nyrere.' And in moves that eerily foretold of events that would occur over two decades later in the Iraqi capital of Baghdad, government buildings were looted, shops were plundered, windows were smashed and several of Amin's soldiers, having been caught by citizens, were beaten to death. In the following days, Tanzanian forces liberated many of the prisoners from Amin's jails, although those held in Makindye prison weren't as fortunate as the rest, for they were either shot or bludgeoned to death by troops still loyal to Amin before the Tanzanians could reach them.

Miraculously, however, Idi Amin escaped from Kampala in a convoy of five limousines and for a short time it seemed as if he had disappeared off the face of the earth. Dora Bloch's relatives offered a reward for his capture, in addition to which Samuel Flatto-Sharon, an Israeli millionaire, hired twelve private investigators to track the ex-dictator down. Eventually, it was discovered that this most hated of men had found sanctuary firstly in Libya where he stayed for approximately ten years, then in Saudi Arabia where he was given asylum by the Royal Family. Amin was also given a house in the Red Sea port of Jeddah and a generous allowance, in return for his promise to keep clear of any kind of political posturing.

In 1999 the Ugandan *Sunday Vision* newspaper then mounted a coup of its own by landing an interview with the exiled 'Butcher of Africa' who told them that, ' I am leading a quiet life and committed to my religion, Islam, and Allah. I don't have problems with anyone…But I am satisfied with what I am getting and even paying school fees for a number of my orphaned relatives in Uganda and helping needy people.'[8]

On 21 July 2003, Idi Amin fell into a coma, having suffered over a period of years from long spells of hypertension combined with kidney problems. He was taken to the King Faisal Specialist Hospital in Jeddah, where he was put on a life-support machine. He briefly regained consciousness but eventually died on 16 August.

Where his remains should be disposed of is now the only outstanding question mark hovering over his name. Some people, including several of his wives and children, believe he should be returned to Uganda for proper burial while others, still haunted by the carnage he made of their lives, wish him only to hell.

[1]   *Lust to Kill: The Rise and Fall of Idi Amin* by Joseph Kamau & Andrew Cameron, Corgi Books, 1979.
[2]   Ibid.
[3]   Ibid.
[4]   Ibid.
[5]   Ibid.
[6]   Ibid.
[7]   'Ugandans mourn loss of murderous despot Amin', by Adrian Blomfield, The *Sunday Telegraph*, 17 August 2003.
[8]   news.bbc.co.uk

SADDAM HUSSEIN

A Stalin of the Middle East

'To those who know him personally, Saddam has no sense of
humor and no patience for advice on diplomacy or image-
building. He alternates his image between that of a father figure
and tyrant.'

Nora Boustany, the *Washington Post*, 12 August 1990

If, over the past ten to twenty years, one man could be described as having been a
thorn in the side of America, then that man was surely the former President of
Iraq, Saddam Hussein. During the 1980-88 Iran-Iraq war he ordered the use of
chemical weapons against the Iranian forces (killing between 450,000 and 730,000),
and against Iraq's huge Kurdish population (killing between 150,000 and 340,000). A
few years later, Saddam extended his crimes to include the invasion of Kuwait (1990-
91), killing over 1,000 of that country's citizens, and in 1991 the suppression of both
Kurdish and Shia insurgencies, killing between 30,000 and 60,000 people. He also
ordered the destruction of southern Iraq's marshlands to prevent the marsh Arabs
claiming a homeland and, in 2003, after repeated calls by the US and its allies to
relinquish all weapons of mass destruction, he led his people into a second war with
the West. That Saddam Hussein was a terrifying despot is not in doubt, but what made
him into such a figure, a man so reviled by the West that alongside Hitler and Stalin,
he stands as one of the most hated political figures of the twentieth century?

Saddam Hussein was born on 28 April 1937[1] in the small Sunni Muslim[2] village of
Al Awja, only a few miles east of the town of Tikrit. His mother was a formidable
woman by the name of Subha Tulfah Al Musallat, while his father was Hussein Al
Majid, but by the time of Saddam's birth, his father had disappeared and was
presumed dead.

Saddam's childhood, while not impoverished in terms of the type of society he lived
in, was still very humble. The family home was a one-room mud hut in which the entire
household, along with their animals, had to live and sleep. There would have been no
sanitation to speak of, no electricity, no fresh water. In addition, the village of Al Awja,
being situated in a particularly impoverished region of Iraq, offered little in the way of
opportunities for a young boy.

'... Tikrit was known only for its watermelons and the skin boats called *kalaks* which
carried them down the Tigris to Baghdad. Disease was rampant, in particular malaria,
bilharzias and tapeworm. Most people suffered from one or more of these endemic
maladies... While there are no records on the subject, life expectancy was very short.'[3]

Bearing the above in mind, it is not surprising to discover that the young Saddam

Saddam Hussein declared himself President of Iraq in 1979 when his predecessor resigned due to ill health, although many believe Saddam forced him to step down. Despite his penchant for uniforms and his many public appearances with firearms, Saddam was rejected when he applied to Baghdad Military College as a young man.

spent most of his early years playing in Al Awja's back alleys, gaining a reputation as a bit of a thug. Then, at the age of six, his mother remarried and his new stepfather put the young boy to work in the fields as a general farmhand. It was a tough life, made all the tougher by the abuse he suffered at the hands of his stepfather who refused to let him attend school. In fact, the only person Saddam looked up to or admired was a maternal uncle called Khairallah Tulfah. Tulfah was an educated man who had once been a second lieutenant in the Iraqi Army after which he had become a schoolteacher.

In 1947, at the age of ten, Saddam Hussein left home to live with this much-loved relation. Indeed, according to various sources, the reason behind his sudden departure was because Saddam was not only desperate to gain an education and learn to read and write but more importantly he wanted to find his way out of poverty and make his mark on the world.

Sometime between 1953-1954 Saddam took an entrance exam for the Baghdad Military College, but failed due to his lack of education. Alongside his poverty-stricken peasant background, this setback no doubt added to an already substantial chip he had on his shoulder. Not withstanding this, however, he turned his mind towards politics. Saddam identified with the Sunni minority in Iraq, the poorest of the poor, and began participating in anti-government demonstrations. He persuaded gangs of thugs to join the cause and set them to beating up anyone who didn't agree with their anti-government stance. At the same time, Saddam also began making friends with more organized sections of the opposition, that is to say students who were affiliated with the Ba'ath, a political party that was founded in Syria circa 1940.

On 14 July 1958, the Iraqi army led by Brigadier Abdel Karim Kassem and Colonel Abdel Salam Aref finally overthrew the Iraqi monarchy. Saddam couldn't have been better pleased if he'd perpetrated the act himself. This, or so he thought, would mark a new phase for his country, but by 1959 his attitude had changed so radically that on 7 October he attempted to assassinate Kassem (who had since taken over the presidency). Afterwards, realizing the plot had failed, Saddam fled to Egypt, returning to Iraq only in 1963 when the Ba'ath party, led by Ahmad Hassan Al Bakr, staged a successful coup and finally overthrew Kassem. However, as is the way with Middle Eastern politics, and with Iraq in particular, nothing stayed settled for long and within months of arriving back in Iraq, Saddam was once again jailed after Colonel Abd-al-Salam Muhammad Aref seized power from the Ba'athists. Saddam eventually escaped and later, in 1966, was made Assistant General Secretary of the Ba'ath party which then staged yet another coup in 1968, this time firmly establishing Bakr as president of the country.

Saddam Hussein was now put in charge of the Office of General Relations, a dainty name for a thuggish department, for in reality General Relations stood for Secret Security. In addition, rather like Stalin, Saddam began to gather as many government departments under him as possible, and slowly but surely made himself indispensable to the 'father leader' Bakr. Saddam also ensured that all threats to the party and therefore his position, whether real or imagined, were dealt with swiftly. One man in particular fell victim to this, Colonel Hajj Sirri, who was not a Ba'athist and therefore posed a slight threat to an already neurotic Saddam. Sirri was arrested and accused of being a CIA agent and subjected to endless interrogations and brutal torture. Sirri, however, would not give in, so finally his torturers pulled their trump card and threatened to rape all the female members of his family. It was too much to bear and subsequently Sirri told his interrogators exactly what they wanted to hear; shortly afterwards he was sentenced to death and hanged.

No doubt this wasn't the first brutal act Saddam Hussein had instigated and certainly it wasn't to be his last, for a short time later, thirty men were, on the flimsiest of evidence, accused of spying for Israel. Saddam, who was by this time in charge of all government propaganda, decided to make a huge show of the case and had the accused men's trials televised. The outcome of the trial almost went without saying, each of the accused being found guilty and being sentenced to death. But further to this, after the sentences had been carried out, the corpses were left hanging in Liberation Square for over a day. The public was urged to view the bodies and when President Bakr and Saddam arrived, they enjoyed a huge welcome from the crowd who cheered and clapped their appearance.

Buoyed up by these two successes and knowing that the elderly and ailing Bakr trusted him implicitly, Saddam now turned his attention on the Iraqi army. This was the only real threat to the new regime, but rather than antagonize the regular forces, Saddam instead set up a paramilitary organization called the Popular Army which would fall under his direct control. Other 'reforms' included restricting the activities of all known Ba'athist opponents and, to this end, Saddam had seventeen sons and grandsons of one such man, Sayyed Muhsin Al Hakim, hanged. The longer Saddam was in power, the stronger his stranglehold over the country. As the journalist and author, Säid Aburish, notes, 'Saddam's twin approach to the consolidation of Ba'athist power continued until the end of 1973. First, enemies were neutralized, be they individuals, ethnic or religious groups or political parties. Simultaneously, ambitious social and economic programmes were pursued at breakneck speed.'[4]

With reference to the former, in December 1974 Saddam had five Shia clerics executed for posing a threat to the Ba'athists, and over the following few months expelled more than 200,000 Shias over the border into Iran. But none of that compares to what occurred next, when, in 1979, Saddam forced General Bakr to resign – an act which was officially put down to Bakr's ill health.

Saddam Hussein now declared himself President of Iraq; he had total control over his country and he was not about to relinquish it despite outside calls for the overthrow of his government. And from where did these outside calls originate? From Iraq's neighbour, Iran, whose own government had, in 1979, changed to an anti-Ba'athist regime. Suddenly Ayatollah Khomeini (who had taken over the reins of power from the Shah of Iran) was encouraging the Iraqi Shias to overthrow their Ba'ath leader. It was a recipe that was bound to lead to disaster and sure enough, in

September 1980, Iraq, responding to a series of border invasions by Iran, mounted a full-scale offensive (using over 300,000 troops) against their neighbor. Saddam himself ran the campaign from a bunker under his presidential palace, yet despite appearances he wasn't removed from the action, far from it: he controlled every military decision from bombing campaigns to minor skirmishes. Saddam also kept a close watch on internal affairs, never for a moment releasing his grip over his own government. As the war dragged on, so conditions within Iraq itself deteriorated. (A sure sign of Saddam's nervousness during this period was that he increased the number of people employed by the secret security ten-fold and it is said that between 1981-1982 over 3,000 mainly Shia civilians were executed.) But perhaps the most notorious of all Saddam's actions during this period (apart from implementing a chemical weapons programme) occurred during a cabinet meeting in March 1982 when Saddam, asking his Minister of Health, Riyadh Ibrahim, to step out of the room with him for a moment, took out a gun and shot him, afterwards returning to the meeting as if nothing had happened.

By 1983 the Iran-Iraq war had reached stalemate. Thousands of lives had been lost on both sides and yet nothing had been achieved and neither country was nearer a resolution. Not, that is, until Saddam began using both mustard and nerve gas (in contravention of the 1899 Hague and 1925 Geneva Conventions). But one of the worst hit sites was the Kurdish town of Halabja (population 45,000) in the north of Iraq which had a combination of mustard gas (which affects the skin, eyes and membranes of the nose, throat and lungs) together with nerve agents Sarin, Tabun and VX, dropped on it. It is believed that in these raids, between 3,200 – 5,000 people were killed, but even those who did manage to survive suffered long-term health problems. The use of even more chemical weapons was implemented during what became known as Iraq's *Anfal* (named after the Muslim victory in the battle of Badr which is spoken of in the Koran), once again directed against the Kurds whom Saddam feared wanted to create an independent Kurdistan. During this campaign it has been estimated that between 50,000 – 100,000 Kurdish men, women and children were either killed by chemical weapons, executed, or displaced, while their villages, farms and mosques were razed to the ground.

Finally, in July 1988, after almost nine years of war, Iran was forced to accept defeat and, though a peace treaty wasn't signed, there was an agreement to end hostilities. However, the toll of the war not only on Iran, but more importantly on Iraq, was enormous. Iraq's treasury was practically empty, people's morale was at an all-time low and corruption was rife. Yet despite these setbacks, Saddam believed the best way to strengthen his position in the Middle East and turn his country into the type of force people couldn't ignore, was to continue developing his chemical weapons. To this end he siphoned off as much money as he could from both civil and military projects and despite his people being on the brink of starvation, never stinted when it came to financially supporting his chemical weapons programme. However, when it came to buying equipment from abroad, Saddam's aims were shortly to be

Saddam's son Uday Hussein was known as a brutal sadist and was left paralysed from the waist down and, some said, impotent after an assassination attempt. He died in a gun battle while on the run from Coalition forces during the 2003 invasion of Iraq.

halted, for the West began denying him credit, on top of which the US started intercepting various shipments of 'unconventional' weapons to Iraq.

Infuriated, Saddam began to act in an increasingly erratic manner. Similarly, his son Uday Hussein[5] (whom several commentators have described as being mentally deficient) also began behaving in an unpredictable way. In October 1988, Uday gatecrashed a party that was being attended by the wife of the Egyptian President, Hosni Mubarak, shooting dead a man by the name of Hanna Geogo. Initially Saddam, in an attempt to make an example of his son, had him imprisoned and then sent into exile in Switzerland, but less than four months after Geogo was murdered, Uday returned to Iraq and was given a presidential pardon. Not long afterwards, Uday then initiated a fight with his cousin and not only damaged his liver, but also left him in a coma. This time Saddam did nothing to punish his son and no doubt it was because of this lack of patriarchal disapproval that Uday then proceeded to gather a band of thugs around him and began trafficking in drugs and arms.

But Saddam was no less outrageous or vicious than his tearaway son, for it was during this period (with his country still on the brink of poverty) that he began to spend vast amounts of money building palaces. One such building, which was started in 1988, took a further eight years to construct. Another had blue marble floors imported from Argentina at a cost of $3,000-4,000 per square metre and, in addition, Saddam also designed and built an Iraqi equivalent to the French Arc de Triomphe in order to celebrate the end of the *Anfal* programme. But at the back of Saddam's mind was the constant pressure of where to find more money, how to make Iraq's oil fields pay greater dividends.

At this time the small kingdom of Kuwait, whose territory bordered Iraq's was, to Saddam's way of thinking, exceeding its oil production quotas as set by OPEC and therefore lowering the price Iraq could charge for its own resources. Saddam also accused the Kuwaiti government of stealing oil from the Rumailah fields and establishing both military and civilian installations and bases on Iraqi territory. Angered by these so-called outrages, Saddam began threatening to invade Kuwait and despite a meeting in Jeddah held on 31 July 1990 between Saudi, Kuwaiti and Iraqi officials who had come together with the sole intention of averting war, Saddam would not be pacified. In the early hours of 2 August 1990 the Iraqi army marched on its neighbor and within less than half a day had occupied Kuwait whose Emir, Sheik Jaber al-Ahmed al-Sabah, fled into exile in Saudi Arabia.

What followed were seven nightmarish months for the Kuwaitis, whose lives were turned upside down as Iraqi troops indulged in an orgy of looting, pillaging, and torture. In fact, during the first days of the invasion, Amnesty International in London received several reports that hundreds of Kuwaiti military personnel had been taken off to detention and torture centers. Essentially what was occurring in Kuwait was an extension of the type of terror wielded by the Ba'athist regime within Iraq itself. The same instruments of torture were used and, as the following extract demonstrates, the same methods.

'The human rights organization [Amnesty International] has interviewed scores of people who have fled Kuwait,' reported one observer, 'and two of its representatives have just returned from Bahrain, where they talked with victims and eyewitnesses of abuses. "Their testimony builds up a horrifying picture of widespread arrests, torture under interrogation, summary executions and mass extra-judicial killings," Amnesty

International said… Some people have also been arrested or killed for failing to replace photos of the Emir with those of Iraq's President Saddam Hussein…Some have been given electric shocks or suffered prolonged beatings to sensitive parts of their bodies. Others have had their limbs broken, their hair plucked out with pincers, their finger and toe nails pulled out, and were threatened with sexual assault or execution. "We cannot even publish more details on former torture victims, in case they or their families are identified and suffer further reprisals," Amnesty International said.'6

In addition to the human rights abuses, government buildings, alongside hotels, nightclubs, hospitals and schools were ransacked, and foreign nationals had to go into hiding for fear they would be used as part of Saddam's 'human shield' against the threat of retaliation by the West.

And retaliate the West did. Initially the UN Security Council passed a resolution (660) condemning the invasion and demanding an immediate withdrawal by Iraq, otherwise sanctions would be implemented and, when this failed to move Saddam, British Prime Minister Margaret Thatcher, began urging US President George Bush to stand up to Saddam and threaten him with war.

Not long afterwards, on 7 August US Defense Secretary, Richard Cheney met with King Fahd of Saudi Arabia and requested permission to station US troops on Saudi soil as a precaution against an invasion by Iraq. But this threat, far from persuading Saddam to move out of Kuwait, prompted him instead to declare Kuwait the nineteenth province of Iraq, for historically, since the time of the Ottoman Empire, Iraq had always considered Kuwait to be part and parcel of its territory.

Naturally the UN were infuriated and promptly issued another resolution condemning Saddam, only this time the USSR also joined in the condemnation, something which came as a huge blow to the Iraqi leader. Suddenly he was out in the cold, without a friendly face in sight, but due to a combination of stubbornness and arrogance, things were about to grow even worse.

On 1 September 1990, Margaret Thatcher announced that Saddam Hussein would be charged with war crimes against humanity whilst on 9 September President Bush met with Mikhail Gorbachev, the two men jointly agreeing to present a united front against Iraq in accordance with the UN. Subsequently an international coalition was formed after which thousands upon thousands of troops from all over the world gathered within the region and, with General Norman Schwarzkopf at the helm, a battle plan was quickly assembled.

By November all diplomatic approaches to end the crisis had come to an end and the UN, tired of Saddam's dissembling, set a deadline for his country's withdrawal from Kuwait (SCR 678, 29 November 1990), adding that a failure to do so would guarantee the use of 'all necessary means' to oust Iraq from the region. Shortly afterwards, on the morning of 16 January 1991, massive air strikes began against Iraq and the words 'Desert Storm' entered the English language.

To begin with, the strikes were against military targets in both Iraq and Kuwait, as well as singling out bridges, power stations, oil refineries, airports etc. As was his way, in order to avoid being targeted, Saddam moved from one presidential palace to another, sleeping in bunkers specially built in case of war. It was the best he could do in a bad situation, for the Iraqi air force was no match for that of the allies who, night after night, bombarded the country. It was difficult to imagine how Saddam felt he could ever achieve victory and yet, on 26 January, Iraqi soldiers, on the direct instructions of their President, briefly invaded Saudi Arabia and occupied the town of Kafji, only to be ousted two days later. In general, the Iraqi troops were tired and hungry. Some troops claimed they had gone without food for several days and because some of the bombing had taken out hospitals, medical provisions were also in short supply. President Bush did not let up the pressure on Saddam, demanding that he withdraw his troops from Kuwait by 23 February or else face a ground war. In retaliation, Saddam set the Kuwaiti oilfields alight, which began an oil spill of biblical proportions. Suddenly the air was filled with mile-wide clouds of acrid black smoke.

Unsurprisingly, this was the last act of a desperate man, for shortly afterwards on 3 March 1991 General Schwarzkopf and Saudi General Khalid Bin Sultan met and accepted the surrender of Iraqi Generals Sultan Hashim Ahmad and Salah Abid Mohammed. By this time US and allied forces had already forayed deep into Iraq itself, but they had stopped short of occupying Baghdad and taking out their ultimate target, Saddam Hussein. It was a decision that, over a decade later, would come back to haunt them, but, at the time, instead of finishing the job they had come to do, President Bush together with General Schwarzkopf began inciting the Iraqi people to rise up and remove Saddam from power themselves.

Believing that the US would aid them in this plan, on 5 March 1991 the Shias in southern Iraq did rise up in open rebellion of their defeated leader. Suddenly armed insurrection broke out in Basra and Nassiriya with thousands of Iraqis shouting for Saddam's demise, and by the time the unrest reached the Shia cities of Najjaf and Karbala, it was all-out civil war. Nor were the Shias alone in their fight, for shortly after the insurrection began, Iraqi Kurds in the north of the country joined in the rebellion. Suddenly they were calling on the US to stand behind what they had begun and come to their aid, but President Bush refused. Some people say this was because it was a Shia uprising and if the US helped, then it would be tantamount to approving Shia-controlled Iran, or worse still that Iraq would later become an Islamic fundamentalist state. Whatever the reason, the allies remained stationary; this was going to be a fight between the rebels and Saddam alone.

Initially Saddam appointed his cousin (best known by the soubriquet Chemical Ali) to crush by any means necessary the rebellion in the south while in Baghdad Saddam gave his troops shoot-to-kill orders in case anyone in the capital dared take up arms. Unfortunately for the rebels, who might have expected support from their Shia neighbour Iran, none was forthcoming. The Iranians, all too aware that any show of involvement would only infuriate the Americans, simply sat back and watched.

Chemical Ali swiftly reoccupied Basra while other divisions under his command

Saddam's face appeared on posters and murals all over Iraq and when he was removed from power ordinary Iraqis took great delite in defiling his image. When he was alive, however, this would have led to the severest of punishment. When Iraq invaded Kuwait in 1990 Kuwaitis were reported to have been arrested and killed for failing to replace photographs of Kuwait's Emir with pictures of Saddam.

conquered Karbala and Najjaf. It was a bloodbath, with between 50,000-200,000 killed, hospitals blown to pieces and hundreds of men, women and children tortured. One report told of an entire family being taken up in a helicopter and thrown out alive to their deaths. Other reports described how anyone thought to be a rebel sympathizer had their ears cut off. And that was only in southern Iraq. Suddenly the Kurds in the north came under attack and, with no sign that the allies would lift a finger to help, Iraqi troops let loose their most base instincts and began a killing spree which ended in over 100,000 Kurds dead or wounded and in the region of 2 million either missing or displaced. These were statistics that the world couldn't ignore and thankfully (albeit too late for many) it didn't.

On 10 April 1991 Operation Provide Comfort was instigated by the allied forces to protect the Kurds and, by creating a no-fly zone in the north, give them a place of safety in which to live. Despite this setback to his plans, Saddam Hussein emerged from the whole sorry tale as the supreme leader of his country and, if it can be believed, he was in an even stronger position politically than when the war had first begun.

The UN now imposed sanctions on Iraq (sanctions which were most strictly upheld by the US and Britain) after which there also began a long campaign to locate Saddam's weapons of mass destruction. As is well-documented, this campaign became a lengthy (stretching over twelve years) game of cat and mouse, with Saddam at first agreeing to UN inspectors then objecting to them, after which he would recant and agree. But tragically, if it was no more than a game to him, for the Iraqi people it proved far more devastating: at the same time as the outside world was imposing strict measures (including food and medical embargoes) against Iraq, so they were also suffering under Saddam's day-to-day oppression. For them it was a no-win situation; the more his people suffered, the more Saddam could turn round to the world at large and say that, for humanity's sake, the sanctions ought to be lifted. But nothing was about to happen unless the UN inspectors were allowed to go about their business so the result was, for twelve years, stalemate. In the interim Saddam's crimes against his own people continued, most notably in the case of the Marsh Arabs whose land Saddam drained by diverting water, which should have run into the marshes, into a third river (alongside the Euphrates and Tigris). When the Marsh Arabs rebelled at what they saw as a direct threat to their way of life, Saddam ordered his Republican Guard to go in and quash the uprising. This they did, killing thousands in their wake and displacing tens of thousands more. Further to this Saddam continued to wreak havoc, not only on the civilian population, but also on members of his own government and extended family. With respect to the former, even though the majority were from his own region of Tikrit, he had many of them executed for fear they were plotting against him. And with respect to the latter, in 1996 the husbands of two of his daughters defected to Saudi Arabia in fear of their lives, only to be wooed back to Iraq by Saddam and consequently executed.

And so the killing continued, until that is 11 September 2001, which as in the case of Osama bin Laden and the Taliban, proved a watershed date.

Immediately after 11 September the US directed the full force of its wrath against those it saw as the main perpetrators i.e. the *al-Qaeda* network and Osama bin Laden. However, shortly after the war in Afghanistan, attention focused on Saddam Hussein. In his State of the Union speech, George W. Bush declared a War on Terror targeting Iraq, alongside Iran, North Korea and Syria, as major players in the Axis of Evil. America was determined to show who was boss and although Prime Minister Tony Blair persuaded Bush to take the UN route, finally on 20 March 2003, war began.

By 3 April US troops had reached Saddam International airport, a mere ten miles outside Baghdad city center, and by 8 April they were operating from inside Baghdad itself. Yet despite a concerted effort to track down and kill Saddam (just like that other enemy of the US Osama bin Laden), he evaded capture. What couldn't be denied the allied forces, however, was the uncovering of a mass grave in which it was believed lay the corpses of up to 15,000 people, missing since the Shiite uprising in 1991. Tragically, similar mass graves were found throughout the country.

'Each cut of the workers' spades unearths another collection of reddened bones and soiled clothing,' wrote Ed Vulliamy for The *Observer* on 25 May 2003 – 'some of the dead were wearing military fatigues, others were clad in sports or everyday clothes when they were killed, a track suit here, a pin-striped-suit there…This is what happened to the victims of Musayyib: in the wake of the insurrection, anyone suspected with taking part was ordered or taken to an outdoor space, and boarded onto trucks and buses. The vehicles were then driven from the river valley out into nowhere. There, the captives were lined up – hands tied and blindfolded – and pushed into the bottom of the pits. And in the earthy tomb, they were machine-gunned and the dirt replaced by bulldozer, by way of crude cover.'

But despite these and other gruesome discoveries including torture chambers and Secret Security files bulging with photographs of dead Iraqis, some with their necks and faces slashed, others with their eyes gouged out and their genitals blackened, still no one could locate either the Iraqi president, nor his weapons of mass destruction. The former, it was thought, might have slipped over the border into Syria, but as for the latter it is (at the time this book was being written) still a matter of some embarrassment for the coalition forces that nothing has, to date, come to light.

And what next for Iraq? For the foreseeable future it appears that America together with Britain is to occupy the country with a view to establishing some kind of stability. Whether this is possible given the Iraqi peoples' (some might argue, justifiable) distrust of the West is yet to be seen, but on recent evidence the outlook is bleak. On 24 June 2003 six Royal British military police were slaughtered and a further eight injured in two attacks in the southeastern town of Majar al-Kabir. Further attacks against the military forces occupying Iraq continued with the US suffering most the casualties. On November 2, 2003, one of the worst incidents occured. Fifteen US soldiers were killed and twenty-one injured when their Chinook helicopter was shot down by Iraqi guerilla fighters. Doubtless reports of this incident, along with all the other recent tragedies, put a smile on the dictator's face. After all, when he was in power Saddam enjoyed nothing better than raining down pain and torment on all those who surrounded him.

In December 2003, eight months after the war ended, Saddam Hussein was finally captured, without a struggle, by US troops near his home town of Tikrit.

1 Some people doubt this date, believing instead that Saddam was born on
     1 July 1939.
2 Put simply, Iraq is split into two main factions i.e. the Sunni and Shia Muslims.
     This schism began as far back as AD680 and accounts for much of the bloodshed
     in Iraq over the centuries.
3 From *Saddam Hussein The Politics of Revenge* by Säid K. Aburish,
     published by Bloomsbury Publishing plc, 2000.
4 From *Saddam Hussein The Politics of Revenge* by Säid K. Aburish,
     published by Bloomsbury Publishing plc, 2000.
5 Saddam has two sons, Uday and Qusay Hussein, both of whom have
     followed in their father's footsteps to become men of violence.
6 www.kuwait-info.org/Gulf_War/amnesty_international.html

ROBERT MUGABE
Zimbabwe's Strongman

My fellow Zimbabweans: I thank you for your courage as you
continue to vote in your millions. We see your determination.
We hear your support. We share your impatience. The power is
in your hands. What the people of Zimbabwe now deserve
is a celebration.
But there are those who say that dark clouds threaten the horizon
of our country...Rarely in the history of mankind have a people
faced such brutality while retaining such gracious exuberance.
Press statement by Morgan Tsvangirai while awaiting the results
of the 2002 presidential elections in Zimbabwe.

When Robert Mugabe first came to power in 1980 he symbolized all the optimism of the newly renamed nation of Zimbabwe (formerly known as Rhodesia). Mugabe spoke of peace, democracy and above all else reconciliation with the past decades of white colonial rule. But early on in his presidency, shadows began to build, in particular with the brutal crushing of the Matabelelands uprising, together with the elimination of several key political opponents. Worse was to follow as his strong authoritarianism came to the fore and corruption overtook any real political ideals. Today Zimbabwe is facing economic collapse, HIV/AIDS is in the ascendant, white-owned farms are being seized while white farmers and their families are either being driven from their homes or are savagely murdered.

Robert Gabriel Mugabe was born on 21 February 1924 at the Kutama Mission, approximately fifty miles from Zimbabwe's capital city, Harare. He had a lonely childhood: one of five siblings, his mother, Bona Mugabe (nee Shonhiwa), didn't spend a great deal of time nurturing her son, added to which at the age of ten, Robert's father, Gabriel Mugabe, deserted the family home. For most of his childhood Robert was brought up by an Irish Jesuit priest called Father O'Hea, subsequent to which he attended several different missionary schools. By 1945, at the age of twenty-one, Robert Mugabe acquired a teaching qualification, but rather than pursuing this profession and settling down, he applied for a scholarship to South Africa's Fort Hare University. Robert Mugabe, even at this early stage, was a highly motivated and ambitious individual. He duly won the scholarship and traveled to South Africa to begin his new studies. This was perhaps the first time Mugabe came in contact with political ideas on a world-side scale and with Communist literature in particular. His imagination was set on fire and by the time he left South Africa to return to Rhodesia in 1952, he was determined to mount a revolution, throw out the white government (headed by Ian Smith – leader of the Rhodesian Front) and turn his home country into a model communist state. But really, it was only after having taken a job at the Takoradi Teacher Training College in Ghana that Mugabe realized his ambitions were possible, for Ghana was the first African colony to achieve independence. At the same time, it was while in Ghana that he met his future wife, Sally Hayfron.

Mugabe returned to Rhodesia in 1960 only to find the country in a state of political turmoil. This was the beginning of the Black Nationalist movement and huge demonstrations were being held on the streets of Rhodesia's capital city, Salisbury (now known as Harare). In response Ian Smith passed a new act called the Law and Order Maintenance Act, which in effect meant that anyone could be arrested and jailed without trial. The nationalists were incensed and responded swiftly by forming two opposition parties: the first led by Joshua Nkomo called the Zimbabwe African People's National Union (ZAPU) and the Zimbabwe African National Union (ZANU) headed by Ndabaningi Sithole. To begin with, Mugabe joined the first of these groups, but three years later, he left to become Secretary General of Sithole's party. There now proceeded several years of internecine warfare between the two groups as each tried to assert itself, but this only gave Ian Smith a greater hold over Rhodesia, a hold he put to good use when in 1964 he jailed Nkomo, Sithole and Mugabe for ten years without trial. Furthermore, less than a year afterwards, on 11 November 1965, Ian Smith issued a Unilateral Declaration of Independence, in the hope that this would finally remove Rhodesia from under Britain's thumb. Sanctions were immediately placed on the country, which brought Rhodesia to its knees, however in 1971 the then British secretary, Sir Alec Douglas-Home arrived in Salisbury to make peace with Ian Smith and his government. A deal was struck, but as it favored white Rhodesians this infuriated the black population and once again the country was subjected to an unprecedented amount of rioting, followed by an all-out guerrilla war.

By 1974 Robert Mugabe was a free man, but instead of staying in Rhodesia he left for Mozambique where he set up and led one of the largest guerrilla factions fighting Ian Smith. Things were not looking good for the Rhodesian leader and though the South African government eventually sent in troops to help quell the unrest, soon even they were disenchanted with Smith. Finally, in 1979 after months of negotiations, the Lancaster House Agreement was signed signalling a Rhodesian peace deal and oncoming black rule. Robert Mugabe returned home to a rapturous welcome. A year earlier he had been elected president of the ZANU party and within a year of his return to Rhodesia he had been elected (after a highly questionable campaign of violence and intimidation) as President of the newly named Zimbabwe. He didn't have to form a coalition government with anyone, yet he decided to set up a political partnership with Joshua Nkomo who, alongside his ZAPU guerrilla forces, had also fought long and hard against Ian Smith. However the Mugabe/Nkomo combination was not a match made in heaven as the following extract humorously makes clear.

'Mugabe did not take to Nkomo with great kindness. Reliable enough legend has it that once, when both men were summoned to President Nyerere of Tanzania – who wanted increased cooperation between them – and they saw the President separately and by turn, that Mugabe, when it was his turn, marched into Nyerere's office and scorned the gestured offer of a chair with the words, "If you're expecting me to sit where that fat bastard just sat, you'll have to think again."'[1]

Indeed so great was the acrimony between the two men that when a sizeable arms cache was discovered hidden in the homes of nine ZAPU supporters in 1982, it led to Nkomo's dismissal from government. His passport was confiscated and he was restricted to living within Bulawayo. In addition Mugabe ordered a crackdown on ZAPU supporters, which led to the total collapse of the coalition.

Mugabe now ruled Zimbabwe alone; a position he had no doubt coveted since his earliest days as a political activist. It was the ideal situation for a power-hungry

When Robert Mugabe met with British Prime Minister Margaret Thatcher in 1989, he already had the blood of up to 20,000 of his countrymen from Matabeleland on his hands, and his brutally repressive regime was still in its infancy.

President, but not for the majority of people living under his rule, as was soon discovered, particularly by those living in Matabeleland.

Between 1983-1984 Mugabe set in motion a concerted military campaign to crush political opposition (in the shape of the Ndebele, Zimbabwe's minority tribe headed by Joshua Nkomo) in Matabeleland, as a consequence of which thousands were beaten, tortured and/or slaughtered. A prime example of the above occurred in February 1983 when the Fifth Brigade (made up entirely of Shona tribesmen loyal only to Mugabe who is also Shona) of the Zimbabwean army went to a village in the south of Matabeleland and corralled hundreds of citizens for interrogation. What they wanted to know was the whereabouts of a group of rebels who were fighting against, and spreading rumors about, the Mugabe government. Amongst the group of arrested civilians were two pregnant girls. The Fifth Brigade (who had been trained to commit gratuitously cruel acts by the North Koreans) immediately segregated them and without further ceremony executed the two girls in front of the rest of the group. It was further reported (by the Catholic Commission for Justice and Peace together with the Legal Resources Foundation) that, not satisfied with shooting the girls, the soldiers then further defiled their bodies by splitting open their stomachs. In fact during Mugabe's brutal Matabeleland campaign thousands of atrocities (including men and women being forced to dig their own graves and whole families being told to dance on the graves of their own dead) were committed and it is widely believed that anywhere between 10,000-20,000 unarmed civilians were massacred.

Thankfully, however, by 1988 a peace accord was signed between Mugabe and Nkomo, the latter being given a new position in the government as one of two acting vice-presidents. However, though this went some way to calming previously troubled waters, the majority of Ndebeles maintained that the treaty only benefited the Shona and that Joshua Nkomo had sold out to the opposition.

'Our former leaders have betrayed us,' said Vusa Manyathela, a former freedom fighter, 'and have been bought with ministerial posts and a lot of money. If we had known that they would desert us, we wouldn't have taken part in the war of liberation with such fervour.'[2]

However if the war was, for the moment, at an end then Robert Mugabe's personal problems had only just begun for on 27 January 1992 his first wife, Sally, died unexpectedly. This was an enormous blow to Mugabe who, though never one to display personal affection in public, was said to have been very close to his wife. In addition, by March of that year drought, followed by inevitable famine, reared its head.

Zimbabwe had, up until this point, always been regarded as Africa's 'bread basket'; in other words as a rich, fertile land capable of producing enough home-grown cereals, fruit and vegetables to sustain its own people. Indeed when Mugabe first came to power, approximately seventy per cent of the land was arable however there was one small fact that stuck in Mugabe's throat and that was that most of this land was owned by white farmers.

In May 2003 human rights campaigners staged a protest outside Lord's Cricket Ground in London on the first day of the first Test Match between England and Zimbabwe, and more than 100 British Members of Parliament called for the Zimbawean team to be banned from playing in England. The English players later refused to play in Zimbabwe.

On 19 March 1992 Robert Mugabe passed the Zimbabwean Land Acquisition Act, which in effect allowed the government to confiscate any farm it so wished. Governments from across the world condemned Mugabe's new law, pointing out that, with an oncoming famine, it was necessary to safeguard food production, not jeopardise it in this cavalier fashion. And to a great extent the critics were right, for as far as Mugabe was concerned, this new law was nothing to do with increasing food production or any other agricultural aim, instead it was to do with what Mugabe regarded as 'social justice' i.e. the redistribution of land from black to white.

Naturally his new policy, despite the famine, played very well with the majority of Zimbabweans; Mugabe had never looked more populist, added to which he began to buy in food from the international market, thus avoiding mass deaths (despite over 150,000 head of cattle dying). But every silver lining has a cloud and, as a result of his spending on foreign imports, Mugabe was slowly emptying his government's coffers. In an article written by Christopher Gregory, the writer noted that 'mounting unemployment, increasing levels of inflation, persistent shortages of consumer goods, declining real wage rates,'[3] and a multitude of other problems both economic and social, beset Zimbabwe during this period. On top of this, those who opposed Mugabe began to voice the opinion that his redistribution of land policy was nothing more than a means to consolidate his increasingly dictatorial rule by distributing farms to his loyal supporters. Worse still, some black leaders also pointed out that Robert Mugabe was in fact establishing a new elitist regime, as bad as anything the nation had suffered during white colonial rule. Sadly, however, the opposition voices weren't strong enough or well enough established to make even the tiniest dent in Mugabe's increasing ego. Indeed at this point the opposition was so disparate (there was the ZANU-Ndonga party, the United African National Congress, the National Democratic Union, the Conservative Alliance of Zimbabwe and the National Front of Zimbabwe, to name but a few) it couldn't mount a concerted attack on anyone, let alone as wily a politician as Robert Mugabe.

Disregarding all criticism, therefore, Mugabe continued with his redistribution programme, subdividing what had once been highly productive sections of farmland into uneconomic holdings, which in turn led to a drastic drop in productivity.

By 1994 Mugabe's hold over the country was that of near-strangulation, but with elections looming the following year, there was some (if not much) hope that an end might be in sight. For instance, one opposition leader by the name of Edgar Tekere stated, 'Let us build an opposition army of Angels with Swords to put down the Mugabe-ZANU-PF evil.'[4] But the phrase 'sticks and stones might break my bones, but words will never hurt me,' could not have been better applied as Mugabe simply laughed off this and other, similar statements. After all, this was the man who had sanctioned the slaughter of thousands of civilians in Matabeleland; why would he worry about angels and swords?

Mugabe was also safe in the knowledge that Joshua Nkomo and his Ndebele supporters in the south of the country would display loyalty and vote for him, for they depended on Mugabe for reinvestment and, more crucially, for water. Bearing all this in mind, the 1995 elections were somewhat lop-sided, added to which the opposition parties were so disorganized that they failed to field candidates for 55 seats out of 150. There was only one glitch in Robert Mugabe's otherwise seamless campaign. Having pointed for quite some time to the fact that he had been brought up a Catholic and therefore enjoyed the highest morals, Mugabe suddenly announced that he had recently married his former private secretary, who was not only half his age, but with whom he had sired two children out of wedlock. The scandal ran for weeks in Zimbabwean newspapers with page-to-page coverage, however even this did nothing to wreck Mugabe's chances at the polls. And nor did his highly questionable racist and sexist comments. Mugabe kept up a constant slur against Zimbabwe's white citizens, as well as singling out homosexuals for particularly vitriolic abuse, calling them 'worse than dogs and pigs'. When the votes were finally cast and the counting was finished, ZANU-PF had won 148 out of 150 seats. It was a landslide victory, yet despite allegations of corruption and vote rigging, Mugabe didn't seem concerned that the election had been, and was being, questioned. As if to illustrate this complete arrogance, on 16 October 1995, only weeks after the elections, Mugabe arrested one of the two opposition leaders who had won a seat in the new parliament. Ndabaningi Sithole was charged with plotting to murder Mugabe. In fact, Sithole was said to have plotted the assassination alongside three other men who all belonged to a Manicaland dissident group. The three men had been arrested while in possession of arms and, during interrogation, had implicated Sithole, or so the story went. Whatever the case, Sithole did not come to trial until 1997. In 1996 Mugabe ran for re-election as President (in Zimbabwe party and presidential elections are separate entities), which led to the claim that Sithole had been arrested so that he couldn't run against Mugabe in this latest poll. Finally, when Sithole did come to trial, he was acquitted, but by then of course it was too late, for Robert Mugabe had polled 90.2 per cent of the country's vote.

In Britain there had also been an election, one in which Tony Blair soundly defeated John Major to become Britain's new Prime Minister. Mugabe, never one to miss an opportunity, now decided to declare his new aims for his country in general and for land reform in particular. Undoubtedly his speech, which was printed verbatim in The *Guardian* newspaper, was meant for the attention of Tony Blair, who was just then about to attend a Commonwealth summit in Edinburgh.

'We are going,' said Mugabe, 'to take the land and we are not going to pay for the soil. This is our set policy. Our land was never bought (by the colonialists) and there is no way we could buy back the land. However, if Britain wants compensation they should give us money and we will pass it on to their children.'[5]

Immediately after the Commonwealth summit, Mugabe then drew up a list of 1,732 white-owned properties, which he wished to confiscate and 'give back' to the people. But if Mugabe thought this populist move would alleviate other problems within the country and endear him to Zimbabweans, he was to a certain extent wrong, for there was growing unrest, signalled by riots and strikes, due for the most part to food shortages and the economic decline of the country as a whole. Nor was that the only trouble that Mugabe had to deal with, for on 1 July 1999, Joshua Nkomo died at the age of eighty-two, leaving Matabeleland in a state of deep mourning and shock. Mugabe, speaking at his funeral, said, 'Do not be afraid that my government will neglect you [the Ndebeles] now that your great leader has gone. My government will treat Matabeleland just as it did when Mr Nkomo was alive.'[6] Of course, no one who was alive during Mugabe's1983-84 campaign could forget just how he had indeed treated the Ndebeles and nor were they about to let him forget it, for after Joshua Nkomo's death, most of Matabeleland began siding with opposition forces, thus strengthening them to a point which not even Mugabe could ignore.

Added to these troubles, it was also apparent that Zimbabwe was suffering a massive economic crisis. In 1997-98, Robert Mugabe had gone to war in the Congo in support of that country's new President, Laurent Kabila. Zimbabwe, Namibia and Angola all supported Kabila as opposed to Rwanda, Uganda and part of the Congo itself who wanted Kabila out. But war is costly and Zimbabwe, which was already on its knees economically, now found itself spending over $1.6 million a day supporting its troops and bombing opposition forces. In addition, apart from the obvious decline in living standards due to a lack of foreign goods and food, other areas began to suffer, in particular people's health.

During the 1980s and 1990s HIV/AIDS had swept through southern Africa and by 1997 Zimbabwe topped the list of countries that were worst affected. 'In Zimbabwe,' wrote Nana Poku, 'by 2001 the likelihood of a 15-year-old woman dying before the end of her productive years will quadruple from around 11 per cent in the early 1980s to over 40 per cent. More than 2,000 Zimbabweans die of AIDS each year.'[7]

True to form, however, Mugabe did nothing to alleviate this tragedy, but instead tried to influence public opinion by deflecting attention away from high inflation and almost total economic collapse, and concentrating it instead on his favourite pet subject, land reforms. Suddenly white farmers were under attack again, only this time there was a vicious edge to the procedure as the issue of 'war veterans' reared its ugly head.

In 1997, in what might well have been one of his rashest statements, Mugabe said he was willing to pay war veterans something in the region of $240 million as a 'thank you' for their services to the country. Naturally this payment would deepen Zimbabwe's already perilous economic situation, but as yet the war veterans and land reforms were not linked. Then, in 1998, at the height of civil unrest, a white female farmer was attacked and her farm put to the torch by what were then known as 'black squatters'.

Despite intimidation of opposition MDC party supporters by his ZANU-PF party activists and the shortage of polling stations in MDC stronghold areas, Mugabe's 2002 election victory was far from a landslide when he polled 1,685,212 votes against his rival Morgan Tsvangirai's 1,258,401.

Anyone else might have found this last act enough to withdraw statements to the effect that it was black Africa's right to regain white farmland, whatever the cost. But not Robert Mugabe. Instead he and his wife travelled to Britain, where they were seen shopping at Harrods. Meanwhile back in Zimbabwe, Morgan Tsvangirai (who would later become Mugabe's chief opposition by leading the Movement for Democratic Change) was pleased to report that many soldiers had begun to desert the war in the Congo. 'Inflation is sky high,' Tsvangirai said, 'the economy is a mess. People question why we are in the war, when we have so many pressing problems here. We cannot afford this.'[8]

Mugabe flew home amongst growing international concern, only to start a concerted campaign to stamp out the freedom of the press. Journalists began to be arrested and beaten, more threats were made against the white farmers, but even these acts could not stop Mugabe suffering the first truly great political defeat of his career when, on 15 February 2000, he lost a referendum on a new constitution which in effect would have further enhanced Mugabe's stranglehold over the country.

Licking his wounds, Mugabe returned to his favourite subject – the white farming problem – and on 16 February, only two days after he'd lost the above vote, black 'squatters' began invading white farms en masse. Led by Chenjerai Hunzvi, a Polish-trained physician who had nicknamed himself 'Hitler', the squatters now became better known as 'war veterans' and, with Hunzvi leading the way, threatened Mugabe with all-out civil unrest if he didn't succumb to their demands and begin paying out gratuities and war pensions.

Mugabe, realizing that he would have to give way or face political suicide, chose the former route and agreed to pay the veterans in the region of Zim. $50,000 each, but in order to foot this bill, money had to be printed, as a result of which inflation rocketed.

Even then, events had still not hit rock bottom, for back in March, the Zimbabwean High Court had ruled that the farm invasions were illegal and that all the squatters should be removed, by force if necessary. But despite this declaration, the court's orders were ignored, leading directly to tragedy when, on 15 April 2000, a white farmer by the name of David Stevens was shot dead at point-blank range by squatters on his farm at Macheke, just south of Harare.

'It was the worst outbreak of violence since the start of the invasion of hundreds of white-owned farms two months ago. Mr Mugabe, returning from a week-long trip to Cuba, was greeted at Harare airport by more than 1,000 war veterans, who have been leading the invasions.

'Leaders of the embattled farming community had hoped that he would use the occasion to call for an end to turmoil. Instead, he and his henchmen said that eviction of the squatters would only cause greater loss of life.'[9]

Ironically, however, it would be Mugabe's 'non-action' which led to a greater loss of life, in addition to a sustained campaign of intimidation and violence. For instance, three days after the Stevens' murder, another white farmer, Martin Olds, died having been besieged on his farm near Bulawayo by approximately 100 war veterans. In desperation Olds had telephoned for assistance, saying that he had been wounded, but the authorities could not reach the farm until the squatters had left, by which time Olds was dead and his farm set alight.

A BBC correspondent by the name of Ben Brown said that although Olds had tried to defend himself he hadn't stood a chance. First he was shot in the leg after which he had retreated into his house, but the squatters threw Molotov cocktails inside and, once the house was on fire, Olds could do nothing but exit the building whereupon he was promptly gunned down. Of course these weren't the only deaths and, tragically, by 15 May over 1,000 farms had been invaded and over 19 people had been killed due to the increasing political violence.

In June Mugabe faced fresh parliamentary elections, but fearing that opposition forces (in the shape of the MDC – Movement for Democratic Change – led by Morgan Tsvangirai) were in the ascendant, he decided to revert to guerrilla tactics in order to win. Mugabe pressed even harder for land reforms, forced many white judges to resign, and portrayed the white farmers as wanting to return Zimbabwe back to a British-run colony. He also used Hunzvi to support his campaign. Hunzvi gloried in violence and on several occasions declared, 'I am the biggest terrorist in Zimbabwe.' It was not surprising therefore that as a campaigner for ZANU-PF, numerous witnesses came forward to identify him as being one of several members of the same gang who had severely beaten and tortured Mugabe's opponents. Indeed 14 members of the MDC were killed during this period, but despite the bloodshed Morgan Tsvangirai declared he was not going to throw in the towel, but fight the election to the last.

In an attempt to deflect international attention away from the intimidation of MDC supporters, more white-owned farms were invaded and more white farmers murdered, but at the same time Mugabe, conscious that the killings were disenfranchising vast sections of the black rural vote from ZANU-PF (owing to the fact that these workers depended on white farm owners for a job and an income), insisted that white farmers now begin campaigning for ZANU-PF in order to win back these votes. 'One provincial governor said, "We are not happy with the attitude of some white commercial farmers who are supporting the opposition. We do not want another war. If you want peace you should support me and the ruling party. If you want trouble, then vote for another party."'[10]

But the violence was nowhere near at an end, and right up until the elections opposition supporters were being beaten and tortured in an effort to dissuade them from voting. Patson Muzuwa, who was involved in founding the MDC, was one such. 'Arrested nine times, the 36-year-old motor mechanic was electrocuted by the police during interrogation, beaten on the ribs and soles of his feet and put under house arrest for seven months.'[11] Muzuwa then woke up one night when several armed militiamen broke into his house and attempted to kidnap him. Fortunately his neighbors came to the rescue otherwise Muzuwa is certain he would have been dragged out to a remote location and been buried alive. Indeed the statistics for the intimidation and bullying of all strata of Zimbabwean society two weeks prior to the elections makes for chilling reading. For instance, an estimated 1,400 farms were occupied by war veterans and at least 29 opposition workers were killed, all of which illustrated Mugabe's utter contempt (if any illustration was indeed needed) for the democratic process and, more importantly, for his people. Winning the election, which Mugabe finally did (although by the narrowest of margins), was all that mattered.

Of course the elections didn't end there, for after the parliamentary elections came the presidential elections which were to take place sometime early in 2002. Tsvangirai regrouped and planned yet another campaign to beat Mugabe at the hustings whilst Mugabe's Finance Minister, Simba Makoni, publicly, and not before time, declared an economic crisis and further warned that the country was about to face a serious shortage of food. At the same, time most western countries who had donated vast sums of money and aid to Zimbabwe, including the World Bank and the IMF, cut their losses and refused to send any more, due for the most part to Mugabe's land seizure programme. Europe also began threatening sanctions if the violence didn't end, but Mugabe, rather than acting to save his country from almost certain economic disaster, instead continued to infuriate Britain by having the Supreme Court of Zimbabwe (now peopled by Mugabe supporters) declare his land 'reform' laws legal. Mugabe also began a concerted effort to silence foreign reporters and repress Zimbabwean journalists from reporting anything that didn't toe the ZANU-PF party line.

Youth brigades were set up, with recruits mainly taken from poor rural areas being promised military training in return for complete loyalty to the government. The youths were then sent to camps and instructed in groups of fifty so that they would bond with one another. Subsequent to training, they were then used as a type of rural militia for the express purpose of intimidating rural MDC areas, thereby furthering ZANU-PF's stranglehold over the country. Nothing was beyond Robert Mugabe, he would go to any lengths to stay in power, to terrorize his people and if the country wasn't connvinced that he was still in control and didn't intend to relinquish his presidency, in January 2002 he introduced three new bills of law. One of these, a public order bill, banned the opposition from holding rallies or demonstrations without first gaining 'police approval'. As the police were, to a man, in the government's pay, it went without saying that no such approval would be forthcoming. Simultaneously, Mugabe made a series of bizarre statements to the press, stating amongst other things that Morgan Tsvangirai was nothing more than a puppet of Tony Blair's and that Blair's government was populated with gay and lesbian ministers. With reference to this last outburst, Mugabe had always displayed contempt for gay and lesbian activities and had gone so far as to state that neither group should, or in the future would, enjoy the same human rights as 'normal' Zimbabweans.

The build-up to the 2002 presidential elections was fraught with accusations of corruption and police brutality. European Union observers, who were supposed to be keeping a close eye on procedures to ensure there was no vote-rigging or intimidation, were pulled out of the country after Mugabe declared a whole list of them were hostile to both him and his government. These countries included Britain, Sweden, Germany, Finland, the Netherlands and Denmark. Immediately after their withdrawal, Mugabe then cut the number of polling stations in MDC strongholds at the same time as increasing the number of stations in rural areas which supported ZANU-PF. Mugabe also stated that if white Zimbabweans didn't relinquish the British part of their dual nationality then they wouldn't be allowed to vote. But none of the above measures would necessarily guarantee Mugabe victory, a fact he knew only too well, for Morgan Tsvangirai was riding very high in the opinion polls. True to form, Mugabe decided to resort to baser tactics i.e. those of intimidation and undisguised brutality. Thousands of MDC supporters were thereafter subjected to ZANU-PF attacks (usually in the form of beatings). 'In many rural areas, citizens suspected of harboring MDC sympathies were abducted by youth brigades, taken to their camps and assaulted. Flesh wounds were inflicted as a visible warning to others. In one case, a youth had the MDC initials carved into his back with a dagger. There were reports of some huts being torched.'[12]

The intimidation was nation-wide. In the cities, gangs of ZANU-PF groups would break into MDC rallies and intimidate the participants. Nor were the police much better, for more often than not they would join in the violence, firing tear gas, and clubbing and battering people with their rifle butts.

At the hustings Mugabe would appear all smiles and promises. His country was on the brink of starvation yet his main message was still one of land redistribution, as if this was going to feed his people and avert a national crisis. By 9 March, polling day, the tension in the country was palpable. In those areas where the polling stations had been reduced, the queues were enormous. This was exactly what Mugabe had hoped for; that MDC supporters would soon grow fed up of waiting and return home without voting; what is more, the bureaucratic procedures were so complicated that at one point it was estimated that for every seven minutes only one vote was being cast. By the last night thousands upon thousands of MDC supporters were still waiting at the polling stations so the MDC went to the High Court to ask for a third day of voting. Much to Mugabe's disgust, the High Court agreed, but when the third day began there was so much confusion with stations first opening and then closing that the whole process was an unmitigated disaster. Finally, on 13 March 2002, the results were announced. Robert Mugabe had taken 1,685,212 of the votes to Morgan Tsvangirai's 1,258,401. It wasn't a landslide victory by any stretch of the imagination, but it *was* a victory and once again Robert Mugabe had clung on to the reins of power, albeit he had had to engineer the results.

Today hundreds of white-owned farms are still occupied by the war veterans together with bands of government supporters. Opposition party leaders, their families and their homes continue to be attacked. Food and fuel shortages are a daily occurrence and, perhaps worst of all, 200 people die daily of HIV/AIDS. Millions of Zimbabweans are suffering under Robert Mugabe, yet he is not doing anything to ease their predicament. The only thing of interest to either Mugabe or his government is the desire to stay in power, whatever the cost.

1 *Robert Mugabe: A Life of Power and Violence*, by Stephen Chan, published by I.B. Tauris & Co Ltd, 2003.
2 *African News*, July, 1997.
3 *Zimbabwe's Second Decade: Little Room for Manoeuvre?*, Larry Benjamin and Christopher Gregory (eds), *Southern Africa at the Crossroads?*, Rivonia: Justified Press, 1992.
4 *Robert Mugabe: A Life of Power and Violence*, by Stephen Chan, published by I.B. Tauris & Co Ltd, 2003.
5 The *Guardian*, 15 October, 1997.
6 The *Guardian*, 6 July, 1999
7 *The Crisis of AIDS in Africa and the Politics of Response*, Nana Poku, 2001.
8 The *Guardian*, 14 November, 1998.
9 www.telegraph.co.uk
10 *Robert Mugabe: A Life of Power and Violence*, by Stephen Chan, published by I.B. Tauris & Co Ltd, 2003.
11 From 'Exile Files', by Sue Summers, The *Observer* Magazine, 10 August 2003.
12 *Robert Mugabe: A Life of Power and Violence*, by Stephen Chan, published by I.B. Tauris & Co Ltd, 2003.

PICTURE ACKNOWLEDGEMENTS

Camera Press: 167 CAMERA PRESS/G/P, 181 CAMERA PRESS/Thabo Jaiyesimi

Corbis: pp. 19, 83, 86 © Hulton-Deutsch Collection/CORBIS; 23, 72, 89, 95, 98, 101. 154, 157 © Bettmann/CORBIS; 29 © Stapleton Collection/CORBIS; 41 © David Turnley/CORBIS; 114 © Miroslav Zajic/CORBIS; 119 © Collection CORBIS KIPA; 122 ©Touhig Sion/CORBIS SYGMA; 125 ©Michael Freeman/CORBIS; 132 © Peter Turnley/CORBIS; 135 © Bernard Bisson/CORBIS SYGMA; 141 © Pablo San Juan/CORBIS; 165 © Mike Stewart/CORBIS SYGMA

Dover Illustrations: p. 16

Getty Images/Hulton Archive: pp. 13, 105, 109, 159

Getty Images/News and Sport: p. 165

Illustrated London News Picture Library: pp. 56, 59, 63, 71

PA Photos/Abaca: p. 173

Mary Evans Picture Library: pp. 24, 33, 37

TopFoto.co.uk: pp. 46, 49, 50, 76, 129, 143, 149, 177, 185

ACKNOWLEDGEMENTS

In writing this book help came from many different quarters, but
in particular I am grateful for the help of the London Library,
my editor Rod Green and Albert Clack at Lubbly Jubbly Books.